PROBLEMS OF THE MODERN ECONOMY

Pollution, Resources, and the Environment

PROBLEMS OF THE MODERN ECONOMY

General Editor: EDMUND S. PHELPS, *Columbia University*

Each volume in this series presents
prominent positions in the debate of
an important issue of economic policy

Pollution, Resources, and the Environment

Edited with an introduction by
ALAIN C. ENTHOVEN
STANFORD UNIVERSITY

and

A. MYRICK FREEMAN III
BOWDOIN COLLEGE

NEW YORK
W · W · NORTON & COMPANY · INC ·

24579-2
GF
41
E39
1973

✗✗ 673520

FIRST EDITION

Library of Congress Cataloging in Publication Data
Enthoven, Alain C   1930–   comp.
    Pollution, resources, and the environment.
    (Problems of the modern economy)
    Bibliography: p.
    1. Human ecology—Addresses, essays, lectures.
2. Conservation of natural resources—Addresses,
essays, lectures.   3. Pollution—Economic aspects—
Addresses, essays, lectures.   I. Freeman, A. Myrick,
1936–   joint comp.   II. Title.
    GF41.E39   1973   301.31'08   73–12091
    ISBN 0–393–05502–7;
    ISBN 0–393–09933–4 (pbk.)

"The Tragedy of the Commons," by Garrett Hardin, from *Science*, vol. 162 (December 13, 1968), pp. 1243–48. Copyright © 1968 by the American Association for the Advancement of Science.
"The Economics of the Coming Spaceship Earth," by Kenneth E. Boulding, from Henry Jarrett, ed., *Environmental Quality in a Growing Economy* (1966), pp. 3–14. Published for Resources for the Future, Inc., by The Johns Hopkins Press.
"Economics and the Environment: A Materials Balance Approach," by Allen V. Kneese, Robert U. Ayres, and Ralph C. D'Arge, adapted from chap. 1 of their book of the same title, published by Resources for the Future, Inc., 1970.
"The Economic Common Sense of Pollution," by Larry E. Ruff, from *The Public Interest*, no. 19 (Spring 1970). Copyright © National Affairs, Inc., 1970.
"Property Rights and Amenity Rights," by Ezra J. Mishan, from *Technology and Growth: The Price We Pay*, Praeger Publishers, Inc., and Staples Press, Ltd.
"Side Effects of Resource Use," by Ralph Turvey, from Henry Jarrett, ed., *Environmental Quality in a Growing Economy* (1966), pp. 3–14. Published for Resources for the Future, Inc., by The Johns Hopkins Press.
"Economics and the Quality of the Environment: Some Empirical Experiences," by Allen V. Kneese, from Morris E. Garnsey and James R. Gibbs, eds., *Social Sciences and the Environment* (1967), pp. 165–82. Used by permission of the Colorado Associated University Press, Boulder, Colorado 80302.
"Air Pollution and Human Health," by Lester B. Lave and Eugene P. Seskin, from *Science*, vol. 169 (August 21, 1970), pp. 723–31. Copyright © 1970 by the American Association for the Advancement of Science.
"Standard-Setting," from *The Politics of Pollution*, by J. Clarence Davies III. Copyright © 1970 by Western Publishing Company, Inc.; reprinted by permission of the Bobbs-Merrill Company, Inc.
"The Delaware Estuary Study: Effluent Charges, Least-Cost Treatment, and Efficiency," by Allen V. Kneese and Blair T. Bower, from *Managing Water Quality: Economics, Technology, and Institutions* (1968), pp. 159–64, 224–34. Published for Resources for the Future, Inc., by The Johns Hopkins Press.

Contents

Introduction

ECOLOGY IS THE STUDY of biological systems of interdependence. The principles governing ecological systems can be illustrated with a simple example. Consider some snails, a tank of water, and algae living in the water. The snails and algae can live in an interdependent balance in which the snails absorb inputs of algae and oxygen from the water, and produce outputs of carbon dioxide and excreta. The algae on the other hand absorb nutrients from the excreta and carbon dioxide from the water and return oxygen and part of their own mass as food to the snails. There is a natural recycling of nutrients and wastes within the system; and the system can indefinitely maintain a state of balance or equilibrium so long as the number of snails is neither too large nor too small relative to the algae.

The human species also interacts with the physical and biological systems of its environment. In this ecological system, man takes in oxygen from the air, water from the rivers and lakes, food and fiber from the biological sphere, and minerals from the land. And man, like a snail, produces waste products which return to the environment. This system can be in balance, like the snail-algae system, as long as there are natural systems which absorb the wastes and transform them into new inputs for man.

Although this book is about economics, this discussion of ecology is pertinent, for we will find that the ecologist's perspective is essential to a better understanding of how man interacts with his environment, and how man can best cope with the problems that he has created.

The ecologist's view of man focuses on the dependence of the human community on the natural environment and the exchanges and flows of food, materials, energy, and waste products between man and nature—or the interdependence and exchange relationships between man and nature. The economist's view of man focuses on the flows of goods and services which take place within the human community among its members. The economic activities of production and consumption lead to interdependence and exchange within the community.

Both points of view are characterized by an attention to specialization of function, exchange relationships, equilibrium or balance of the system, and the more complex dynamic phenomena of growth and succession. However, both points of view are incomplete. In each case insights of considerable richness and value can be gained by adopting the perspective of the other discipline.

The economist focuses on flows among members of the human community. The ecological perspective tells him that these flows of materials and energy come from and inevitably return to the natural environment. The growing problems of pollution and environmental degradation are forcing the economist to study man's exchanges with the environment as well as exchanges with his fellows.

The ecologist focuses on flows between the environment and the human community. The economic perspective teaches him that the nature and magnitude of these flows are determined by the level and nature of economic activity within the human community. Ultimately these flows are determined by the kinds of institutions and mechanisms which man has developed for governing and managing his economic activity.

In Part One three essays by an ecologist and two economists explain and highlight the interconnections between the ecologists' and economists' perspectives on the world. They focus on two dimensions of the environmental problem—the interrelatedness of economic activity and environmental quality, and the failure to develop institutions or mechanisms for managing and controlling the environment.

Garrett Hardin, an ecologist, deals primarily with this second dimension. As Hardin makes clear, the "tragedy of the commons" stems from the absence of any set of institutions or social mechanisms to control our use of or access to scarce environmental resources. The consequence of unrestricted entry is overuse and, ultimately, the destruction of the commons. The tragedy of the commons appears in many forms—the overgrazing of federal lands, crowding in our national parks, and overfishing of the ocean. Pollution is another form, since pollution stems from the unregulated use of the environment as a waste dump. Hardin believes that world population levels are too high now, and continued population growth is unacceptable. Thus, for Hardin, the ultimate commons is existence itself, and the tragedy is the freedom to breed. Several readings in Part Three deal explicitly with the population issues raised by Hardin.

Turning from causes to solutions, Hardin recommends "Mutual coercion, mutually agreed upon by the majority of the people affected." But this prescription leaves unanswered two practical but significant questions. The first is, Can our present political system obtain a majority agreement on an effective plan of coercion? Subsequent readings by Freeman and Haveman and Robert Heilbroner raise some doubts on this question. The second question concerns the forms which coercion can take. Granted that the tragedy arises from the absence of mechanisms for coercion or regulation, what kinds of institutions and mechanisms will be effective in averting the tragedy of the commons? This is one of the major questions posed for environmental policy analysis; and most of the remaining readings touch upon it in varying degrees.

Since its origins, economic thought has been based, implicitly, on the assumption that the economy is an "open system" in which man takes resources from the environment, transforms them, derives services from them, and discards them, and where the resulting changes in the environment can be ignored. But we are becoming painfully aware that our economy does not operate in an open system, and the assumption that it does is no longer tenable or useful. The economics of a "closed system" must be developed. Kenneth Boulding was probably the first economist to appreciate the implications of an ecological perspective for economic thought. He prophesies the fundamental change in our way of looking at the economy and the environment by contrasting the images of the "cowboy economy" of the past and the "spaceman economy" of the future.

Boulding also has some provocative comments on the ultimate objective of economic activity. He suggests that this objective is the maintenance of desirable states or conditions, rather than consumption *per se*. Thus as consumption becomes more costly, both because of increasing scarcity of things to consume and increasing scarcity of places to dispose of the waste products, our objective will be to minimize consumption rather than maximize it. These speculations on the future might well be read again in company with Ayres' and Kneese's discussion of the stationary economy in Part Three.

The third reading of Part One represents an attempt to work out some of the practical implications of the perspectives brought to the environmental problem by Hardin and Boulding. Kneese, Ayres, and D'Arge view the environment as a resource providing many services to man—the air and water essential for life, food and materials, the absorption and carrying off of the waste products of our economic activity, and a variety of recreation and amenity values. Our use of these environmental resources is governed by, among other things, the principle of material balance, which states that when the economy absorbs resources from the environment, it must ultimately return an equal mass of materials to the environment as waste products.

Although private ownership and markets work well in managing and allocating many resources, they fail to work effectively with respect to the environmental resources. Kneese *et al.* provide this volume's first discussion of the concept of externalities or spillover effects and why their presence results in market failure. This is the concept which underlies Hardin's tragedy of the commons; and it is central to the discussion of pollution in Part Two.

POLLUTION

Larry Ruff provides a clear review of several important economic concepts and an overview of the economic aspects of environmental pollution. Taken with the next two papers by Mishan and Turvey, the following tale emerges. The basic institutional mechanism for allocating or managing resources is the system of markets. Markets operate where property rights or rights to ownership are clearly defined. But where property rights are vague, undefined (the commons, again), or unenforceable, there are spillover effects or externalities; social costs diverge from private costs; and market prices fail to provide accurate signals to buyers and sellers to govern their resource allocation decisions. Pollution arises because firms and individuals with waste products to dispose of see the environment as a dump with a zero price. Yet those whose uses of the environment are impaired by the dumping of wastes cannot communicate their desires for a cleaner environment to the polluters. They have no *effective* property rights in the environment.

Ezra Mishan urges that this situation be rectified by granting property rights or amenity rights in a pleasant environment to individuals. However, as the more careful working out of several examples by Ralph Turvey suggests, the problem is not so simple. A major question is the enforceability of property rights. My property rights to my watch and my wallet may be meaningless if there are no police to deter the mugger. Similarly individuals' amenity rights to a clean environment would require a police force to catch and deter those who would steal that clean environment by dumping wastes into it. Turvey describes several methods for dealing with spillover effects, including granting property rights and permitting exchange, direct regulation or coercion, and various tax and subsidy schemes. The important points to consider are that each method has an implied allocation of property rights and associated benefits and costs, and that each situation must be considered in the light of the fairness or equity of this allocation as well as other factors such as the effectiveness and ease of enforceability.

Pollution control is costly. It absorbs resources which could be used to produce other things of value. In a world of scarce resources, it is possible to have too little pollution, i.e., to buy too much pollution control. This would be the case if the last unit of pollution control bought imposed costs which were greater than the benefits received. This point makes clear the necessity for trying to identify and measure the benefits of pollution control. The Council on Environmental Quality has estimated that continued public and private spending for pollution control between 1973 and 1980 will have to total almost $200 billion in order to achieve present air and water quality standards.[1] What will we have bought with this expenditure? Was this a bargain? And should we have spent more? Allen Kneese outlines a conceptual basis for approaching this question. Since man is the measure of all things economic, we must attempt to measure or infer man's willingness to pay for improvements in his environment. Willingness to pay for conventional goods is recorded more or less automatically in the marketplace as a consequence of exchange. But where there are no markets, considerable ingenuity and detective work is necessary for developing willingness-to-pay measures. Kneese outlines some of the difficulties and pitfalls in this work

1. President's Council on Environmental Quality, *Environmental Quality, 1972: 3rd Annual Report* (Washington, D.C., 1972).

and describes some of the limited successes which have been achieved so far.

A major component of pollution damages is the illness and premature death associated with air pollution. At the time that Kneese wrote (1966) very little was known about the relationships between air pollution on the one hand and illness and increased mortality on the other. Significant and pioneering research in this area is reported by Lester Lave and Eugene Seskin. Prior to their work, most of what is known about the effects of air pollution on human beings stemmed from laboratory and clinical work in which subjects were exposed to high levels of air pollution for fairly short periods of time. Clinical effects such as increased heartbeat, high blood pressure, and tissue irritation were noted. But this cumulative body of experimental results bears almost no relationship to what is happening to residents of our polluted cities. They are exposed more or less continuously to levels of air pollution far below those used in the laboratory and for which the immediate effects may not be perceptible even to the individuals or to examining physicians. Only after long periods of exposure do the cumulative effects make themselves known, and then often in subtle and unexpected ways. For example, one of Lave and Seskin's findings is that higher air pollution levels are as likely to be associated with cancer of the stomach as with cancer of the lungs. The Lave-Seskin paper is significant both for its accumulation of a considerable weight of evidence that higher air pollution levels such as those experienced in our dirtier cities is associated with and perhaps causes ill health and higher death rates and for their attempt to put a dollar price tag on these pollution damages.

In addition to identifying and measuring the aggregate levels of damages from various pollutants, we should also be concerned with the incidence of these damages, i.e., who gets hurt. Freeman finds evidence to support the proposition that high income enables its recipients to buy protection from environmental insults such as air pollution, leaving the poor to bear the relatively greater burden. He also examines the likely incidence of pollution control costs and discusses policies to spread these costs more equitably.

Public pressures for pollution control are not waiting while economists develop and refine their monetary measures of pollution control benefits. In the absence of usable monetary measures of damages which can be compared with the cost of pollution control to determine the best level of control, public policy has proceeded by establishing air and water quality standards. Davies explains these standards, shows that they reflect implicit weighing of benefits and costs, and discusses some of the considerations which go into their establishment in practice.

Kneese and Bower report a study which shows: (a) that the establishment of water quality standards can be based on a crude weighing of benefits and costs; (b) that it is possible to calculate the level of effluent charges which is necessary to achieve the desired levels of water quality; (c) that large amounts of money can be saved by achieving these water quality standards at the lowest possible cost; and (d) that effluent charges are likely to achieve water quality standards at much lower costs than alternatives such as uniform treatment.

The two most significant methods for coping with spillover effects from air and water pollution are direct regulation with enforcement and economic incentives such as a tax on pollution. This country's policies for controlling both air and water pollution are based on the regulation-enforcement strategy. Freeman and Haveman review our experience with this strategy in controlling water pollution. They find the strategy lacking both in terms of effectiveness and ability to achieve pollution control at least cost (i.e., economic efficiency). They advocate a switch to the alternative of effluent charges. Their analysis of why regulation-enforcement has failed and their suggestion as to why the effluent charge strategy has not been adopted in its place both have some bearing on the question of "mutual coercion, mutually agreed upon" raised by Hardin.

The two papers by Zwick and Zwick and Benstock can be viewed as a rebuttal to Freeman and Haveman. Both pairs of authors see the discretionary power of enforcers as one of the major villains in the failure to make progress against pollution. But while Freeman and Haveman urge a change in strategies, Zwick and Benstock favor tougher enforcement, and in particular, making prosecution of polluters mandatory.[2]

2. But for a very critical view of this recommendation from another law-yer, see Joseph L. Sax, "Flaws in Public Citizen No. 1," *New Republic*, February 5, 1972, pp. 27–29.

RESOURCES AND POPULATION

Part Three takes up some important long-run questions. As population and economic activity grow over time, how will the associated resource demands from and flows of waste products back to the environment affect the environment and ultimately the human community whose survival is dependent upon it? And how will the physical ecological relationships and the constraints of a finite environment affect the economy over the long run?

The National Academy of Science's Committee on Resources and Man three years ago set out to assess the ultimate capacity of our planet. They state the problem as follows: "Since resources are finite, then, as population increases, the ratio of resources to man must eventually fall to an unacceptable level. This is the crux of the Malthusian dilemma, often evaded but never invalidated." The Committee concludes with pleas for population control and improved resource management programs without delay.

Ansley Coale discusses the role of markets and the price system in managing scarce resources. Of course spillover effects may impede the functioning of the price system. But as Coale points out, the evidence suggests that, except for common property resources, the market has worked well, and that so far technology has succeeded in making resources less scarce rather than more scarce. This suggests that the Malthusian ratio must be expanded to include a growing technology in the numerator. Coale also discusses the question of population policy in the context of the U.S. situation. He argues that there is no urgency in moving to zero population growth.

Most of the developed, industrialized nations have made the "demographic transition" from a state of low population growth with high but matching birth and death rates to a state of low population growth with low birth and death rates. This transition had two important characteristics. It was slow and gradual—taking 150 to 200 years—and the interim was a period of fairly rapid population growth as death rates fell more rapidly than birth rates. This experience stands in contrast to the Malthusian prediction that improved well-being would lead to excessive breeding, with population outstripping resources and pushing the society back to a subsistence level. Richard Easterlin examines the United States experience and tests a hypothesis which seeks to explain why birth rates confounded the Malthusian prediction by falling. Easterlin's analysis suggests that the economic and social factors associated with urbanization and rising real income levels were important influences on fertility in the United States.

In contrast to Ansley Coale, who limited his discussion to the United States, Robert Heilbroner takes a global view of the population question and comes to a much more gloomy conclusion. A doubling of the world population by the turn of the century is unavoidable in the absence of world-wide famine or catastrophe. If all of the world population in the year 2000 were raised to the present levels of income and consumption experienced in the United States, Heilbroner believes that the burdens placed on the environment by the demand for food production, resources, and pollution would greatly exceed the earth's capacity to meet them. But this is an unlikely situation. The real question is whether the population growth of the less developed countries can be slowed sufficiently and the technology and capital stock of these countries expanded sufficiently to provide some expansion in real income and welfare per capita. Questions like this are discouragingly difficult to answer, and the immensity of the task has so far discouraged many of those who have made serious attempts to seek an answer.

Heller discusses, among other things, the costs and benefits of economic growth. In his view the costs are misunderstood and often overstated, while the benefits are ignored or given insufficient weight. And it is the form that economic growth takes rather than the mere fact of growth that is important in assessing the impact of growth on the environment.

The crucial question concerning economic growth and resource adequacy is the role of technology. Has technological change reduced our economic dependency on the natural resource base? Or, as Nordhaus and Tobin pose the question, has technology permitted the substitution of capital for resources on favorable terms? Their econometric analysis of the data leads them to an affirmative answer. And they suggest that the next fifty years is not likely to be radically different from the past fifty years in this regard.

This conclusion stands in stark contrast with the conclusions of Donella and Dennis Meadows. Another stark contrast is in the methods by which they reached their conclusions. The Meadows group constructed a model of the world in which mathematical equations depicted relationships among population, capital stock, technology, pollution, and the resource base. These equations are based on assumptions rather than on detailed empirical estimates of the relationships involved. Their model world is doomed to collapse and death within the next one hundred years. What they regard as massive transfusions of technology in the form of improved pollution control or increased resource base are insufficient to stave off the crisis for more than a few years, and in some cases are counterproductive.

As the review of their book by Passell, Roberts, and Ross suggests, their development and use of the model and the conclusions they reached are highly questionable. The crucial question is, how accurately does their model reflect the real world? For example, contrast the role of technology in the Meadows model with the results of Nordhaus and Tobin. Furthermore it appears that relatively minor changes in the structure of the model can result in significant changes in the results.[3] In other words, the Meadowses' results are far more sensitive to the assumptions made than they let on. On the other hand, they describe a set of policies and adjustments to the model which are required to prevent a crisis and bring the world system into a stable equilibrium. It would be a valuable exercise to speculate on the role of prices and economic adjustment mechanisms in bringing about these changes.

Also it is interesting to contrast the Meadowses' and Heller's views on the effects of growth on equality. Heller argues that continued economic growth is a prerequisite to reducing inequality. But as the Meadowses put it, "One of the most · commonly accepted myths in our present society is the promise that a continuation of our present patterns of growth will lead to human equality." Heller is clearly concerned only with the United States. He assumes that growth will be accompanied by improved mechanisms for redistributing income from the haves to the have-nots within the country. To what extent this will happen in the United States is still an open question. But no such redistributive mechanisms exist on a world-wide basis. Nor is it likely that they will be developed on an adequate scale in the near future. Hence,

3. For example, see Robert Boyd, "World Dynamics: A Note," *Science* 177 (August 11, 1972), 516–19.

the Meadowses, and Heilbroner too, are on solid ground in fear-
ing the consequence of a continuation of the present world-wide
patterns of economic growth.

The Ayres and Kneese contribution to this section is a sober
reflection on the possibilities for and likely consequences of the
long-run evolution to the inevitable zero-growth (in physical
terms) economy. In contrasting the Meadowses and Ayres-Kneese
points of view, it becomes clear that the real differences are
quantitative rather than qualitative in nature. Ayres and Kneese
recognize limitations in technological development. There are
diminishing returns to technology. But the question is, do we run
into these quickly or slowly? There are economic adjustment
mechanisms based on prices and markets. But do these operate
smoothly to reallocate resources, change consumption patterns,
call for products of greatly increased durability, and so on? Or
are the mechanisms too weak to accomplish the needed readjustments in time? And what changes do we need to make in our
institutional structures and policies to make the adjustment mechanisms work better and facilitate the necessary changes? These
are the difficult questions. And now that they have been asked,
we must start the hard work of finding answers.

PRESERVATION

The three papers in the concluding section deal with some of
the issues that arise when narrow economic pressures for development collide with the environmentalist's preservation values.
When scenic areas, unique biological and ecological communities,
or wilderness areas are threatened with destruction through economic development, the controversies can become quite heated.
But in many cases, such as the supersonic transport (SST) and
the Cross-Florida Barge Canal, it is not economic necessity inexorably destroying environmental values. Rather, it is often considerations such as national prestige or the aggrandizement of a
particular bureaucracy that motivate large-scale environmental
insults. Careful and objective economic analysis, which includes
environmental benefits and costs, often shows such projects to be
unjustified on economic grounds.

Krutilla outlines some of the economic benefits which can be
realized by preserving natural environments and ecological sys-

tems. Although it may be difficult to place monetary values on these benefits, the problem is conceptually no different from that of measuring the monetary benefits of pollution control. Krutilla goes on to show how private markets are likely to fail in allocating resources to preservation. Then he suggests that governments may also fail if they tend to make such decisions case by case wholly on the basis of majority rule. Majority rule applied this way may be bad economics. If a 60 percent majority prefers dams and lakes to free-flowing streams, on a case-by-case basis the majority would eventually dam all the streams in the country. But the diminishing marginal utility of the lakes and the increasing scarcity value of rare free-flowing streams provide an economic reason for preserving the minority interest. In this case good economics leads to good ecology.

Alan Carlin shows how the logic and techniques of benefit-cost analysis can be perverted when the analysts overstate benefits and understate costs in an effort to justify a project already selected on other grounds. Of course, this does not mean that benefit-cost analysis is not a potentially valuable contributor to decision-making in the public sector. The results of such an analysis should not be believed merely because they come from an analysis. Benefit-cost analyses published by government agencies should be scrutinized and challenged. They ought to be open and explicit so that their critics can review and possibly refute them. Benefit-cost analysis does not guarantee good answers. At its best, it should provide logical ground rules for constructive debate on the real issues.

The final reading by Charles Cicchetti and A. Myrick Freeman III could be viewed as demonstrating that Carlin's point about benefit-cost analysis also applies to the environmental impact analyses prepared by federal agencies. The authors show how one can use a general conceptual framework for bringing together data on economic benefits and environmental costs in order to make better-informed decisions on issues such as the development of the Alaskan North Slope oil field. Development of that oil would result in substantial economic benefits, but would also have adverse effects on the Arctic environment. Any decision as to whether and how to develop this oil involves a weighing of economic benefits against environmental costs.

The Department of the Interior's environmental impact analysis of the Trans-Alaska Pipeline and its most likely alternative, a pipeline through Canada, concluded that although neither route could be said to be superior in terms of environmental effects, there was a strong case for choosing the Alaskan route on economic and other grounds. Yet Cicchetti and Freeman's analysis, based in large part on the same data, concludes that the economic benefits of the Canadian route are greater and the environmental costs are less, and thus the Canadian route is to be preferred. The authors then suggest that the oil companies continue to press for the Alaskan route because of some special conditions which create a divergence between what is good for the nation and what is good for the oil companies. These conditions were minimized or ignored in the Department of the Interior's Environmental Impact Statement.

This points up the difference between pseudo-analysis for the purpose of justifying decisions already made on other grounds and objective analysis meant to illuminate the problem of choice. And it also indicates that improved environmental management decisions require not only more and better information on benefits and costs, but also improved political and administrative institutions for making these decisions.

PROBLEMS OF THE MODERN ECONOMY

Pollution, Resources, and the Environment

PART ONE Ecology and Economics: Some Perspectives on the Problem

The Tragedy of the Commons

GARRETT HARDIN

Garrett Hardin is professor of biology at the University of California, Santa Barbara. This article, which first appeared in Science *in 1968, is based on a presidential address before the Pacific Division of the American Association for the Advancement of Science.*

AT THE END of a thoughtful article on the future of nuclear war, Wiesner and York[1] concluded that: "Both sides in the arms race are . . . confronted by the dilemma of steadily increasing military power and steadily decreasing national security. *It is our considered professional judgment that this dilemma has no technical solution.* If the great powers continue to look for solutions in the area of science and technology only, the result will be to worsen the situation."

I would like to focus your attention not on the subject of the article (national security in a nuclear world) but on the kind of conclusion they reached, namely that there is no technical solution to the problem. An implicit and almost universal assumption of discussions published in professional and semipopular scientific journals is that the problem under discussion has a technical solution. A technical solution may be defined as one that requires a change only in the techniques of the natural sciences, demand-

1. J. B. Wiesner and H. F. York, *Scientific American* 211, no. 4 (1964), 27.

ing little or nothing in the way of change in human values or ideas of morality.

Because of previous failures in prophecy, it takes courage to assert that a desired technical solution is not possible. Wiesner and York exhibited this courage. Whether they were right or not is not the concern of the present article. Rather, the concern here is with the important concept of a class of human problems which can be called "no technical solution problems," and, more specifically, with the identification and discussion of one of these.

The class of "no technical solution problems" has members. My thesis is that the "population problem," as conventionally conceived, is a member of this class. How it is conventionally conceived needs some comment. It is fair to say that most people who anguish over the population problem are trying to find a way to avoid the evils of overpopulation without relinquishing any of the privileges they now enjoy. They think that farming the seas or developing new strains of wheat will solve the problem—technologically. I try to show here that the solution they seek cannot be found. The population problem cannot be solved in a technical way, any more than can the problem of winning the game of tick-tack-toe.

Population, as Malthus said, naturally tends to grow "geometrically," or, as we would now say, exponentially. In a finite world this means that the per capita share of the world's goods must steadily decrease. Is ours a finite world?

A fair defense can be put forward for the view that the world is infinite; or that we do not know that it is not. But, in terms of the practical problems that we must face in the next few generations with the foreseeable technology, it is clear that we will greatly increase human misery if we do not, during the immediate future, assume that the world available to the terrestrial human population is finite. "Space" is no escape.[2]

A finite world can support only a finite population; therefore, population growth must eventually equal zero. When this condition is met, what will be the situation of mankind? Specifically, can Bentham's goal of "the greatest good for the greatest number" be realized?

No—for two reasons, each sufficient by itself. The first is a

2. G. Hardin, *Journal of Heredity* 50 (1959), 68; S. von Hoernor, *Science* 137 (1962), 18.

theoretical one. It is not mathematically possible to maximize for two (or more) variables at the same time. The second reason springs directly from biological facts. To live, any organism must have a source of energy (for example, food). This energy is utilized for two purposes: mere maintenance and work. For man, maintenance of life requires about 1,600 kilocalories a day ("maintenance calories"). Anything that he does over and above merely staying alive will be defined as work, and is supported by "work calories" which he takes in. Work calories are used not only for what we call work in common speech; they are also required for all forms of enjoyment, from swimming and automobile racing to playing music and writing poetry. If our goal is to maximize population it is obvious what we must do: We must make the work calories per person approach as close to zero as possible. No gourmet meals, no vacations, no sports, no music, no literature, no art. I think that everyone will grant, without argument or proof, that maximizing population does not maximize goods. Bentham's goal is impossible.

In reaching this conclusion I have made the usual assumption that it is the acquisition of energy that is the problem. The appearance of atomic energy has led some to question this assumption. However, given an infinite source of energy, population growth still produces an inescapable problem. The problem of the acquisition of energy is replaced by the problem of its dissipation, as J. H. Fremlin has so wittily shown.[3] The arithmetic signs in the analysis are, as it were, reversed; but Bentham's goal is still unobtainable.

The optimum population is, then, less than the maximum. The difficulty of defining the optimum is enormous; so far as I know, no one has seriously tackled this problem. Reaching an acceptable and stable solution will surely require more than one generation of hard analytical work—and much persuasion. . . .

Has any cultural group solved this practical problem at the present time, even on an intuitive level? One simple fact proves that none has: there is no prosperous population in the world today that has, and has had for some time, a growth rate of zero. Any people that has intuitively identified its optimum point will soon reach it, after which its growth rate becomes and remains zero.

3. J. H. Fremlin, *New Science*, no. 415 (1964), p. 285.

Of course, a positive growth rate might be taken as evidence that a population is below its optimum. However, by any reasonable standards, the most rapidly growing populations on earth today are (in general) the most miserable. This association (which need not be invariable) casts doubt on the optimistic assumption that the positive growth rate of a population is evidence that it has yet to reach its optimum.

We can make little progress in working toward optimum population size until we explicitly exorcise the spirit of Adam Smith in the field of practical demography. In economic affairs, *The Wealth of Nations* (1776) popularized the "invisible hand," the idea that an individual who "intends only his own gain," is, as it were, "led by an invisible hand to promote . . . the public interest." [4] Adam Smith did not assert that this was invariably true, and perhaps neither did any of his followers. But he contributed to a dominant tendency of thought that has ever since interfered with positive action based on rational analysis, namely, the tendency to assume that decisions reached individually will, in fact, be the best decisions for an entire society. If this assumption is correct it justifies the continuance of our present policy of laissez-faire in reproduction. If it is correct we can assume that men will control their individual fecundity so as to produce the optimum population. If the assumption is not correct, we need to reexamine our individual freedoms to see which ones are defensible.

TRAGEDY OF FREEDOM IN A COMMONS

The rebuttal to the invisible hand in population control is to be found in a scenario first sketched in a little known pamphlet [5] in 1833 by a mathematical amateur named William Forster Lloyd (1794–1852). We may well call it "the tragedy of the commons," using the word "tragedy" as the philosopher Whitehead used it: [6] "The essence of dramatic tragedy is not unhappi-

4. A. Smith, *The Wealth of Nations* (New York: Modern Library, 1937), p. 423.

5. W. F. Lloyd, *Two Lectures on the Checks to Population* (Oxford: Oxford University Press, 1833), reprinted (in part) in *Population, Evolution, and Birth Control*, G. Hardin, ed. (San Francisco: Freeman, 1964), p. 37.

6. A. N. Whitehead, *Science and the Modern World* (New York: Mentor, 1948), p. 17.

ness. It resides in the solemnity of the remorseless working of things." He then goes on to say, "This inevitableness of destiny can only be illustrated in terms of human life by incidents which in fact involve unhappiness. For it is only by them that the futility of escape can be made evident in the drama."

The tragedy of the commons develops in this way. Picture a pasture open to all. It is to be expected that each herdsman will try to keep as many cattle as possible on the commons. Such an arrangement may work reasonably satisfactorily for centuries because tribal wars, poaching, and disease keep the numbers of both man and beast well below the carrying capacity of the land. Finally, however, comes the day of reckoning, that is, the day when the long desired goal of social stability becomes a reality. At this point, the inherent logic of the commons remorselessly generates tragedy.

As a rational being, each herdsman seeks to maximize his gain. Explicitly or implicitly, more or less consciously, he asks, "What is the utility *to me* of adding one more animal to my herd?" This utility has one negative and one positive component.

1) The positive component is a function of the increment of one animal. Since the herdsman receives all the proceeds from the sale of the additional animal, the positive utility is nearly + 1.

2) The negative component is a function of the additional overgrazing created by one more animal. Since, however, the effects of overgrazing are shared by all the herdsmen, the negative utility for any particular decision-making herdsman is only a fraction of −1.

Adding together the component partial utilities, the rational herdsman concludes that the only sensible course for him to pursue is to add another animal to his herd. And another; and another. But this is the conclusion reached by each and every rational herdsman sharing a commons. Therein is the tragedy. Each man is locked into a system that compels him to increase his herd without limit—in a world that is limited. Ruin is the destination toward which all men rush, each pursuing his own best interest in a society that believes in the freedom of the commons. Freedom in a commons brings ruin to all.

Some would say that this is a platitude. Would that it were! In a sense, it was learned thousands of years ago, but natural selection favors the forces of psychological denial.[7] The individual benefits as an individual from his ability to deny the truth even though society as a whole, of which he is a part, suffers. Education can counteract the natural tendency to do the wrong thing, but the inexorable succession of generations requires that the basis for this knowledge be constantly refreshed.

In an approximate way, the logic of the commons has been understood for a long time, perhaps since the discovery of agriculture or the invention of private property in real estate. But it is understood mostly only in special cases which are not sufficiently generalized. Even at this late date, cattlemen leasing national land on the western ranges demonstrate no more than an ambivalent understanding, in constantly pressuring federal authorities to increase the head count to the point where overgrazing produces erosion and weed-dominance. Likewise, the oceans of the world continue to suffer from the survival of the philosophy of the commons. Maritime nations still respond automatically to the shibboleth of the "freedom of the seas." Professing to believe in the "inexhaustible resources of the oceans," they bring species after species of fish and whales closer to extinction.[8]

The National Parks present another instance of the working out of the tragedy of the commons. At present, they are open to all, without limit. The parks themselves are limited in extent—there is only one Yosemite Valley—whereas population seems to grow without limit. The values that visitors seek in the parks are steadily eroded. Plainly, we must soon cease to treat the parks as commons or they will be of no value to anyone.

What shall we do? We have several options. We might sell them off as private property. We might keep them as public property, but allocate the right to enter them. The allocation might be on the basis of wealth, by the use of an auction system. It might be on the basis of merit, as defined by some agreed-upon standards. It might be by lottery. Or it might be on a first-come, first-served basis, administered to long queues. These, I think, are all the reasonable possibilities. They are all objectionable. But we must choose—or acquiesce in the destruction of the commons that we call our National Parks.

7. G. Hardin, ed., *Population, Evolution, and Birth Control,* p. 56.
8. S. McVay, *Scientific American* 216, no. 8 (1966), 13.

POLLUTION

In a reverse way, the tragedy of the commons reappears in problems of pollution. Here it is not a question of taking something out of the commons, but of putting something in—sewage, or chemical, radioactive, and heat wastes into water; noxious and dangerous fumes into the air; and distracting and unpleasant advertising signs into the line of sight. The calculations of utility are much the same as before. The rational man finds that his share of the cost of the wastes he discharges into the commons is less than the cost of purifying his wastes before releasing them. Since this is true for everyone, we are locked into a system of "fouling our own nest," so long as we behave only as independent, rational, free-enterprisers.

The tragedy of the commons as a food basket is averted by private property, or something formally like it. But the air and waters surrounding us cannot readily be fenced, and so the tragedy of the commons as a cesspool must be prevented by different means, by coercive laws or taxing devices that make it cheaper for the polluter to treat his pollutants than to discharge them untreated. We have not progressed as far with the solution of this problem as we have with the first. Indeed, our particular concept of private property, which deters us from exhausting the positive resources of the earth, favors pollution. The owner of a factory on the bank of a stream—whose property extends to the middle of the stream—often has difficulty seeing why it is not his natural right to muddy the waters flowing past his door. The law, always behind the times, requires elaborate stitching and fitting to adapt it to this newly perceived aspect of the commons.

The pollution problem is a consequence of population. It did not much matter how a lonely American frontiersman disposed of his waste. "Flowing water purifies itself every ten miles," my grandfather used to say, and the myth was near enough to the truth when he was a boy, for there were not too many people. But as population became denser, the natural chemical and biological recycling processes became overloaded, calling for a redefinition of property rights. . . .

FREEDOM TO BREED IS INTOLERABLE

The tragedy of the commons is involved in population problems in another way. In a world governed solely by the principle of "dog eat dog"—if indeed there ever was such a world—how many children a family had would not be a matter of public concern. Parents who bred too exuberantly would leave fewer descendants, not more, because they would be unable to care adequately for their children. David Lack and others have found that such a negative feedback demonstrably controls the fecundity of birds.[9] But men are not birds, and have not acted like them for millenniums, at least.

If each human family were dependent only on its own resources; if the children of improvident parents starved to death; if, thus, overbreeding brought its own "punishment" to the germ line—then there would be no public interest in controlling the breeding of families. But our society is deeply committed to the welfare state,[10] and hence is confronted with another aspect of the tragedy of the commons.

In a welfare state, how shall we deal with the family, the religion, the race, or the class (or indeed any distinguishable and cohesive group) that adopts overbreeding as a policy to secure its own aggrandizement?[11] To couple the concept of freedom to breed with the belief that everyone born has an equal right to the commons is to lock the world into a tragic course of action.

Unfortunately this is just the course of action that is being pursued by the United Nations. In late 1967, some thirty nations agreed to the following:

The Universal Declaration of Human Rights describes the family as the natural and fundamental unit of society. It follows that any choice and decision with regard to the size of the family must irrevocably rest with the family itself, and cannot be made by anyone else.[12]

9. D. Lack, *The Natural Regulation of Animal Numbers* (Oxford: Clarendon Press, 1954).
10. H. Girvetz, *From Wealth to Welfare* (Stanford, Calif.: Stanford University Press, 1950).
11. G. Hardin, *Perspectives in Biological Medicine* 6 (1963), 366.
12. U Thant, *International Planned Parenthood News*, no. 168 (February 1968), p. 3.

It is painful to have to deny categorically the validity of this right. However, let us not forget what Robert Louis Stevenson said: "The truth that is suppressed by friends is the readiest weapon of the enemy." If we love the truth we must openly deny the validity of the Universal Declaration of Human Rights, even though it is promoted by the United Nations. We should also join with Kingsley Davis [13] in attempting to get Planned Parenthood–World Population to see the error of its ways in embracing the same tragic ideal.

CONSCIENCE IS SELF-ELIMINATING

It is a mistake to think that we can control the breeding of mankind in the long run by an appeal to conscience. Charles Galton Darwin made this point when he spoke on the centennial of the publication of his grandfather's great book. The argument is straightforward and Darwinian.

People vary. Confronted with appeals to limit breeding, some people will undoubtedly respond to the plea more than others. Those who have more children will produce a larger fraction of the next generation than those with more susceptible consciences. The difference will be accentuated, generation by generation.

In C. G. Darwin's words: "It may well be that it would take hundreds of generations for the progenitive instinct to develop in this way, but if it should do so, nature would have taken her revenge, and the variety *Homo contracipiens* would become extinct and would be replaced by the variety *Homo progenitivus*." [14]

The argument assumes that conscience or the desire for children (no matter which) is hereditary—but hereditary only in the most general formal sense. The result will be the same whether the attitude is transmitted through germ cells, or exosomatically, to use A. J. Lotka's term. (If one denies the latter possibility as well as the former, then what's the point of education?) The argument has here been stated in the context of the population problem, but it applies equally well to any instance

13. K. Davis, *Science* 158 (1967), 730.
14. S. Tax, ed., *Evolution after Darwin* (Chicago: University of Chicago Press, 1960), vol. 2, p. 469.

in which society appeals to an individual exploiting a commons to restrain himself for the general good—by means of his conscience. To make such an appeal is to set up a selective system that works toward the elimination of conscience from the race.

The long-term disadvantage of an appeal to conscience should be enough to condemn it, but it has serious short-term disadvantages as well. If we ask a man who is exploiting a commons to desist "in the name of conscience," what are we saying to him? What does he hear?—not only at the moment but also in the wee small hours of the night when, half asleep, he remembers not merely the words we used but also the nonverbal communication cues we gave him unawares? Sooner or later, consciously or subconsciously, he senses that he has received two communications, and that they are contradictory:

(1) (intended communication) "If you don't do as we ask, we will openly condemn you for not acting like a responsible citizen"; (2) (unintended communication) "If you *do* behave as we ask, we will secretly condemn you for a simpleton who can be shamed into standing aside while the rest of us exploit the commons."

To conjure up a conscience in others is tempting to anyone who wishes to extend his control beyond the legal limits. Leaders at the highest level succumb to this temptation. Has any president during the past generation failed to call on labor unions to moderate voluntarily their demands for higher wages, or to steel companies to honor voluntary guidelines on prices? I can recall none. The rhetoric used on such occasions is designed to produce feelings of guilt in noncooperators. . . .

We hear much talk these days of responsible parenthood: the coupled words are incorporated into the titles of some organizations devoted to birth control. Some people have proposed massive propaganda campaigns to instill responsibility into the nation's (or the world's) breeders. But what is the meaning of the word responsibility in this context? Is it not merely a synonym for the word conscience? When we use the word responsibility in the absence of substantial sanctions are we not trying to browbeat a free man in a commons into acting against his own interest? Responsibility is a verbal counterfeit for a substantial *quid pro quo*. It is an attempt to get something for nothing.

If the word responsibility is to be used at all, I suggest that it be in the sense Charles Frankel uses it.[15] "Responsibility," says this philosopher, "is the product of definite social arrangements." Notice that Frankel calls for social arrangements—not propaganda.

MUTUAL COERCION, MUTUALLY AGREED UPON

The social arrangements that produce responsibility are arrangements that create coercion, of some sort. Consider bank-robbing. The man who takes money from a bank acts as if the bank were a commons. How do we prevent such action? Certainly not by trying to control his behavior solely by a verbal appeal to his sense of responsibility. Rather than rely on propaganda we follow Frankel's lead and insist that a bank is not a commons; we seek the definite social arrangements that will keep it from becoming a commons. That we thereby infringe on the freedom of would-be robbers we neither deny nor regret.

The morality of bank-robbing is particularly easy to understand because we accept complete prohibition of this activity. We are willing to say "Thou shalt not rob banks," without providing for exceptions. But temperance also can be created by coercion. Taxing is a good coercive device. To keep downtown shoppers temperate in their use of parking space we introduce parking meters for short periods, and traffic fines for longer ones. We need not actually forbid a citizen to park as long as he wants to; we need merely make it increasingly expensive for him to do so. Not prohibition, but carefully biased options are what we offer him. A Madison Avenue man might call this persuasion; I prefer the greater candor of the word coercion.

Coercion is a dirty word to most liberals now, but it need not forever be so. As with the four-letter words, its dirtiness can be cleansed away by exposure to the light, by saying it over and over without apology or embarrassment. To many, the word coercion implies arbitrary decisions of distant and irresponsible bureaucrats; but this is not a necessary part of its meaning. The only kind of coercion I recommend is mutual coercion, mutually agreed upon by the majority of the people affected.

To say that we mutually agree to coercion is not to say that

15. C. Frankel, *The Case for Modern Man* (New York: Harper, 1955), p. 203.

we are required to enjoy it, or even to pretend we enjoy it. Who enjoys taxes? We all grumble about them. But we accept compulsory taxes because we recognize that voluntary taxes would favor the conscienceless. We institute and (grumblingly) support taxes and other coercive devices to escape the horror of the commons. . . .

RECOGNITION OF NECESSITY

Perhaps the simplest summary of this analysis of man's population problems is this: the commons, if justifiable at all, is justifiable only under conditions of low-population density. As the human population has increased, the commons has had to be abandoned in one aspect after another.

First we abandoned the commons in food gathering, enclosing farm land and restricting pastures and hunting and fishing areas. These restrictions are still not complete throughout the world.

Somewhat later we saw that the commons as a place for waste disposal would also have to be abandoned. Restrictions on the disposal of domestic sewage are widely accepted in the Western world; we are still struggling to close the commons to pollution by automobiles, factories, insecticide sprayers, fertilizing operations, and atomic energy installations.

In a still more embryonic state is our recognition of the evils of the commons in matters of pleasure. There is almost no restriction on the propagation of sound waves in the public medium. The shopping public is assaulted with mindless music, without its consent. Our government is paying out billions of dollars to create supersonic transport which will disturb 50,000 people for every one person who is whisked from coast to coast three hours faster. Advertisers muddy the airwaves of radio and television and pollute the view of travelers. We are a long way from outlawing the commons in matters of pleasure. Is this because our Puritan inheritance makes us view pleasure as something of a sin, and pain (that is, the pollution of advertising) as the sign of virtue?

Every new enclosure of the commons involves the infringement of somebody's personal liberty. Infringements made in the distant past are accepted because no contemporary complains of a loss. It is the newly proposed infringements that we vigorously oppose; cries of "rights" and "freedom" fill the air. But what does "freedom" mean? When men mutually agreed to pass laws against robbing, mankind became more free, not less so. Individuals locked into the logic of the commons are free only to bring on universal ruin; once they see the necessity of mutual coercion, they become free to pursue other goals. I believe it was Hegel who said, "Freedom is the recognition of necessity."

The most important aspect of necessity that we must now recognize is the necessity of abandoning the commons in breeding. No technical solution can rescue us from the misery of overpopulation. Freedom to breed will bring ruin to all. At the moment, to avoid hard decisions many of us are tempted to propagandize for conscience and responsible parenthood. The temptation must be resisted, because an appeal to independently acting consciences selects for the disappearance of all conscience in the long run, and an increase in anxiety in the short.

The only way we can preserve and nurture other and more precious freedoms is by relinquishing the freedom to breed, and that very soon. "Freedom is the recognition of necessity"— and it is the role of education to reveal to all the necessity of abandoning the freedom to breed. Only so can we put an end to this aspect of the tragedy of the commons.

The Economics of the Coming Spaceship Earth

KENNETH E. BOULDING

Kenneth Boulding was elected president of the American Economic Association in 1968. He has written a number of books on economics. Professor Boulding teaches economics at the University of Colorado. This article was published in Environmental Quality in a Growing Economy, *edited by Henry Jarrett.*

WE ARE NOW in the middle of a long process of transition in the nature of the image which man has of himself and his environment. Primitive men, and to a large extent also men of the early civilizations, imagined themselves to be living on a virtually illimitable plane. There was almost always somewhere beyond the known limits of human habitation, and over a very large part of the time that man has been on earth, there has been something like a frontier. That is, there was always some place else to go when things got too difficult, either by reason of the deterioration of the natural environment or a deterioration of the social structure in places where people happened to live. The image of the frontier is probably one of the oldest images of mankind, and it is not surprising that we find it hard to get rid of.

Gradually, however, man has been accustoming himself to the notion of the spherical earth and a closed sphere of human activity. A few unusual spirits among the ancient Greeks perceived that the earth was a sphere. It was only with the circumnavigations and the geographical explorations of the fifteenth and sixteenth centuries, however, that the fact that the earth was a sphere became at all widely known and accepted. Even in the nineteenth century, the commonest map was Mercator's projection, which visualizes the earth as an illimitable cylinder, essentially a plane wrapped around the globe, and it was not until the Second World War and the development of the air age that the global nature of the planet really entered the popular imagination. Even now we are very far from having made the moral,

14

political, and psychological adjustments which are implied in this transition from the illimitable plane to the closed sphere.

Economists in particular, for the most part, have failed to come to grips with the ultimate consequences of the transition from the open to the closed earth. One hesitates to use the terms "open" and "closed" in this connection, as they have been used with so many different shades of meaning. Nevertheless, it is hard to find equivalents. The open system implies that some kind of structure is maintained in the midst of a throughput from inputs to outputs. In a closed system, the outputs of all parts of the system are linked to the inputs of other parts. There are no inputs from outside and no outputs to the outside; indeed, there is no outside at all. . . . All living organisms, including man himself, are open systems. They have to receive inputs in the shape of air, food, water, and give off outputs in the form of effluvia and excrement. Deprivation of input of air, even for a few minutes, is fatal. Deprivation of the ability to obtain any input or to dispose of any output is fatal in a relatively short time. All human societies have likewise been open systems. They receive inputs from the earth, the atmosphere, and the waters, and they give outputs into these reservoirs; they also produce inputs internally in the shape of babies and outputs in the shape of corpses. Given a capacity to draw upon inputs and to get rid of outputs, an open system of this kind can persist indefinitely. . . .

Systems may be open or closed in respect to a number of classes of inputs and outputs. Three important classes are matter, energy, and information. The present world economy is open in regard to all three. We can think of the world economy or "econosphere" as a subset of the "world set," which is the set of all objects of possible discourse in the world. We then think of the state of the econosphere at any one moment as being the total capital stock; that is, the set of all objects, people, organizations, and so on, which are interesting from the point of view of the system of exchange. This total stock of capital is clearly an open system in the sense that it has inputs and outputs, inputs being production which adds to the capital stock, outputs being consumption which subtracts from it. From a material point of view, we see objects passing from the noneconomic into the economic set in the process of production, and we similarly see products passing out of the economic set as their value becomes zero. Thus we see the econosphere as a material process involving the discovery and mining of fossil fuels, ores, etc., and at the other end a process by which the effluents of the system are passed out into noneconomic reservoirs—for instance, the atmosphere and the oceans—which are not appropriated and do not enter into the exchange system.

From the point of view of the energy system, the econosphere involves inputs of available energy in the form, say, of water power, fossil fuels, or sunlight, which are necessary in order to create the material throughput and to move matter from the noneconomic set into the economic set or even out of it again; and energy itself is given off by the system in a less available form, mostly in the form of heat. These inputs of available energy must come either from the sun or from the earth itself, either through its internal heat or through its energy or rotation or other motions, which generate, for instance, the energy of the tides. Agriculture, a few solar machines, and water power use the current available energy income. In advanced societies this is supplemented very extensively by the use of fossil fuels, which represent as it were a capital stock of stored-up sunshine. Because of this capital stock of energy, we have been able to maintain an energy input into the system, particularly over the last two centuries, much larger than we would have been able to do with existing techniques if we had had to rely on the current input of available energy from the sun or the earth itself. This supplementary input, however, is by its very nature exhaustible.

The inputs and outputs of information are more subtle and harder to trace, but also represent an open system, related to, but not wholly dependent on, the transformations of matter and energy. By far the larger amount of information and knowledge is self-generated by the human society, though a certain amount of information comes into the sociosphere in the form of light from the universe outside. . . .

From the human point of view, knowledge or information is by far the most important of the three systems. Matter only acquires significance and only enters the sociosphere or the econosphere insofar as it becomes an object of human knowledge. We can think of capital, indeed, as frozen knowledge or knowledge imposed on the material world in the form of improbable arrangements. A machine, for instance, originated in the mind of man, and both its construction and its use involve information processes imposed on the material world by man himself. The cumulation of knowledge, that is, the excess of its production over its consumption, is the key to human development of all kinds, especially to economic development. We can see this preeminence of knowledge very clearly in the experiences of countries where the material capital has been destroyed by a war, as in Japan and Germany. The knowledge of the people was not destroyed, and it did not take long, therefore, certainly not more than ten years, for most of the material capital to be reestablished again. In a country such as Indonesia, however, where the knowledge did not exist, the material capital did not come into being either. By "knowledge" here I mean, of course, the whole cognitive structure, which includes valuations and motivations as well as images of the factual world.

The concept of entropy, used in a somewhat loose sense, can be applied to all three of these open systems. In the case of material systems, we can distinguish between entropic processes, which take concentrated materials and diffuse them through the oceans or over the earth's surface into the atmosphere, and anti-entropic processes, which take diffuse materials and concentrate them. Material entropy can be taken as a measure of the uniformity of the distribution of elements and, more uncertainly, compounds and other structures on the earth's surface. There is, fortunately, no law of increasing material entropy, as there is in the corresponding case of energy, as it is quite possible to concentrate diffused materials if energy inputs are allowed. Thus the processes for fixation of nitrogen from the air, processes for the extraction of magnesium or other elements from the sea, and processes for the desalinization of sea water are anti-entropic in the material sense, though the reduction of material entropy has to be paid for by inputs of energy and also inputs of information, or at least a stock of information in the system. In regard to matter, therefore, a closed system is conceivable; that is, a system in which there is neither increase nor decrease in material entropy. In such a system all outputs from consumption would constantly be recycled to become inputs for production, as, for instance, nitrogen in the nitrogen cycle of the natural ecosystem.

In regard to the energy system there is, unfortunately, no escape from the grim Second Law of Thermodynamics; and if there were no energy inputs into the earth, any evolutionary or developmental process would be impossible. The large energy inputs which we have obtained from fossil fuels are strictly temporary. Even the most optimistic predictions would expect the easily available supply of fossil fuels to be exhausted in a mere matter of centuries at present rates of use. If the rest of the world were to rise to American standards of power consumption, and still more if world population continues to increase, the exhaustion of fossil fuels would be even more rapid. The development of nuclear energy has improved this picture, but has not fundamentally altered it, at least in present technologies, for fissionable material is still relatively scarce. If we should achieve the economic use of energy through fusion, of course, a much larger source of energy materials would be available, which would expand the time horizons of supplementary energy input into an open social system by perhaps tens to hundreds of thousands of years. Failing this, however, the time is not very far distant, historically speaking, when man will once more have to retreat to his current energy input from the sun, even though this could be used much more effectively than in the past with increased knowledge. Up to now, certainly, we have not got very far with the technology of using current solar energy, but the possibility of substantial improvements in the future is certainly high. It may be, indeed, that the biological revolution which is just beginning will produce a solution to this problem, as we develop artificial organisms which are capable of much more efficient transformation of solar energy into easily available forms than any that we now have. As Richard Meier has suggested, we may run our machines in the future with methane-producing algae. . . .[1]

The closed earth of the future requires economic principles which are somewhat different from those of the open earth of the past. For the sake of picturesqueness, I am tempted to call the open economy the "cowboy economy," the cowboy being symbolic of the illimitable plains and also associated with reckless, exploitative, romantic, and violent behavior, which is char-

1. Richard L. Meier, *Science and Economic Development* (New York: Wiley, 1956).

acteristic of open societies. The closed economy of the future might similarly be called the "spaceman economy," in which the earth has become a single spaceship, without unlimited reservoirs of anything, either for extraction or for pollution, and in which, therefore, man must find his place in a cyclical ecological system which is capable of continuous reproduction of material form even though it cannot escape having inputs of energy. The difference between the two types of economy becomes most apparent in the attitude toward consumption. In the cowboy economy, consumption is regarded as a good thing and production likewise; and the success of the economy is measured by the amount of the throughput from the "factors of production," a part of which, at any rate, is extracted from the reservoirs of raw materials and noneconomic objects, and another part of which is output into the reservoirs of pollution. If there are infinite reservoirs from which material can be obtained and into which effluvia can be deposited, then the throughput is at least a plausible measure of the success of the economy. The gross national product is a rough measure of this total throughput. It should be possible, however, to distinguish that part of the GNP which is derived from exhaustible and that which is derived from reproducible resources, as well as that part of consumption which represents effluvia and that which represents input into the productive system again. Nobody, as far as I know, has ever attempted to break down the GNP in this way, although it would be an interesting and extremely important exercise, which is unfortunately beyond the scope of this paper.

By contrast, in the spaceman economy, throughput is by no means a desideratum, and is indeed to be regarded as something to be minimized rather than maximized. The essential measure of the success of the economy is not production and consumption at all, but the nature, extent, quality, and complexity of the total capital stock, including in this the state of the human bodies and minds included in the system. In the spaceman economy, what we are primarily concerned with is stock maintenance, and any technological change which results in the maintenance of a given total stock with a lessened throughput (that is, less production and consumption) is clearly a gain. This idea that both production and consumption are bad things rather than good things is very strange to economists, who have been obsessed with the income-flow concepts to the exclusion, almost, of capital-stock concepts.

There are actually some very tricky and unsolved problems involved in the questions as to whether human welfare or well-being is to be regarded as a stock or a flow. Something of both these elements seems actually to be involved in it, and as far as I know there have been practically no studies directed toward identifying these two dimensions of human satisfaction. Is it, for instance, eating that is a good thing, or is it being well fed? Does economic welfare involve having nice clothes, fine houses, good equipment, and so on, or is it to be measured by the depreciation and the wearing out of these things? I am inclined myself to regard the stock concept as most fundamental; that is, to think of being well fed as more important than eating, and to think even of so-called services as essentially involving the restoration of a depleting psychic capital. Thus I have argued that we go to a concert in order to restore a psychic condition which might be called "just having gone to a concert," which, once established, tends to depreciate. When it depreciates beyond a certain point, we go to another concert in order to restore it. If it depreciates rapidly, we go to a lot of concerts; if it depreciates slowly, we go to few. On this view, similarly, we eat primarily to restore bodily homeostasis, that is, to maintain a condition of being well fed, and so on. On this view, there is nothing desirable in consumption at all. The less consumption we can maintain a given state with, the better off we are. If we had clothes that did not wear out, houses that did not depreciate, and even if we could maintain our bodily condition without eating, we would clearly be much better off.

It is this last consideration, perhaps, which makes one pause. Would we, for instance, really want an operation that would enable us to restore all our bodily tissues by intravenous feeding while we slept? Is there not, that is to say, a certain virtue in throughput itself, in activity itself, in production and consumption itself, in raising food and in eating it? It would certainly be rash to exclude this possibility. Further interesting problems are raised by the demand for variety. We certainly do not want a constant state to be maintained; we want fluctuations in the state. Otherwise there would be no demand for variety in food, for variety in scene, as in travel, for variety in social contact, and so on. The demand for variety can, of course, be costly, and sometimes it seems to be too costly to be tolerated or at least legitimated, as in the case of marital partners, where the maintenance of a homeostatic state in the family is usually regarded as much more desirable than the variety and excessive throughput of the libertine. There are problems here which the economics profession has neglected with astonishing singlemindedness. My own attempts to call attention to some of them, for instance, in two articles,[2] as far as I can judge, produced no response whatever; and economists continue to think and act as if production, consumption, throughput, and the GNP were the sufficient and adequate measure of economic success.

It may be said, of course, why worry about all this when the spaceman economy is still a good way off (at least beyond the lifetimes of any now living), so let us eat, drink, spend, extract, and pollute, and be as merry as we can, and let posterity worry about the spaceship earth. It is always a little hard to find a convincing answer to the man who says, "What has posterity ever done for me?" . . . Should we just go on increasing the GNP and indeed the gross world product, or GWP, in the expectation that the problems of the future can be left to the future, that when scarcities arise, whether this is of raw materials or of pollutable reservoirs, the needs of the then present will determine the solutions of the then present, and there is no use giving ourselves ulcers by worrying about problems that we really do not have to solve? There is even high ethical authority for this point of view in the New Testament, which advocates that we should take no thought for tomorrow and let the dead bury their dead. There has always been something rather refreshing in the view that we should live like the birds, and perhaps posterity is for the birds in more senses than one; so perhaps we should all call it a day and go out and pollute something cheerfully. As an old taker of thought for the morrow, however, I cannot quite accept this solution; and I would argue, furthermore, that tomorrow is not only very close, but in many respects it is already here. The shadow of the future spaceship, indeed, is already falling over our spendthrift merriment. Oddly enough,

2. K. E. Boulding, "The Consumption Concept in Economic Theory," *American Economic Review* 35, no. 2 (May 1945), 1–14; and "Income or Welfare?," *Review of Economic Studies* 17 (1949–50), 77–86.

it seems to be in pollution rather than in exhaustion that the problem is first becoming salient. Los Angeles has run out of air, Lake Erie has become a cesspool, the oceans are getting full of lead and DDT, and the atmosphere may become man's major problem in another generation, at the rate at which we are filling it up with gunk. It is, of course, true that at least on a microscale, things have been worse at times in the past. The cities of today, with all their foul air and polluted waterways, are probably not as bad as the filthy cities of the pretechnical age. Nevertheless, that fouling of the nest which has been typical of man's activity in the past on a local scale now seems to be extending to the whole world society; and one certainly cannot view with equanimity the present rate of pollution of any of the natural reservoirs, whether the atmosphere, the lakes, or even the oceans.

I would argue strongly also that our obsession with production and consumption to the exclusion of the "state" aspects of human welfare distorts the process of technological change in a most undesirable way. We are all familiar, of course, with the wastes involved in planned obsolescence, in competitive advertising, and in poor quality of consumer goods. These problems may not be so important as the "view with alarm" school indicates, and indeed the evidence at many points is conflicting. New materials especially seem to edge toward the side of improved durability, such as, for instance, neolite soles for footwear, nylon socks, wash and wear shirts, and so on. The case of household equipment and automobiles is a little less clear. Housing and building construction generally almost certainly has declined in durability since the Middle Ages, but this decline also reflects a change in tastes toward flexibility and fashion and a need for novelty, so that it is not easy to assess. What is clear is that no serious attempt has been made to assess the impact over the whole of economic life of changes in durability, that is, in the ratio of capital in the widest possible sense to income. I suspect that we have underestimated, even in our spendthrift society, the gains from increased durability, and that this might very well be one of the places where the price system needs correction through government-sponsored research and development. The problems which the spaceship earth is going to present, therefore, are not all in the future by any means, and a strong case can be made for paying much more attention to them in the present than we now do.

It may be complained that the considerations I have been putting forth relate only to the very long run, and they do not much concern our immediate problems. There may be some justice in this criticism, and my main excuse is that other writers have dealt adequately with the more immediate problems of deterioration in the quality of the environment. It is true, for instance, that many of the immediate problems of pollution of the atmosphere or of bodies of water arise because of the failure of the price system, and many of them could be solved by corrective taxation. If people had to pay the losses due to the nuisances which they create, a good deal more resources would go into the prevention of nuisances. These arguments involving external economies and diseconomies [3] are familiar to economists, and there is no need to recapitulate them. The law of torts is quite inadequate to provide for the correction of the price system which is required, simply because where damages are widespread and their incidence on any particular person is small, the ordinary remedies of the civil law are quite inadequate and inappropriate. There needs, therefore, to be special legislation to cover these cases, and though such legislation seems hard to get in practice, mainly because of the widespread and small personal incidence of the injuries, the technical problems involved are not insuperable. If we were to adopt in principle a law for tax penalties for social damages, with an apparatus for making assessments under it, a very large proportion of current pollution and deterioration of the environment would be prevented. There are tricky problems of equity involved, particularly where old established nuisances create a kind of "right by purchase" to perpetuate themselves, but these are problems again which a few rather arbitrary decisions can bring to some kind of solution.

The problems which I have been raising in this paper are of larger scale and perhaps much harder to solve than the more practical and immediate problems of the above paragraph. Our success in dealing with the larger problems, however, is not un-

---

3. [These concepts are explained in the next reading. *Editors.*]

related to the development of skill in the solution of the more immediate and perhaps less difficult problems. One can hope, therefore, that as a succession of mounting crises, especially in pollution, arouse public opinion and mobilize support for the solution of the immediate problems, a learning process will be set in motion which will eventually lead to an appreciation of and perhaps solutions for the larger ones. My neglect of the immediate problems, therefore, is in no way intended to deny their importance, for unless we at least make a beginning on a process for solving the immediate problems we will not have much chance of solving the larger ones. On the other hand, it may also be true that a long-run vision, as it were, of the deep crisis which faces mankind may predispose people to taking more interest in the immediate problems and to devote more effort for their solution. This may sound like a rather modest optimism, but perhaps a modest optimism is better than no optimism at all.

Economics and the Environment:
A Materials Balance Approach

ALLEN V. KNEESE, ROBERT U. AYRES, and
RALPH C. D'ARGE

*Allen V. Kneese is director of the Environmental Quality Program
at Resources for the Future, Inc., a Washington-based research
organization. Dr. Ayres is a physicist with International Research
and Technology Corporation, Washington. Professor D'Arge is at
the University of California, Riverside. This paper is adapted from
the first chapter of their book of the same title.*

PRELUDE—ECONOMIC THEORY AND MATERIAL THINGS

THE HUNTER is camped on a great plain with a small fire providing a flickering light and intermittent warmth. Tiny wisps of smoke ascend into a vast, clear night sky. Tomorrow the hunter will move, leaving behind ashes, food scraps, and his own excreta. After ten steps these are lost from sight and smell, probably forever. With them he leaves too his brief speculation about sky and earth, brought on by the loneliness of night, and he peers toward the horizon in search of prey.

The Administrator of the World Environment Control Authority sits at his desk. Along one wall of the huge room are real-time displays, processed by computer from satellite data, of developing atmospheric and ocean patterns, as well as the flow, and quality conditions of the world's great river systems. In an instant, the Administrator can shift from real-time mode to simulation to test the larger effects of changes in emissions of material residuals and heat to water and atmosphere at control points generally corresponding to the locations of the world's great cities and the transport movements among them. In a few seconds the computer displays information in color code for various time periods—hourly, daily, or yearly phases at the Administrator's option. It automatically does this for current steady state and simulated future conditions of emissions, water flow regulation, and atmospheric conditions. Observing a dangerous reddish glow in the eastern Mediterranean, the Administrator dials sub-control station Athens and orders a step-up of removal by the liquid residuals handling plants there. Over northern Europe, the brown smudge of a projected air quality standards violation appears and sub-control point Essen is ordered to take the Ruhr area off sludge incineration for 25 hours but is advised that temporary storage followed by accelerated incineration—but with muffling—after 24 hours will be admissible. The CO_2 simulator now warns the Administrator that another upweller must be brought on line in the Murray Fracture Zone within two years if the internationally agreed balance of CO_2 and oxygen is to be maintained in the atmosphere.

These are extremes of interactions of man with his natural environment. But surely everyone would agree that actuality is much closer to the latter than to the former end of this spectrum. It appears, however, that our concepts of law and economics are somewhere in the middle. These are rooted in the idea that property and private two-party exchange can satisfactorily solve almost all resources allocation problems. Instances of air and water pollution have been regarded as somewhat unusual aberrations which can be satisfactorily treated in an ad hoc and specific way—not as problems of resources allocation on a massive scale.

EXTERNALITIES AND ECONOMIC THEORY

Economic theory has long recognized in a limited way the existence of "common property" problems and resource misallocations associated with them. It was early appreciated that when property rights to a valuable resource could not be parceled out in such a way that one participant's activities in the use of that resource would leave the others unaffected, except through market exchange, unregulated private exchange would lead to inefficiencies. These inefficiencies were of two types: those associated with "externalities" and those associated with "user costs." The former term refers to certain broader costs (or benefits) of individual action which are not taken into account in deciding to take that action. For instance, the individual crude petroleum producer, pumping from a common pool, has no market incentive to take account of the increased cost imposed on others because of reduced gas pressure resulting from his own pumping. Also, because he cannot be sure that a unit of petroleum he does not exploit now will be available for his later use, acting individually he has no reason to conserve petroleum for his later and possibly higher value use. Thus he has no incentive to take account of his true user cost. The only limit to his current exploitation is current cost—not the opportunity cost of future returns. Consequently the resource will be exploited at an excessively rapid rate in the absence of some sort of collective action. While these problems were recognized with respect to such resources as petroleum, fisheries, and groundwater, still private property and exchange have been regarded as the keystones of an efficient allocation of resources.

It is the main thesis of this book that at least one class of externalities—those associated with the disposal of residuals resulting from modern consumption and production activities—must be viewed as a normal, indeed inevitable, part of these processes. Their economic significance tends to increase as economic development proceeds, and the ability of the natural environment to receive and assimilate them is an important natural resource of rapidly increasing value. We suggest below that the common failure to recognize these facts in economic theory may result from viewing the production and consumption processes in a manner which is somewhat at variance with the fundamental physical law of conservation of mass.

Modern welfare economics concludes that if (1) preference orderings of consumers and production functions of producers are independent and their shapes appropriately constrained, (2) consumers maximize utility subject to given income and price parameters, and (3) producers maximize profits subject to these price parameters, then a set of prices exists such that no individual can become better off without making some other individual worse off. For a given distribution of income this is an efficient state. Given certain further assumptions concerning the structure of markets, this "Pareto optimum" can be achieved via a pricing mechanism and voluntary decentralized exchange.

If the capacity of the environment to assimilate residuals is scarce, the decentralized voluntary exchange process cannot be free of uncompensated technological external diseconomies unless

(1) all inputs are fully converted into outputs, with no unwanted material and energy residuals along the way,[1] and all final outputs are utterly destroyed in the process of consumption, or (2) property rights are so arranged that all relevant environmental attributes are in private ownership and these rights are exchanged in competitive markets. Neither of these conditions can be expected to hold in an actual economy, and they do not.

Nature does not permit the destruction of matter except by annihilation with antimatter, and the means of disposal of unwanted residuals which maximizes the internal return of decentralized decision units is by discharge to the environment, principally watercourses and the atmosphere. Water and air are traditionally examples of free goods in economics. But in reality in developed economies they are common property resources of great and increasing value, which present society with important and difficult allocation problems that exchange in private markets cannot solve. These problems loom larger as increased population and industrial production put more pressure on the environment's ability to dilute, chemically degrade, and simply accumulate residuals from production and consumption processes. Only the crudest estimates of present external costs associated with residuals discharge exist, but it would not be surprising if these costs were already in the tens of billions of dollars annually.[2] Moreover, as we shall emphasize again, technological means for processing or purifying one or another type of residuals do not destroy the residuals but only alter their form. Thus, given the level, patterns, and technology of production and consumption, recycle of materials into productive uses or discharge into an alternative medium are the only general operations for protect-

1. Or any residuals which occur must be stored on the producer's premises.
2. It is interesting to compare this with estimates of the cost of another well-known misallocation of resources that has occupied a central place in economic theory and research. In 1954, Harberger published an estimate of the welfare cost of monopoly which indicated that it amounted to about 0.07 percent of GNP. A. C. Harberger, "Monopoly and Resources Allocation," *American Economic Review* 44 (May 1954), 77–87. In a later study, Schwartzman calculated the allocative cost at only 0.01 percent of GNP. D. Schwartzman, "The Burden of Monopoly," *Journal of Political Economy* 68 (December 1960), 627–30. Leibenstein generalized studies such as these to the statement that 'in a great many instances the amount to be gained by increasing allocative efficiency is trivial." H. Leibenstein, "Allocative Efficiency vs. 'X-Efficiency,'" *American Economic Review* 56 (June 1966), 392–415. But Leibenstein did not consider the allocative costs associated with environmental pollution.

ing a particular environmental medium such as water. Residual problems must be seen in a broad regional or economy-wide context rather than as separate and isolated problems of disposal of gaseous, liquid, solid, and energy waste products.

Frank Knight perhaps provides a key to why these elementary facts have played so small a role in economic theorizing and empirical research: "The basic economic magnitude (value or utility) is service, not good. It is inherently a stream or flow in time . . ." [3]

Standard economic allocation theory is in truth concerned with services. Material objects are merely the vehicles which carry some of these services, and they are exchanged because of consumer preferences for the services associated with their use or because they can help to add value in the manufacturing process. Yet we persist in referring to the "final consumption" of goods as though material objects such as fuels, materials, and finished goods somehow disappear into a void—a practice which was comparatively harmless only so long as air and water were almost literally "free goods." [4] Of course, residuals from both the production and consumption processes remain, and they usually render disservices (like killing fish, increasing the difficulty of water treatment, reducing public health, soiling and deteriorating buildings, etc.) rather than services. These disservices flow to consumers and producers whether they want them or not, and except in unusual cases they cannot control them by engaging in individual exchanges.

THE FLOW OF MATERIALS

To elaborate on these points, we find it useful to view environmental pollution and its control from the perspective of a ma-

3. F. H. Knight, *Risk, Uncertainty, and Profit* (New York: A. M. Kelley, 1921). The point was also clearly made by Fisher: "The only true method, in our view, is to regard uniformly as income the *service* of a dwelling to its owner (shelter or money rental), the *service* of a piano (music), and the *service* of food (nourishment) . . ." (emphasis in original). I. Fisher, *Nature of Capital and Income* (New York: A. M. Kelley, 1906).

4. We are tempted to suggest that the word "consumption" be dropped entirely from the economist's vocabulary as being basically deceptive. It is difficult to think of a suitable substitute, however. At least, the word consumption should not be used in connection with goods, but only with regard to services or flows of "utility."

terials balance problem for the entire economy.[5] The inputs of the system are fuels, foods, and raw materials which are partly converted into final goods and partly become residuals. Except for increases in inventory, final goods also ultimately enter the residuals stream. Thus, goods which are "consumed" really only render certain services. Their material substance remains in existence and must be either reused or discharged to the natural environment.

In an economy which is closed (no imports or exports) and where there is no net accumulation of stocks (plants, equipment, inventories, consumer durables, or buildings), the amount of residuals which is inserted into the natural environment must be approximately equal to the weight of basic fuels, food, and raw materials entering the processing and production system, plus oxygen taken from the atmosphere.[6] This result, while obvious upon reflection, leads to the at first rather surprising corollary that residuals disposal involves a greater tonnage of materials than basic materials processing, although many of the residuals, being gaseous, require comparatively little physical "handling."

Chart 1 shows a materials flow of the type we have in mind. In an open (regional or national) economy, it would be necessary to add flows representing imports and exports. In an economy undergoing stock or capital accumulation, the production of residuals in any given year would be less by that amount than the basic inputs. In the entire U.S. economy, accumulation ac-

5. As far as we know, the idea of applying materials balance concepts to waste disposal problems was first expressed by Smith. F. A. Smith, "The Economic Theory of Industrial Waste Production and Disposal," draft of a doctoral dissertation, Northwestern University, 1967. We also benefited from an unpublished paper by Joseph Headley in which a pollution "matrix" is suggested. We have also found suggestive references by Boulding to a "spaceship economy" ("The Economics of the Coming Spaceship Earth," pp. 3–14). One of the authors has previously used a similar approach in ecological studies of nutrient interchange among plants and animals; see R. U. Ayres, "Stability of Biosystems in Sea Water," Technical Report No. 142, Hudson Laboratories, Columbia University, 1967. As we note later, residual energy is another major source of external costs and could be analyzed analogously in terms of "energy balance."

6. To simplify our language, we will not repeat this essential qualification at each opportunity, but assume it applies through the following discussion. In addition, we must include residuals such as NO and NO_2 arising from reactions between components of the air itself but occurring as combustion by-products.

CHART 1. *Schematic Depiction of Materials Flow*

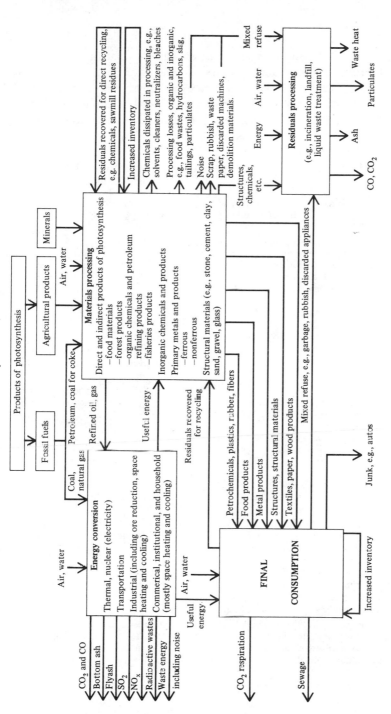

counts for about 10–15 percent of basic annual inputs, mostly in the form of construction materials, and there is some net importation of raw and partially processed materials, amounting to 4 or 5 percent of domestic production. Table 1 shows estimates of the weight of raw materials produced in the United States in several recent years, plus net imports of raw and partially processed materials.

Of the "active" inputs,[7] perhaps three-quarters of the over-all

TABLE 1. *Weight of Basic Materials Production in the United States plus Net Imports, 1963–65*

Material	1963	1964	(10^6 tons) 1965
Agricultural (including fishery, wildlife, and forest) products:			
Food and fiber:			
Crops	350	358	364
Livestock and dairy	23	24	23.5
Fishery	2	2	2
Forestry products (85% dry wt. basis):			
Sawlogs	107	116	120
Pulpwood	53	55	56
Other	41	41	42
Total	576	596	607.5
Mineral fuels	1,337	1,399	1,448
Other minerals:			
Iron ore	204	237	245
Other metal ores	161	171	191
Other nonmetals	125	133	149
Total	490	541	585
Grand total[a]	2,403	2,536	2,640.5

[a] Excluding construction materials, stone, sand, gravel, and other minerals used for structural purposes, ballast, fillers, insulation, etc. Gangue and mine tailings are also excluded from this total. These materials account for enormous tonnages but undergo essentially no chemical change. Hence, their use is more or less tantamount to physically moving them from one location to another. If this were to be included, there is no logical reason to exclude material shifted in highway cut and fill operations, harbor dredging, landfill, plowing, and even silt moved by rivers. Since a line must be drawn somewhere, we chose to draw it as indicated above.

SOURCE: R. U. Ayres and A. V. Kneese, "Environmental Pollution," in *Federal Programs for the Development of Human Resources,* a compendium of papers submitted to the Subcommittee on Economic Progress of the Joint Economic Committee, U.S. Congress, vol. 2 (Washington, D.C., 1968).

7. See footnote to Table 1.

weight is eventually discharged to the atmosphere as carbon (combined with atmospheric oxygen in the form of CO or CO_2) and hydrogen (combined with atmospheric oxygen as H_2O) under current conditions. This discharge results from combustion of fossil fuels and from animal respiration. Discharge of carbon dioxide can be considered harmless in the short run. There are large "sinks" (in the form of vegetation and large water bodies, mainly the oceans) which reabsorb this gas, although there is some evidence of its net accumulation in the atmosphere. Some experts believe that CO_2 is likely to show a large relative increase—as much as 50 percent—by the end of the century, possibly giving rise to significant and probably, on balance, adverse weather changes.[8] Thus, continued combustion of fossil fuels at a high rate could produce externalities affecting the entire world. The effects associated with most residuals will normally be more confined, however, usually limited to regional air and water sheds.

The remaining residuals are either gases (like carbon monoxide, nitrogen dioxide, and sulfur dioxide—all potentially harmful even in the short run), dry solids (like rubbish and scrap), or wet solids (like garbage, sewage, and industrial residuals suspended or dissolved in water). In a sense, the dry solids and gases are the irreducible, limiting forms of residuals. By the application of appropriate equipment and energy, most undesirable substances can, in principle, be removed from water and air streams,[9] but what is left must be disposed of in solid form, transformed, or reused. Looking at the matter in this way clearly reveals a primary interdependence between the various residuals streams which casts into doubt the traditional classification of air, water, and land pollution as individual categories for purposes of planning and control policy.

Material residuals do not necessarily have to be discharged to the environment. In many instances it is possible to recycle them back into the productive system. The materials balance view underlines the fact that the throughput of new materials

8. *Implications of Rising Carbon Dioxide Content of the Atmosphere*, Conservation Foundation, New York, 1963. There is strong evidence that discharge of residuals has already affected the climate of individual cities. W. P. Lowry, "The Climate of Cities," *Scientific American* 217 (August 1967), 15–23.

9. Except CO_2, which may be harmful in the long run, as noted.

necessary to maintain a given level of production and consumption decreases as the technical efficiency of energy conversion and materials utilization increases. Similarly, other things being equal, the longer cars, buildings, machinery, and other durables remain in service, the fewer new materials are required to compensate for loss, wear, and obsolescence—although the use of old or worn machinery (e.g., automobiles) tends to increase other residuals problems. Technically efficient combustion of (desulfurized) fossil fuels would leave only water, ash, and carbon dioxide as residuals, while nuclear energy conversion need leave only negligible quantities of material residuals, although pollution from discharge of heat—an energy residual—and of radiative materials cannot be dismissed by any means.

Given the population, industrial production, and transport services in an economy (a regional rather than a national economy would normally be the relevant unit), it is possible to visualize combinations of social policy which could lead to quite different relative burdens placed on the various residuals-receiving environmental media. And, given the possibilities for recycle and less residual-generating production processes, a lighter over-all burden can be placed upon the environment as a whole. To take one extreme, a region which went in heavily for electric space heating and wet scrubbing of stack gases (from steam plants and industries), which ground up its garbage and delivered it to the sewers and then discharged the raw sewage to watercourses, would protect its air resources to an exceptional degree. But this would come at the sacrifice of placing a heavy residuals load upon water resources. On the other hand, a region which treated municipal and industrial liquid residuals streams to a high level but relied heavily on the incineration of sludges and solid residuals would protect its water and land resources but at the expense of discharging residuals predominantly to the air. Finally, a region which practiced high-level recovery and recycle of residuals and fostered low residuals production processes to a far-reaching extent in each of the economic sectors might discharge very few residuals to any of the environmental media.

Further complexities are added by the fact that sometimes it is possible to modify an environmental medium through investment in control facilities so as to improve its assimilative capacity.

The clearest, but far from only, example is with respect to watercourses where reservoir or groundwater storage can be used to augment low river flows which ordinarily are associated with critical water quality levels (high external cost situations).[10] Thus, internalization of external cost associated with particular discharges by means of other restrictions, even if done perfectly, cannot guarantee Pareto optimality. Investments involving public good aspects must enter into an optimal solution.

CONCLUSION

Air and water used to be the economist's favorite examples of "free goods" (goods so abundant that their marginal value to any user, or potential user, is zero). It was historically fortunate for conventional economic theorizing about the efficiency of market processes that this was approximately true in fact. These media served the function of "infinite sinks" for most of the residuals which are, as the materials balance view so clearly shows, an inevitable accompaniment of production and consumption activities.

What is appearing now, however, is a vast asymmetry in the adequacy of our property institutions (which, of course, underlie all private exchange) to handle resources allocation problems. On the one hand, in the production of basic natural resources commodities, property institutions with some controls and adjustments, in general, serve quite well to lead production into highest productivity channels now and in the future. On the other hand, the flow of residuals back to the environment is heavily weighted to media where private property institutions can function imperfectly, if at all. Once these media become overloaded on a significant scale, they are free goods no more but, rather, *natural resources* of ever increasing value as economic development proceeds.

To recapitulate briefly our main points:

1. Technological external diseconomies are not freakish anomalies in the processes of production and consumption but inherent and normal parts of them.

10. Careful empirical work has shown that this technique can fit efficiently into water quality management systems. See R. K. Davis, *The Range of Choice in Water Management* (Baltimore: Johns Hopkins Press, 1968).

2. These external diseconomies are quantitatively negligible in a low-population economically undeveloped setting, but they become progressively (nonlinearly) more important as the population rises and the level of output increases (i.e., as the natural reservoirs of dilution and assimilative capacity become exhausted).[11]

3. They cannot be properly dealt with by considering environmental media such as air and water in isolation.

4. Isolated and ad hoc taxes and other restrictions are not sufficient for their optimum control, although such policy instruments are essential elements in a more systematic and coherent program of environmental quality management.

5. Public investment programs, particularly including transportation systems, sewage disposal, and river flow regulation, are intimately related to the amounts and effects of residuals and must be planned in light of them.

11. Externalities associated with residuals discharge may appear at certain threshold values which are relevant only at some stage of economic development and industrial and population concentrations. This may account for their general treatment as "exceptional" cases in the economics literature. These threshold values truly would be exceptional cases for less developed agrarian economies.

PART TWO Environmental Pollution

The Economic Common Sense of Pollution

LARRY E. RUFF

Larry Ruff has taught at the University of California, San Diego, and is now an economist with the U.S. Environmental Protection Agency. This article was published in The Public Interest.

WE ARE GOING to make very little real progress in solving the problem of pollution until we recognize it for what, primarily, it is: an economic problem, which must be understood in economic terms. Of course, there are *noneconomic* aspects of pollution, as there are with all economic problems, but all too often, such secondary matters dominate discussion. Engineers, for example, are certain that pollution will vanish once they find the magic gadget or power source. Politicians keep trying to find the right kind of bureaucracy; and bureaucrats maintain an unending search for the correct set of rules and regulations. Those who are above such vulgar pursuits pin their hopes on a moral regeneration or social revolution, apparently in the belief that saints and socialists have no garbage to dispose of. But as important as technology, politics, law, and ethics are to the pollution question, all such approaches are bound to have disappointing results, for they ignore the primary fact that pollution is an economic problem.

Before developing an economic analysis of pollution, however, it is necessary to dispose of some popular myths.

First, pollution is not new. Spanish explorers landing in the sixteenth century noted that smoke from Indian campfires hung in the air of the Los Angeles basin, trapped by what is now called the inversion layer. Before the first century B.C., the drinking waters of Rome were becoming polluted.

Second, most pollution is not due to affluence, despite the current popularity of this notion. In India, the pollution runs in the streets, and advice against drinking the water in exotic lands is often well taken. Nor can pollution be blamed on the self-seeking activities of greedy capitalists. Once beautiful rivers and lakes which are now open sewers and cesspools can be found in the Soviet Union as well as in the United States, and some of the world's dirtiest air hangs over cities in Eastern Europe, which are neither capitalist nor affluent. In many ways, indeed, it is much more difficult to do anything about pollution in noncapitalist societies. In the Soviet Union, there is no way for the public to become outraged or to exert any pressure, and the polluters and the courts there work for the same people, who often decide that clean air and water, like good clothing, are low on their list of social priorities.

In fact, it seems probable that affluence, technology, and slow-moving, inefficient democracy will turn out to be the cure more than the cause of pollution. After all, only an affluent, technological society can afford such luxuries as moon trips, three-day weekends, and clean water, although even our society may not be able to afford them all; and only in a democracy can the people hope to have any real influence on the choice among such alternatives.

What *is* new about pollution is what might be called the *problem* of pollution. Many unpleasant phenomena—poverty, genetic defects, hurricanes—have existed forever without being considered problems; they are, or were, considered to be facts of life, like gravity and death, and a mature person simply adjusted to them. Such phenomena become problems only when it begins to appear that something can and should be done about them. It is evident that pollution has advanced to the problem stage. Now the question is, what can and should be done?

Most discussions of the pollution problem begin with some startling facts. Did you know that 15,000 tons of filth are dumped into the air of Los Angeles County every day? But by themselves, such facts are meaningless, if only because there is no way to know whether 15,000 tons is a lot or a little. It is much more important for clear thinking about the pollution problem to understand a few economic concepts than to learn a lot of sensational-sounding numbers.

MARGINALISM

One of the most fundamental economic ideas is that of *marginalism*, which entered economic theory when economists became aware of the differential calculus in the nineteenth century and used it to formulate economic problems as problems of "maximization." The standard economic problem came to be viewed as that of finding a level of operation of some activity which would maximize the net gain from that activity, where the net gain is the difference between the benefits and the costs of the activity. As the level of activity increases, both benefits and costs will increase; but because of diminishing returns, costs will increase faster than benefits. When a certain level of the activity is reached, any further expansion increases costs more than benefits. At this "optimal" level, "marginal cost"—or the cost of expanding the activity—equals "marginal benefit," or the benefit from expanding the activity. Further expansion would cost more than it is worth, and reduction in the activity would reduce benefits more than it would save costs. The net gain from the activity is said to be maximized at this point.

This principle is so simple that it is almost embarrassing to admit it is the cornerstone of economics. Yet intelligent men often ignore it in discussion of public issues. Educators, for example, often suggest that, if it is better to be literate than illiterate, there is no logical stopping point in supporting education. Or scientists have pointed out that the benefits derived from "science" obviously exceed the costs and then have proceeded to infer that their particular project should be supported. The correct comparison, of course, is between *additional* benefits created by the proposed activity and the *additional* costs incurred.

The application of marginalism to questions of pollution is simple enough conceptually. The difficult part lies in estimating the cost and benefits functions, a question to which I shall return. But several important qualitative points can be made immediately. The first is that the choice facing a rational society is *not* between clean air and dirty air, or between clear water and polluted water, but rather between various *levels* of dirt and pollution. The aim must be to find that level of pollution abatement where the costs of further abatement begin to exceed the benefits.

The second point is that the optimal combination of pollution control methods is going to be a very complex affair. Such steps as demanding a 10 percent reduction in pollution from all sources, without considering the relative difficulties and costs of the reduction, will certainly be an inefficient approach. Where it is less costly to reduce pollution, we want a greater reduction, to a point where an additional dollar spent on control anywhere yields the same reduction in pollution levels.

MARKETS, EFFICIENCY, AND EQUITY

A second basic economic concept is the idea—or the ideal—of the self-regulating economic system. Adam Smith illustrated this ideal with the example of bread in London: the uncoordinated, selfish actions of many people—farmer, miller, shipper, baker, grocer—provide bread for the city dweller, without any central control and at the lowest possible cost. Pure self-interest, guided only by the famous "invisible hand" of competition, organizes the economy efficiently.

The logical basis of this rather startling result is that, under certain conditions, competitive prices convey all the information necessary for making the optimal decision. A builder trying to decide whether to use brick or concrete will weigh his requirements and tastes against the prices of the materials. Other users will do the same, with the result that those whose needs and preferences for brick are relatively the strongest will get brick. Further, profit-maximizing producers will weigh relative production costs, reflecting society's productive capabilities, against relative prices, reflecting society's tastes and desires, when deciding how much of each good to produce. The end result is that users get brick and cement in quantities and proportions that reflect their individual tastes and society's production opportunities. No other solution would be better from the standpoint of all the individuals concerned.

This suggests what it is that makes pollution different. The efficiency of competitive markets depends on the identity of *private* costs and *social* costs. As long as the brick-cement producer must compensate somebody for every cost imposed by his production, his profit-maximizing decisions about how much to produce, and how, will also be socially efficient decisions. Thus, if a producer dumps wastes into the air, river, or ocean; if he pays nothing for such dumping; and if the disposed wastes have no noticeable effect on anyone else, living or still unborn; then the private and social costs of disposal are identical and nil, and the producer's private decisions are socially efficient. *But if these wastes do affect others, then the social costs of waste disposal are not zero. Private and social costs diverge, and private profit-maximizing decisions are not socially efficient.* Suppose, for example, that cement production dumps large quantities of dust into the air, which damages neighbors, and that the brick-cement producer pays these neighbors nothing. In the social sense, cement will be overproduced relative to brick and other products because users of the products will make decisions based on market prices which do not reflect true social costs. They will use cement when they should use brick, or when they should not build at all.

This divergence between private and social costs is the fundamental cause of pollution of all types, and it arises in any society where decisions are at all decentralized—which is to say, in any economy of any size which hopes to function at all. Even the socialist manager of the brick-cement plant, told to maximize output given the resources at his disposal, will use the People's Air to dispose of the People's Wastes; to do otherwise would be to violate his instructions. And if instructed to avoid pollution "when possible," he does not know what to do: how can he decide whether more brick or cleaner air is more important for building socialism? The capitalist manager is in exactly the same situation. Without prices to convey the needed information, he does not know what action is in the public interest, and certainly would have no incentive to act correctly even if he did know.

Although markets fail to perform efficiently when private and social costs diverge, this does not imply that there is some inherent flaw in the idea of acting on self-interest in response to market prices. Decisions based on private cost calculations are typically correct from a social point of view; and even when they are not quite correct, it often is better to accept this inefficiency than to turn to some alternative decision mechanism, which may be worse. Even the modern economic theory of socialism is based on the high correlation between managerial self-interest and public good. There is no point in trying to find something—some omniscient and omnipotent *deus ex machina*—to replace markets and self-interest. Usually it is preferable to modify existing institutions, where necessary, to make private and social interest coincide.

And there is a third relevant economic concept: the fundamental distinction between questions of efficiency and questions of equity or fairness. A situation is said to be efficient if it is not possible to rearrange things so as to benefit one person without harming any others. That is the *economic* equation for efficiency. *Politically,* this equation can be solved in various ways; though most reasonable men will agree that efficiency is a good thing, they will rarely agree about which of the many possible efficient states, each with a different distribution of "welfare" among individuals, is the best one. Economics itself has nothing to say about which efficient state is the best. That decision is a matter of personal and philosophical values, and ultimately must be decided by some political process. Economics can suggest ways of achieving efficient states, and can try to describe the equity considerations involved in any suggested social policy; but the final decisions about matters of "fairness" or "justice" cannot be decided on economic grounds.

ESTIMATING THE COSTS OF POLLUTION

Both in theory and practice, the most difficult part of an economic approach to pollution is the measurement of the cost and benefits of its abatement. Only a small fraction of the costs of pollution can be estimated straightforwardly. If, for example, smog reduces the life of automobile tires by 10 percent,. one component of the cost of smog is 10 percent of tire expenditures. It has been estimated that, in a moderately polluted area of New York City, filthy air imposes extra costs for painting, washing, laundry, etc., of $200 per person per year. Such costs must be included in any calculation of the benefits of pollution abatement, and yet they are only a part of the relevant costs—and often a small part. Accordingly it rarely is possible to justify a measure like river pollution control solely on the basis of costs to individuals or firms of treating water because it usually is cheaper to process only the water that is actually used for industrial or municipal purposes, and to ignore the river itself.

The costs of pollution that cannot be measured so easily are often called "intangible" or "noneconomic," although neither term is particularly appropriate. Many of these costs are as tangible as burning eyes or a dead fish, and all such costs are relevant to a valid economic analysis. Let us therefore call these costs "nonpecuniary."

The only real difference between nonpecuniary costs and the other kind lies in the difficulty of estimating them. If pollution in Los Angeles harbor is reducing marine life, this imposes costs on society. The cost of reducing commercial fishing could be estimated directly: it would be the fixed cost of converting men and equipment from fishing to an alternative occupation, plus the difference between what they earn in fishing and what they earn in the new occupation, plus the loss to consumers who must eat chicken instead of fish. But there are other, less straightforward costs: the loss of recreation opportunities for children and sportsfishermen and of research facilities for marine biologists, etc. Such costs are obviously difficult to measure and may be very large indeed; but just as surely as they are not zero, so too are they not infinite. Those who call for immediate action and damn the cost, merely because the spiny starfish and furry crab populations are shrinking, are putting an infinite marginal value on these creatures. This strikes a disinterested observer as an overestimate.

The above comments may seem crass and insensitive to those who, like one angry letter-writer to the Los Angeles *Times,* want to ask: "If conservation is not for its own sake, then what in the world *is* it for?" Well, what *is* the purpose of pollution control? Is it for its own sake? Of course not. If we answer that it is to make the air and water clean and quiet, then the question arises: what is the purpose of clean air and water? If the answer is, to please the nature gods, then it must be conceded that all pollution must cease immediately because the cost of angering the gods is presumably infinite. But if the answer is that the purpose of clean air and water is to further human enjoyment of life on this planet, then we are faced with the economists' basic question: given the limited alternatives that a niggardly nature allows, how can we best further human enjoyment of life? And the answer is, by making intelligent marginal decisions on the basis of costs and benefits. Pollution control is for lots of things: breathing comfortably, enjoying mountains, swimming in water, for health, beauty, and the general delectation. But so are many other things, like good food and wine, comfortable housing and fast transportation. The question is not which of these desirable things we should have, but rather what combination is most desirable. To determine such a combination, we must know the rate at which individuals are willing to substitute more of one desirable thing for less of another desirable thing. Prices are one way of determining those rates.

But if we cannot directly observe market prices for many of the costs of pollution, we must find another way to proceed. One possibility is to infer the costs from other prices, just as we infer the value of an ocean view from real estate prices. In principle, one could estimate the value people put on clean air and beaches by observing how much more they are willing to pay for property in nonpolluted areas. Such information could be obtained; but there is little of it available at present.

Another possible way of estimating the costs of pollution is to ask people how much they would be willing to pay to have pollution reduced. A resident of Pasadena might be willing to pay $100 a year to have smog reduced 10 to 20 percent. In Barstow, where the marginal cost of smog is much less, a resident might not pay $10 a year to have smog reduced 10 percent. If we knew how much it was worth to everybody, we could add up these amounts and obtain an estimate of the cost of a marginal amount of pollution. The difficulty, of course, is that there is no way of guaranteeing truthful responses. Your response to the question, how much is pollution costing *you,* obviously will depend on what you think will be done with this information. If you think you will be compensated for these costs, you will make a generous estimate; if you think that you will be charged for the control in proportion to these costs, you will make a small estimate.

In such cases it becomes very important how the questions are asked. For example, the voters could be asked a question of the form: Would you like to see pollution reduced x percent if the result is a y percent increase in the cost of living? Presumably a set of questions of this form could be used to estimate the costs of pollution, including the so-called unmeasurable costs. But great care must be taken in formulating the questions. For one thing, if the voters will benefit differentially from the activity, the questions should be asked in a way which reflects this fact. If, for example, the issue is cleaning up a river, residents near the river will be willing to pay more for the cleanup and should have a means of expressing this. Ultimately, some such political procedure probably will be necessary, at least until our more direct measurement techniques are greatly improved.

Let us assume that, somehow, we have made an estimate of the social cost function for pollution, including the marginal cost associated with various pollution levels. We now need an estimate of the benefits of pollution—or, if you prefer, of the costs of pollution abatement. So we set the Pollution Control Board (PCB) to work on this task.

The PCB has a staff of engineers and technicians, and they begin working on the obvious question: for each pollution source, how much would it cost to reduce pollution by 10 percent, 20 percent, and so on. If the PCB has some economists, they will know that the cost of reducing total pollution by 10 percent is *not* the total cost of reducing each pollution source by 10 percent. Rather, they will use the equimarginal principle and find the pattern of control such that an additional dollar spent on control of any pollution source yields the same reduction. This will minimize the cost of achieving any given level of abatement. In this way the PCB can generate a "cost of abatement" function, and the corresponding marginal cost function.

While this procedure seems straightforward enough, the practical difficulties are tremendous. The amount of information needed by the PCB is staggering; to do this job right, the PCB would have to know as much about each plant as the operators of the plant themselves. The cost of gathering these data is obviously prohibitive, and, since marginal principles apply to data collection too, the PCB would have to stop short of complete information, trading off the resulting loss in efficient control against the cost of better information. Of course, just as fast as the PCB obtained the data, a technological change would make it obsolete.

The PCB would have to face a further complication. It would not be correct simply to determine how to control existing pollution sources given their existing locations and production methods. Although this is almost certainly what the PCB would do, the resulting cost functions will overstate the true social cost of control. Muzzling existing plants is only one method of control.

Plants can move, or switch to a new process, or even to a new product. Consumers can switch to a less-polluting substitute. There are any number of alternatives, and the poor PCB engineers can never know them all. This could lead to some costly mistakes. For example, the PCB may correctly conclude that the cost of installing effective dust control at the cement plant is very high and hence may allow the pollution to continue, when the best solution is for the cement plant to switch to brick production while a plant in the desert switches from brick to cement. The PCB can never have all this information and therefore is doomed to inefficiency, sometimes an inefficiency of large proportions.

Once cost and benefit functions are known, the PCB should choose a level of abatement that maximizes net gain. This occurs where the marginal cost of further abatement just equals the marginal benefit. If, for example, we could reduce pollution damages by $2 million at a cost of $1 million, we should obviously impose that $1 million cost. But if the damage reduction is only $½ million, we should not and in fact should reduce control efforts.

This principle is obvious enough but is often overlooked. One author, for example, has written that the national cost of air pollution is $11 billion a year but that we are spending less than $50 million a year on control; he infers from this that "we could justify a tremendous strengthening of control efforts on purely economic grounds." That *sounds* reasonable, if all you care about are sounds. But what is the logical content of the statement? Does it imply we should spend $11 billion on control just to make things even? Suppose we were spending $11 billion on control and thereby succeeded in reducing pollution costs to $50 million. Would this imply we were spending too *much* on control? Of course not. We must compare the *marginal* decrease in pollution costs to the *marginal* increase in abatement costs.

DIFFICULT DECISIONS

Once the optimal pollution level is determined, all that is necessary is for the PCB to enforce the pattern of controls which it has determined to be optimal. (Of course, this pattern will not really be the best one, because the PCB will not have all the information it should have.) But now a new problem arises: how should the controls be enforced? The most direct and widely used method is in many ways the least efficient: direct regulation. The PCB can decide what each polluter must do to reduce pollution and then simply require that action under penalty of law. But this approach has many shortcomings. The polluters have little incentive to install the required devices or to keep them operating properly. Constant inspection is therefore necessary. Once the polluter has complied with the letter of the law, he has no incentive to find better methods of pollution reduction. Direct control of this sort has a long history of inadequacy; the necessary bureaucracies rarely manifest much vigor, imagination, or devotion to the public interest. Still, in some situations there may be no alternative.

A slightly better method of control is for the PCB to set an acceptable level of pollution for each source and let the polluters find the cheapest means of achieving this level. This reduces the amount of information the PCB needs, but not by much. The setting of the acceptable levels becomes a matter for negotiation, political pull, or even graft. As new plants are built and new control methods invented, the limits should be changed; but if they are, the incentive to find new designs and new techniques is reduced.

A third possibility is to subsidize the reduction of pollution, either by subsidizing control equipment or by paying for the reduction of pollution below standard levels. This alternative has all the problems of the above methods, plus the classic short-coming which plagues agricultural subsidies: the old joke about getting into the not-growing-cotton business is not always so funny.

The PCB will also have to face the related problem of deciding *who* is going to pay the costs of abatement. Ultimately, this is a question of equity or fairness which economics cannot answer; but economics can suggest ways of achieving equity without causing inefficiency. In general, the economist will say: if you think polluter A is deserving of more income at polluter B's expense, then by all means give A some of B's income; but do *not* try to help A by allowing him to pollute freely. For example, suppose A and B each operate plants which produce identical amounts of pollution. Because of different technologies, however, A can reduce his pollution 10 percent for $100, while

B can reduce his pollution 10 percent for $1,000. Suppose your goal is to reduce total pollution 5 percent. Surely it is obvious that the best (most efficient) way to do this is for A to reduce his pollution 10 percent while B does nothing. But suppose B is rich and A is poor. Then many would demand that B reduce his pollution 10 percent while A does nothing because B has a greater "ability to pay." Well, perhaps B does have greater ability to pay, and perhaps it is "fairer" that he pay the costs of pollution control; but if so, B should pay the $100 necessary to reduce A's pollution. To force B to reduce his own pollution 10 percent is equivalent to taxing B $1,000 and then blowing the $1,000 on an extremely inefficient pollution control method. Put this way, it is obviously a stupid thing to do; but put in terms of B's greater ability to pay, it will get considerable support though it is no less stupid. The more efficient alternative is not always available, in which case it may be acceptable to use the inefficient method. Still, it should not be the responsibility of the pollution authorities to change the distribution of welfare in society; this is the responsibility of higher authorities. The PCB should concentrate on achieving economic efficiency without being grossly unfair in its allocation of costs.

Clearly, the PCB has a big job which it will never be able to handle with any degree of efficiency. Some sort of self-regulating system, like a market, is needed, which will automatically adapt to changes in conditions, provide incentives for development and adoption of improved control methods, reduce the amount of information the PCB must gather and the amount of detailed control it must exercise, and so on. This, by any standard, is a tall order.

PUTTING A PRICE ON POLLUTION

And yet there is a very simple way to accomplish all this. *Put a price on pollution.* A price-based control mechanism would differ from an ordinary market transaction system only in that the PCB would set the prices, instead of their being set by demand-supply forces, and that the state would force payment. Under such a system, anyone could emit any amount of pollution so long as he pays the price which the PCB sets to approximate the marginal social cost of pollution. Under this circumstance, private decisions based on self-interest are efficient. If pollution consists of many components, each with its own social cost, there should be different prices for each component. Thus, extremely dangerous materials must have an extremely high price, perhaps stated in terms of "years in jail" rather than "dollars," although a sufficiently high dollar price is essentially the same thing. In principle, the prices should vary with geographical location, season of the year, direction of the wind, and even day of the week, although the cost of too many variations may preclude such fine distinctions.

Once the prices are set, polluters can adjust to them any way they choose. Because they act on self-interest they will reduce their pollution by every means possible up to the point where further reduction would cost more than the price. Because all face the same price for the same type of pollution, the marginal cost of abatement is the same everywhere. If there are economies of scale in pollution control, as in some types of liquid waste treatment, plants can cooperate in establishing joint treatment facilities. In fact, some enterprising individual could buy these wastes from various plants (at negative prices—i.e., they would get paid for carting them off), treat them, and then sell them at a higher price, making a profit in the process. (After all, this is what rubbish removal firms do now.) If economies of scale are so substantial that the provider of such a service becomes a monopolist, then the PCB can operate the facilities itself.

Obviously, such a scheme does not eliminate the need for the PCB. The board must measure the output of pollution from all sources, collect the fees, and so on. But it does not need to know anything about any plant except its total emission of pollution. It does not control, negotiate, threaten, or grant favors. It does not destroy incentive because development of new control methods will reduce pollution payments.

As a test of this price system of control, let us consider how well it would work when applied to automobile pollution, a problem for which direct control is usually considered the only feasible approach. If the price system can work here, it can work anywhere.

Suppose, then, that a price is put on the emissions of automobiles. Obviously, continuous metering of such emissions is impossible. But it should be easy to determine the average output of pollution for cars of different makes, models, and years, having different types of control devices and using different types of fuel. Through graduated registration fees and fuel taxes, each car owner would be assessed roughly the social cost of his car's pollution, adjusted for whatever control devices he has chosen to install and for his driving habits. If the cost of installing a device, driving a different car, or finding alternative means of transportation is less than the price he must pay to continue his pollution, he will presumably take the necessary steps. But each individual remains free to find the best adjustment to his particular situation. It would be remarkable if everyone decided to install the same devices which some states currently require; and yet that is the effective assumption of such requirements.

Even in the difficult case of auto pollution, the price system has a number of advantages. Why should a person living in the Mojave desert, where pollution has little social cost, take the same pains to reduce air pollution as a person living in Pasadena? Present California law, for example, makes no distinction between such areas; the price system would. And what incentive is there for auto manufacturers to design a less polluting engine? The law says only that they must install a certain device in every car. If GM develops a more efficient engine, the law will eventually be changed to require this engine on all cars, raising costs and reducing sales. But will such development take place? No collusion is needed for manufacturers to decide unanimously that it would be foolish to devote funds to such development. But with a pollution fee paid by the consumer, there is a real advantage for any firm to be first with a better engine, and even a collusive agreement wouldn't last long in the face of such an incentive. The same is true of fuel manufacturers, who now have no real incentive to look for better fuels. Perhaps most important of all, the present situation provides no real way of determining whether it is cheaper to reduce pollution by muzzling cars or industrial plants. The experts say that most smog comes from cars; but *even if true, this does not imply that it is more efficient to control autos rather than other pollution sources.* How can we decide which is more efficient without mountains of information? The answer is, by making drivers and plants pay the same price for the same pollution, and letting self-interest do the job.

In situations where pollution outputs can be measured more or less directly (unlike the automobile pollution case), the price system is clearly superior to direct control. A study of possible control methods in the Delaware estuary, for example, estimated that, compared to a direct control scheme requiring each polluter to reduce his pollution by a fixed percentage, an effluent charge which would achieve the same level of pollution abatement would be only half as costly—a saving of about $150 million. Such a price system would also provide incentive for further improvements, a simple method of handling new plants, and revenue for the control authority.

In general, the price system allocates costs in a manner which is at least superficially fair: those who produce and consume goods which cause pollution, pay the costs. But the superior efficiency in control and apparent fairness are not the only advantages of the price mechanism. Equally important is the ease with which it can be put into operation. It is not necessary to have detailed information about all the techniques of pollution reduction, or estimates of all costs and benefits. Nor is it necessary to determine whom to blame or who should pay. All that is needed is a mechanism for estimating, if only roughly at first, the pollution output of all polluters, together with a means of collecting fees. Then we can simply pick a price—any price—for each category of pollution, and we are in business. The initial price should be chosen on the basis of some estimate of its effects but need not be the optimal one. If the resulting reduction in pollution is not "enough," the price can be raised until there is sufficient reduction. A change in technology, number of plants, or whatever, can be accommodated by a change in the price, even without detailed knowledge of all the technological and economic data. Further, once the idea is explained, the price system is much more likely to be politically acceptable than some method of direct control. Paying for a service, such as garbage disposal, is a well-established tradition, and is much less objectionable than having a bureaucrat nosing around and giving arbitrary orders. When businessmen, consumers, and politicians understand the alternatives, the price system will seem very attractive indeed. . . .

SOME OBJECTIONS AREN'T AN ANSWER

There are some objections that can be raised against the price system as a tool of pollution policy. Most are either illogical or apply with much greater force to any other method of control.

For example, one could object that what has been suggested here ignores the difficulties caused by fragmented political jurisdictions; but this is true for any method of control. The relevant question is: what method of control makes interjurisdictional cooperation easier and more likely? And the answer is: a price system, for several reasons. First, it is probably easier to get agreement on a simple schedule of pollution prices than on a complex set of detailed regulations. Second, a uniform price schedule would make it more difficult for any member of the "cooperative" group to attract industry from the other areas by promising a more lenient attitude toward pollution. Third, and most important, a price system generates revenues for the control board, which can be distributed to the various political entities. While the allocation of these revenues would involve some vigorous discussion, any alternative methods of control would require the various governments to raise taxes to pay the costs, a much less appealing prospect; in fact, there would be a danger that the pollution prices might be considered a device to generate revenue rather than to reduce pollution, which could lead to an overly-clean, inefficient situation.

Another objection is that the Pollution Control Board might be captured by those it is supposed to control. This danger can be countered by having the board members subject to election or by having the pollution prices set by referendum. With any other control method, the danger of the captive regulator is much greater. A uniform price is easy for the public to understand, unlike obscure technical arguments about boiler temperatures and the costs of electrostatic collectors versus low-sulfur oil from Indonesia; if pollution is too high, the public can demand higher prices, pure and simple. And the price is the same for all plants, with no excuses. With direct control, acceptable pollution levels are negotiated with each plant separately and in private, with approved delays and special permits and other nonsense. The opportunities for using political influence and simple graft are clearly much larger with direct control. . . .

"IF WE CAN GO TO THE MOON, WHY . . . ETC?

"If we can go to the moon, why can't we eliminate pollution?" This new, and already trite, rhetorical question invites a rhetorical response: "If physical scientists and engineers approached their tasks with the same kind of wishful thinking and fuzzy moralizing which characterizes much of the pollution discussion, we would never have gotten off the ground." Solving the pollution problem is no easier than going to the moon, and therefore requires a comparable effort in terms of men and resources and the same sort of logical hard-headedness that made Apollo a success. Social scientists, politicians, and journalists who spend their time trying to find someone to blame, searching for a magic device or regulation, or complaining about human nature, will be as helpful in solving the pollution problem as they were in getting us to the moon. The price system outlined here is no magic formula, but it attacks the problem at its roots, and has a real chance of providing a long-term solution.

Property Rights and Amenity Rights

EZRA J. MISHAN

Ezra J. Mishan regularly teaches economics at the London School of Economics and at American University in Washington, D.C. This article is taken from his widely read criticism of the goal of economic growth, Technology and Growth: The Price We Pay.

I

THE COMPETITIVE MARKET has long been recognized by economists as an inexpensive mechanism for allocating goods and services with tolerable efficiency. Once it is observed that the production of "bads," or noxious spillover effects, has begun, increasingly, to accompany the production of goods, one might be excused for talking about a serious failure of the market mechanism. In fact the failure is not to be attributed to the market itself, but to the legal framework within which it operates. In particular, we must remind ourselves that what constitutes a cost to commercial enterprise depends upon the existing law. If the law recognized slavery the costs of labour would be no greater than the costs involved in capturing a man and maintaining him thereafter at subsistence level.

How, then, can the law be altered so as to remove the existing inequities?

In so far as the activities of private industry are in question, the alteration required of the existing law is clear. For private industry, when it troubles at all to justify its existence to society, is prone to do so just on the grounds that the value of what it produces exceeds the costs it incurs—gains exceed losses, in short. But what *are* costs under the law and what *ought* to be counted as costs is just what is in issue. A great impetus would doubtless take place in the expansion of certain industries if they were allowed freely to appropriate, or freely to trespass upon, the land or property of others. Even where they were effectively bought off by the property-owning victims, the owners of these specially licensed industries would certainly become richer. And one could be sure if, after the elapse of some years, the Government sought to revoke this licence there would be a tremendous outcry followed by a determined campaign of opposition alleging that such arbitrary infringement of liberties would inevitably stifle progress, jeopardize employment, and, of course, "lose the country valuable export markets."

Such an example, though admittedly far-fetched, is distinctly relevant. For private property in this country has been regarded as inviolate for centuries. Even if the Government, during a national emergency or in fulfillment of some radical piece of legislation, takes over the ownership of private property it is obliged to compensate the owners. It may well be alleged that in any instance the Government paid too little or too much. But it would not occur to a British Government merely to confiscate private property.

In extending this principle of compensation, largely on the grounds of equity, the law should explicitly recognize also the facts of allocation. Privacy, quiet, and clean air, are scarce goods, far scarcer than they were before the war and sure to become scarcer in the foreseeable future. There is no warrant, therefore, for allowing them to be treated as though they were free goods; as though they were so abundant that a bit more or a bit less made not the slightest difference to anyone. Indeed, if the world were so fashioned that clean air and quiet took on a physically identifiable form, and one that allowed it to be transferred as between people, we should be able to observe whether a man's quantum of the stuff had been appropriated, or damaged, and institute legal proceedings accordingly. The fact that the universe has not been so accommodating in this respect does not in any way detract from the principle of justice involved, or from the principle of economy regarding the allocation of scarce resources. One has but to imagine a country in which men were invested by law with property rights in privacy, quiet, and clean air—simple things, but for many indispensable to the enjoyment of the good life—to recognize that the extent of the compensatory payments that would perforce accompany the operation of industries, of motorized traffic and airlines, would constrain many of them to close down—or else to operate at levels far below those which would prevail in the absence of such legislation, until such time as industry and transport discovered inexpensive ways of controlling their own noxious by-products.

Thus, if the law were altered so that private airport authorities were compelled to fully compensate victims of aircraft noise it is more than possible—even though the decision costs would be very much lower than those which would have to be incurred by the victims under the present law—that most airports would be quite unable to cover such costs with their profits. They would be recognized as uneconomic and would have to close down.

II

The consequence of recognizing such rights in one form or another, let us call them *amenity rights,* would be far-reaching. Such innovations as the invisible electronic bugging devices currently popular in the United States among people eager to "peep in" on other people's conversations could be legally prohibited in recognition of such rights. The case against their use would rest simply on the fact that the users of such devices would be unable to compensate the victims, including all the potential victims, to continue living in a state of unease or anxiety. So humble an invention as the petrol-powered lawn-mower, and other petrol-driven garden implements would come also into conflict with such rights. The din produced by any one man is invariably heard by dozens of families who, of course, may be enthusiastic gardeners also. If they are all satisfied with the current situation or could come to agreement with one another, well and good. But once amenity rights were enacted, at least no man could be forced against his will to absorb these noxious by-products of the activity of others. Of course, compensation that would satisfy the victim (always assuming he tells the truth) may exceed what the offender could pay. In the circumstances, the enthusiast would have to make do with a hand lawn-mower until the manufacturer discovered means of effectively silencing the din.The manufacturer would, of course, have every incentive to do so, for under such legislation the degree of noise-elimination would be regarded as a factor in the measurement of technical efficiency. The commercial prospects of the product would then vary with the degree of noise-elimination achieved.

Admittedly there are difficulties whenever actual compensation payments have to be made, say, to thousands of families disturbed by aircraft noise. Yet once the principle of amenity rights is recognized in law, a rough estimate of the magnitude of compensation payments necessary to maintain the welfare of the number of families affected would be entered as a matter of course into the social cost calculus. And unless these compensatory payments could also be somehow covered by the proceeds of the air service there would be no *prima facie* case for maintaining the air service. If, on the other hand, compensatory payments could be paid (and their payment costs the company less than any technical device that would effectively eliminate the noise) some method of compensation must be devised. . . .

III

What is of importance is that the ethical and economic principles served by amenity rights be accepted by law in the first instance. Once accepted, it will not overtax the wit of man to devise over time the machinery necessary to implement the law. But there should be no mistake about it; such a law will have the most drastic effects on private enterprise which, for too long, has neglected the damage inflicted on society at large in producing its wares. For many decades now, private firms have, without giving it a thought, polluted the air we breathe, poisoned lakes and rivers with their effluence, and produced gadgets that have destroyed the quiet of millions of families, gadgets that range from motorized lawn-mowers and motor-cycles to transistors and private planes. What is being proposed therefore may be regarded as an *alteration of the legal framework within which private firms operate in order to direct their enterprise toward ends that accord more closely with the interests of modern society.*

More specifically, it would provide industry with the pecuniary incentive necessary to undertake prolonged research into methods of removing the potential and existing amenity-destroying features of so many of today's products and services.

The social advantage of enacting legislation embodying amenity rights is further reinforced by a consideration of the regressive nature of the chief spillover effects. The rich have legal protection of their property and have less need, at present, of protection from the disamenity created by others. The richer a man is the wider is his choice of neighbourhood. If the area he happens to choose appears to be sinking in the scale of amenity he can move, if at some inconvenience, to a quieter area. He can select a suitable town house, secluded perhaps, or made soundproof throughout, and spend his leisure and pleasure in the country or abroad, and at times of his own choosing. In contrast, the poorer a family the less opportunity it has for moving from its present locality. To all intents it is stuck in the area and must put up with whatever disamenity is inflicted upon it.

And generalizing from the experience of the last ten years or so, one may depend upon it that it will be the neighbourhoods of the working and lower middle classes that will suffer most from the increased construction of fly-overs and fly-unders and road-widening schemes that inevitably tend to concentrate the traffic and thicken the pollution. Thus the recognition of amenity rights would have favourable distributive effects on the welfare of society. It would promote not only a rise in the standards of environment generally from which all would benefit, it would raise them most for the lower income groups that have suffered more than any other group from unchecked "development" since the war.

Side Effects of Resource Use

RALPH TURVEY

Ralph Turvey is chief economist with Britain's Electricity Council and has published numerous articles on welfare economics and resource economics. This paper appeared in Environmental Quality in a Growing Economy, *edited by Henry Jarrett.*

MANY OF THE PROBLEMS with which this book is concerned involve some sort of failure of the market mechanism as it now functions. The failure arises because decisions concerning the use of natural resources do not always take into account all the effects of that use. The neglected or side effects on the quality of the environment can, however, be very important, and thus need examination.

My purpose here is not to list and evaluate such side effects. It is the more limited one of analyzing their nature and introducing the various possible ways of coping with them. Economists have thought about all this and have produced an extensive and fairly technical literature on the subject. I have endeavored to distill from it the main ideas that are relevant to this volume and to present them in practical terms. Although I shall try to minimize the amount of jargon, I had better begin by stating that the technical terms used include "side-use effects," "spillovers," "externalities" or "external economies and diseconomies." These can be roughly and generally defined as the impacts of the activities of households, public agencies, or enterprises upon the activities of other households, public agencies, or enterprises which are exerted otherwise than through the market. They are, in other words, relationships other than those between buyer and seller.

To make this notion clearer it is best to proceed directly to the examples that I shall use. All seven of them are significant in practice. But it is important to note that they are used only as illustrations and that I do not pretend to deal fully with any of them.

Fisheries constitute the first example. In some kinds of fisheries, once a certain intensity of fishing is reached, the stock of fish is reduced with the result that fishing is made more difficult and costly. This means that each fisherman, by taking fish, is adding to the costs of all the other fishermen. What is more, not only the scale of activity, as measured by the weight of fish caught, but also its nature is relevant, since (in a trawl fishery) the mesh size of the nets used also affects the stock. An increase in mesh size, by raising the minimum size of fish caught, would in some fisheries ultimately result in an increase in the stock, so making fishing easier. Thus by using a smaller mesh instead of a larger one, each fisherman is raising the costs of all the other fishermen.

In this example the impact of each fisherman's activity upon that of others is reciprocal. This feature is shared with the next two examples while, as we shall see, this is not the case with the last four of our seven examples, where the impact of one activity upon another is unidirectional.

The second example consists of traffic congestion on roads or in an urban street network. Once traffic flow exceeds a certain level, vehicles (and pedestrians) get in each other's way and slow down the traffic flow. Thus any one vehicle affects other vehicles by increasing the time spent and the fuel used in the journeys which those other vehicles are making. The relationship is reciprocal because the presence of each vehicle adds to the costs of all the others.

The same is true of the third example: wells which all tap a common source of water. Each well deprives other wells of some water, either by reducing their rate of flow or by bringing nearer the day when their yield diminishes.

Reciprocality is not the only common feature of these three examples. They are also alike in that, usually at least, a large number of households or enterprises are involved: hundreds of fishermen, thousands of vehicles, and dozens of wells. These two features are not logically connected, of course, but just happen to be common to these three examples.

My other cases are unidirectional. The fourth is the adverse effect upon households living round an airport of the noise of jets landing and taking off; the fifth is river pollution by the discharge of industrial effluents, and the sixth is the destruction of visual amenity involved in placing overhead power transmission lines in areas of scenic beauty.

Seventh, and last, is cattle poisoning by the emission of fluorine in the smoke from brickworks. Fluorosis causes cows' teeth to mottle and wear faster than normal. Their bones grow deformed and brittle and may break. The consequence is that milk yields and the values of the animals drop considerably; cows may even have to be slaughtered.

We can now use our examples to show that where side effects —externalities—are involved in resource use, the market mechanism, i.e., buyer-seller relationships, alone may not produce the best possible allocation of resources. Some additional mechanism may produce a better allocation of resources by causing households or firms to alter the scales or the nature of their activities.

This is a rather general statement, so I must use my examples to show what it means. But there is another general statement to make first: the right word is "may" not "will." We should never aim to get rid of absolutely all external effects of one activity upon another, since the net gain from doing so would be negative. A world with no traffic congestion at all, never any noise, no overhead power lines, and not a trace of smoke is a nice thought, but irrelevant to action. Thus the question is not one of abolishing adverse unfavorable effects, but is one of reducing them in some cases where investigation shows that on balance such a reduction is worthwhile.

Let us now list the main activity adjustments that are possible in the seven examples. First, fishing. Here a reduction in the amount of fishing effort and an increase in mesh size will first lower the catch and then raise it and/or make possible a further reduction in the amount of fishing effort. Thus there is an initial loss, in that fewer fish are caught, followed by a continuing gain, in that the catch will rise more or fall less [1] than the number of boats and men engaged in the fishery. In either case, cost per ton of fish caught will end up lower than it was to start with.

Second, roads. A reduction in the number of vehicles would reduce the time and running costs incurred in the journeys of

1. This is a little complicated. I have analyzed the problem and provided references to the literature in my paper "Optimization and Suboptimization in Fishery Regulations," *American Economic Review* (March 1964).

the remaining vehicles. Similarly, a reduction in the amount of on-street parking is a nuisance for the drivers who wish to park but will benefit moving traffic (and pedestrians).

Third, wells. If fewer wells were drilled, drilling costs would be saved while the off-take of water would be reduced less.

Fourth, aircraft noise. In unidirectional cases, such as this, there is usually scope for both the creator of the adverse external effect and the sufferer from it to adjust the scale and the nature of their activity. Thus airlines can reduce the number of night jet take-offs, modify engines to reduce noise, and alter the speed and angle of ascent—all at a cost. The households around the airport, on the other hand, can install soundproofing or move.

Fifth, the emission of effluent into rivers. The enterprise or sewerage authority can treat the effluent before discharging it and possibly install storage facilities in order to reduce the rate of discharge at times when the river is low. In some cases an enterprise can also alter its production process in order to reduce the noxiousness of its effluent or it can even shift its location. Those enterprises or public authorities downstream can also spend money on treating the polluted river water in order to reduce the adverse consequences of the pollution and households can move.

Sixth, power lines. These can be cited differently or put underground.

Seventh, brickworks. Smoke filtering is possible and so is a change of location—two very expensive alternatives. Farmers, on the other hand, can shift from dairy farming to poultry or arable farming.

This review of the examples shows that there are frequently several possible ways in which the nature or scale of activities can be modified in order to reduce the adverse consequences of external effects. In most actual cases, therefore, the problem is a multidimensional one: who should do what how much?

An economic criterion can be used in answering this question. It is simply that the present value of the monetary measure of all gains from modifying activities less the present value of the monetary measure of all losses from these modifications be maximized. Unfortunately, this test is rarely sufficient in itself to provide an answer, and often cannot be applied in practice.

Nobody is going to quarrel with this criterion as a principle;

it is like being against sin! But it is able to give an answer only when all gains and all losses can be satisfactorily measured and expressed in terms of a common denominator, dollars. Gains and losses occurring at different times are rendered comparable by using a discount rate which expresses one's evaluation of futurity to turn them into their equivalent gains and losses at a common reference date. Given satisfactory measurement, given expression in dollar terms, and given an agreed discount rate, to apply the criterion is to choose the best.

The beauty of this criterion, in the eyes of some economists, is that whenever its application indicates that some course of action is desirable—gains exceed losses—the gainers can fully compensate the losers and still remain better off. Thus nobody loses on balance and at least some of the parties end up better off. What can be fairer than that?

The answer is that payment of compensation by gainers to losers is not always considered fair, so that even if it were always practicable it would not always be done. Yet the idea which lies at the root of the criterion (namely, that a course of action can be regarded unequivocally as desirable if it makes some people better off and nobody worse off)' requires that compensation actually be paid.

The brickworks example can be used to illustrate this, if we take it that all that matters are brick costs and farming costs and sales, all of them measurable in monetary terms. Suppose (though it is probably not true at present) that application of the criterion showed the best course of action to be cleansing brickwork smoke.[2] This would mean that the gain to farmers from an improvement in the health of any cows they keep would exceed the cost to the brickworks of cleansing the smoke, so that farmers could fully compensate the brickworks and yet remain net gainers. My point is that many people would not regard it as fair to make the farmers compensate the brickworks; on the contrary, they would claim that fairness requires the brickworks to meet the cost of cleansing the smoke since the brickworks is responsible for the damage.

Let us accept this judgment. Then the introduction of smoke

2. According to a report in *The Times* of London (May 5, 1965), a scheme for cleansing brickwork smoke which uses a wet scrubber and heat exchanger would put up the cost of bricks by 25 percent.

cleansing will not make some people better off and nobody worse off; instead it will harm the brickworks and benefit the farmers. Thus, in deciding whether or not the smoke ought to be cleansed, we are not just comparing total gains with total losses; we are also deciding whether or not it is fair to impose a loss on the brickworks.

What this example shows, then, is that even when all gains and losses can be measured and rendered comparable by expressing them in dollar terms, the economic criterion taken by itself is not always sufficient for choosing the right course of action. Considerations of fairness may also be relevant. In a democratic country this means that the problem may have a political aspect.

When some of the gains and losses cannot be expressed in dollar terms, the choice of the right course of action always has a political aspect, for it always involves judgments about fairness as well as mere calculation. The airport example illustrates this. The cost to airlines of reducing noise and the cost to householders of soundproofing their dwellings can no doubt be calculated in monetary terms. But the gain to householders from a reduction in noise cannot.[3] Hence deciding what measures, if any, should be taken involves:

Ascertaining the cheapest way of achieving various reductions in noise levels;

Choosing the reduction to aim at;

Deciding who should bear the cost;

and the two latter issues, which are interdependent, both involve judgments of fairness or what I am here calling political considerations.

All this goes to show, then, that who should do what how much is often a question which cannot be decided on a purely technical basis by an economic calculation. Political considerations—judgments of what is equitable—are also required. This is the message for economists and technologists. On the other hand, there also is a message for administrators and politicians; namely, that even though an economic calculation of gains and losses is often not sufficient to reach a well-based decision, it is nearly always an essential preliminary.

3. Asking people how much they would pay to obtain a given reduction in noise and comparing the prices of similar houses near and remote from the airport are both impracticable.

We are now ready to go on to discuss possible mechanisms for dealing with external effects. Since these, by definition, are relationships which are not coordinated by the market mechanism, it is a truism to say that these mechanisms are either nonmarket ones or that they involve the creation of a market where none existed before, i.e., the creation of rights which can be bought and sold. These are like the classical alternatives of status or contract.

Regulation is the mechanism of most general appeal, at least to noneconomists. It is easy to find examples:

Specification of a minimum mesh size to be used in a fishery;

Prohibition of parking at certain times in certain streets;

Confining the use of water from wells to certain purposes;

Limitation of the number of night take-offs by jet planes;

Requiring that effluents be treated before discharge into a river;

Forbidding the erection of overhead power lines in areas of natural beauty;

Prohibition of brickworks in certain areas (zoning).

Regulation may either consist of general rules or of specific decisions on individual cases. A good example of the latter is furnished by the British treatment of overhead power lines. The Central Electricity Generating Board, which is responsible for the National Grid, has a statutory responsibility to consider the impact of its activities upon amenity and has to get a statutory consent from the Minister of Power for each new transmission line. . . .

It is scarcely necessary to say that regulation of one sort or another is often the most appropriate way of dealing with external effects. What does need saying, however, is that this is not always true: sometimes the cure is worse than the disease and sometimes other mechanisms of control are better. I do not believe that any general classification can be provided to tell us what is best in any particular case; on the contrary, I think that each case must be examined in some detail. My task is therefore to show by example what alternatives there are and to indicate the circumstances under which they may be feasible.

The first alternative involves creating a contract between the parties. If B carries on an activity which damages A, A can offer to pay B some money in consideration of his reducing the scale or changing the nature of his activity in order to diminish or abolish the damage. Such a bargain will be mutually advantageous when the economic criterion discussed above is fulfilled. If some alteration of B's activity costs B less than it profits A, the latter can afford to pay B enough to meet these costs. Thus suppose that an expenditure of $1,000 by B is worth $1,500 to A. Then if A pays B anything between $1,001 and $1,499, B will gain something between one dollar and $499 and A will gain between $499 and one dollar.

When the point is put in these abstract terms it invites the response that this sort of bargaining is open to blackmailers. Might not B be tempted to bother A solely in order to turn a dishonest penny by getting A to pay him to stop? The answer is, of course, that the parties must act within a legal framework of rights and obligations which determines their bargaining positions. The law of nuisance is particularly relevant here, both because it is an important part of this framework and because it provides a second alternative to the sort of regulations listed above; namely, the award of injunctions by the courts.

Nuisances, in the legal sense, are acts not warranted by law (or failure to discharge legal duties) which obstruct, inconvenience, or damage the public or which, when concerned with the use or occupation of land, damage another person in connection with his occupation or use of land. This latter category constitutes private nuisance and it is only here that a private individual has a right to legal action and may claim damages or an injunction. Whether an act constitutes a nuisance is a matter either of common law or of statute; thus the Public Health Acts specify a number of statutory nuisances where legal proceedings are initiated by public authorities. It is important to note that some acts which would otherwise be wrongful may be authorized by statute. Thus actions for nuisance arising from civil aircraft are prohibited.

The law of nuisance may, however, apply to another of our examples. Certain farmers are taking legal proceedings with the object of obtaining redress for the loss and damage which their farms have suffered due to fluorine. (They are not seeking an injunction; in the case of brickworks because it is not practicable to eliminate the fluorine from the emissions.) An alternative method which has actually been used in one or two cases is for the manufacturer to purchase an affected farm on such terms as to avoid claims in respect of fluorine pollution.

Leaving aside the technical point, yet to be resolved, as to whether damage can be proved to the satisfaction of the courts, this case shows that if the farmers have a right, their bargaining position will be improved. An alternative to payment of damages is a private contract which avoids claims for damages. In this particular case it appears that the cost (to brickworks) of ceasing to emit fluorine exceeds the cost (to farmers) imposed by its continued emission. Thus the economic criterion suggests that the right thing is for the emission to continue, whether or not the farmers have a right against the brickworks. If they do not have such a right, they bear the cost. If they do, the brickworks bears the cost either in the form of damages awarded by the courts or by payment made under a contract. Thus the absence or existence of the right on the part of the farmers does not affect the allocation of resources between activities but only the distribution of the gains and losses between the parties. The law of nuisance is thus only relevant to the fairness of what happens.

Whether or not this result follows in all cases where the parties can make a private bargain is difficult to say. It is easy to imagine circumstances in which civil proceedings might fail to lead to the maximization of net gains, particularly since in British law it is no defense for the person committing a nuisance to prove that the benefit to the public far exceeds the disadvantage!

An actual river-pollution case will serve to illustrate the complexities of the problem and to show why generalization is difficult. This is the Pride of Derby Angling Association and the Earl of Harrington versus Derby Corporation, British Celanese Ltd. and the British Electricity Authority. The plaintiffs' waters have been polluted and the water temperature had been raised, with injurious results to fish, by the discharge of heated trade effluent by British Celanese, by the discharge of insufficiently treated sewage matter by Derby Corporation, and by the discharge of heated water by the (then) British Electricity Authority. An injunction was granted but was suspended for two years to give the defendants time to remedy matters; meanwhile the defendants had to indemnify the plaintiff against the damage.

Three features of this case are of particular interest. The first is that since the two plaintiffs' waters had been polluted by the combined effects of the activities of the defendants, they were entitled to bring an action against all three of them. The second emerges from the following statement made by Lord Evershed in the course of his judgment on the appeal:

> It is, I think, well settled that if A proves that his proprietary rights are being wrongfully interfered with by B, and that B intends to continue his wrong, then A is prima facie entitled to an injunction, and he will be deprived of that remedy only if special circumstances exist, including the circumstance that damages are an adequate remedy for the wrong that he has suffered. In the present case it is plain that damages would be a wholly inadequate remedy for the first-named plaintiffs, who have not been incorporated in order to fish for monthly sums.

Since there was apparently no inquiry into the costs to the defendants of ceasing to pollute one may be forgiven for wondering whether it is clear that gains less losses were maximized.

The third interesting feature of this case is that the interests of the fishermen were looked after by their Angling Association, a voluntary collective body formed precisely for purposes such as this. Economists tend to neglect such voluntary associations, concentrating instead on compulsory associations for collective action—the public authorities. Yet their function is similar: to do collectively what cannot be done by the market or by bargains between individuals.

The public authorities are, of course, able to pursue courses of action which are not open to voluntary associations. They can bring proceedings in respect of public nuisances. Another way, already mentioned, is by regulation—either general or particular. But there is yet a third way, not mentioned so far, which has long interested economists. This is the use of special taxes. The argument runs as follows: If group B's activity adversely affects group A, this means that group B is imposing a cost upon group A so that the cost to society as a whole of group B's activity (its social cost) exceeds its cost to group B itself (its private cost). Thus in looking only at its private cost when deciding upon its activity, group B must fail to maximize the excess of gains over social cost. It can be induced to take social cost rather than private cost into account, however, if it is charged a tax which raises its private cost to equality with social cost. Thus an external diseconomy is viewed as an excess of social over private cost and is to be dealt with by levying a tax equal to this excess.

We have earlier seen how a nonoptimal situation where a single B adversely affects a single A can usually be remedied either if A is able to secure adequate but not excessive damages from B (when he has a right against him) or by his paying B to desist (when he has not). In just the same way, a tax imposed by the public authorities upon a group B could be replaced by the public authorities paying group B to desist. The same allocation of resources can usually be achieved in either case; the difference is thus in most cases only a question of fairness, i.e., of the distribution of the costs and gains between group B on the one hand and the public authority's taxpayers on the other.

Fishery regulation, street congestion, and the use of water from wells are all examples in which economists have urged that a properly designed tax would be superior to any form of regulation. Actually, some combination of both is probably required. Thus, in the case of fish, it can be shown that a tax on catch should be accompanied by regulation of mesh size if the present value of gains minus losses is to be maximized.

The external diseconomies in these three examples are reciprocal. Reflection suggests that this is because all three involve what economists call a common property resource. This is a resource required in production which is significantly limited in availability but whose use is nonetheless free. In the three examples this resource is, respectively, the fish stock, the street system, and the underground water. An increase in the catch, the number of journeys undertaken, and the amount of water abstracted lowers the fish stock, increases street congestion, and reduces water reserves. This raises the costs of all fishermen, all drivers, and all water users by making fish more difficult to catch, slowing down traffic, and lowering the water table. But this effect of an increase in the use of the common property resource by one user is not felt by him; it is felt by his fellows. Thus the social cost of any given increase in the catch, vehicle-miles, or gallons exceeds the private cost of such an increase to the one who provides it. By using up more of the common property resource he leaves less of it for his fellows; this is a cost but it is a social cost only and not a private cost as well because he does not pay for its use. Putting a price on the use of the common property resource, however, could raise private cost to equality with social cost and put an end to the wasteful and excessively intensive use of the common property resource. It is wastefully used because it is free to the user but significantly scarce; it is treated like air but is really like good agricultural land.

This last paragraph aims to set out the essentials of the matter, not to provide a rigorous demonstration. It suffices here to point out that agricultural land would be wastefully exploited if farmers could all use it without buying or renting it—as indeed happens sometimes with common land. Thus the proceeds to be got from a properly designed tax on catch, urban road journeys, or water abstraction constitute the rent which society as a whole could obtain from better utilization of its common property resource.

Urban roads differ from the other two examples in that the amount available is entirely within the control of man. But this does not affect the present issue which is to make the best use of the roads we have at any particular point of time. It should by now be obvious that gasoline taxes paid in respect of a vehicle, being only very loosely related to its utilization in congested conditions, do relatively little to optimize road usage. What is needed are charges for road use which are closely related to the amount of use made of congested roads at times of congestion. Modern technology has made possible several ways of achieving this.

A tax may also be the best method of dealing with unidirectional external diseconomies when the numbers of people or firms concerned is so large that only collective action is possible. On the other hand, it may not be the best method. Writers of economic textbooks like to use the example of smoke nuisance, but none has explained how a smoke tax could in practice be levied or has discussed how its rate should vary with the height of the chimney or the composition of the smoke, though both are relevant to the amount of damage caused. . . .

Regulation, contracts (or legal actions), and taxes are thus three ways of dealing with external economies and diseconomies. A fourth way, which deserves mention for the sake of completeness, is what economists call "internalizing the externalities." The problem to be faced is that of causing one or more separate decision-making units to take account of the impact of their activities upon other such units. Centralizing decision-making for the group of units could clearly achieve this result.

Thus, if a particular fishery were exploited by a single concern rather than by a number of separate fishermen, it could take into account the interaction between the activities of the fishermen acting under its control. This serves to show what is meant by "internalizing" and that is all that is necessary here.

This completes our review. The main points which I have made are that each case must be considered on its merits and that these should be set out in economic terms as far as possible. Administrators should consider alternatives to direct regulation, economists should not exaggerate the applicability of tax devices, and both should remember that, in a democratic country, questions of fairness require legal or political decisions.

Economics and the Quality of the Environment: Some Empirical Experiences

ALLEN V. KNEESE

Allen V. Kneese is one of the pioneers in applying economic theory to the problems of pollution control and environmental quality. He is on the staff of Resources for the Future, Inc., in Washington, D.C. This paper was published in Social Sciences and the Environment *in 1967.*

THE CONTRIBUTIONS economics can make toward improved decisions in regard to environmental quality seem to fall rather naturally into three categories: provision of a conceptual framework for considering environmental problems, empirical information on benefits and costs associated with environmental quality management, and help in the analysis of control systems.

I propose to concentrate on empirical information on benefits and costs and more specifically on some experiences and problems in empirically estimating the benefits of environmental improvement. Benefit evaluation, in many ways, is the most difficult of the three areas and the one in which we most need to develop our capabilities. It is also an area where clear understanding of the natural relationships bearing on human satisfaction must be understood, and therefore one in which joint or parallel work of natural scientists, engineers, and social scientists can be constructive. It seems fair to say that much has already been accomplished and I will stress this. But it is also true that many problems, some of them quite baffling, remain.

Economists interested in public policy problems associated with resources development and use have usually worked within the conceptual framework of welfare economics. Of course, the theory is highly abstract, and it has to be adapted and elaborated considerably to fit particular problems. Nevertheless, the ideas of welfare economics are explicit or implicit in the work of most economists. Mason Gaffney has described the *gestalt* of the practicing welfare economist with respect to environmental deterioration very well:

One of the most important functions of economic analysis is to evaluate public policy. Economics, contrary to common usage, begins with the postulate that man is the measure of all things. Direct damage to human health and happiness is more directly "economic," therefore, than damage to property which is simply an intermediate means to health and happiness. Neither do economists regard "economic" as a synonym for "pecuniary." Rather money is but one of many means to ends, as well as a useful measure of value. "Economic damage" therefore includes damages to human function and pleasure. The economist tries to weigh these direct effects on people in the same balance with other costs and benefits—to the end of making decisions to maximize net social benefits.[1]

The studies of demand for environmental quality cited in this paper are efforts to implement this concept. When a well-functioning market exists, the economist's conceptual framework usually permits him to view prices as indicators of social value or benefit. In very few instances, however, in connection with the various pollution, congestion, recreation, landscape, health, and other environmental problems, will there be any market price clearly and directly applicable to the determination of benefits. There are several reasons for this, which come under such headings as externalities and public goods. These phenomena tend to occur when a resource is held in common—when it cannot be owned in individual parcels and sold on markets.

The ambient air is an illustration. Assume that an air polluter has a legal right to discharge his wastes to the atmosphere (but please *don't* assume that I am advocating this). Assume, too, that he can sell that right to parties damaged by the air pollution. Now, if some party purchases a right to reduced air pollution, he simultaneously and inevitably confers that right on all others who were affected by it. Since the others cannot be kept from enjoying this right whether they help pay or not, they have no incentive to participate in the transaction. Unless it happens that one party's interest in cleaner air is sufficiently large to induce him to buy it whether others contribute or not, market transactions cannot produce a reduction in air pollution even though the damage sustained by the total group would outweigh the cost of reducing the air pollution. Even though something of possibly great value to the persons involved is foregone, no market, and therefore no price, develops.

1. M. Gaffney, "Applying Economic Controls," *Bulletin of the Atomic Scientists,* June 1965, p. 20.

In such cases of market failure, the economist's approach is usually to try to simulate the results of a market if it could function. He tries, for example, to determine how much people would be willing to pay for a reduction in air pollution if they could, in fact, buy their share of it. Thus he searches for a measure of "willingness to pay."

Where market failure occurs, often certain market prices, together with assumptions about human preferences and behavior, can be used in the valuation process, but, as already mentioned, seldom are the prices themselves the appropriate indicator of value. The best-known example of where such an imputation procedure is regularly used in project evaluations is in determining flood control benefits. It is assumed that a rational flood plain occupant would be willing to pay up to what he loses to avoid the loss. This assumption plus information on the value of items in the flood plain, and flow elevations and flow frequencies, are used to compute the mathematical expectation of the loss. The calculation is repeated (perhaps numerous times) with the hydrology altered to reflect the regulating effect of a reservoir or a system of reservoirs. The difference between expected values with and without the reservoir is taken as the benefit of regulation and this, of course, corresponds to the concept of willingness to pay.

The benefit of environmental control programs such as flood and pollution control may be viewed as reduction in damages or losses that would otherwise occur. The measure of the benefit can therefore be taken as the avoidance of the loss.

AIR POLLUTION DAMAGES

A few studies have attempted to calculate the damages that occur when the air becomes contaminated. Usually they have been based on slender evidence and one cannot have great confidence in their numerical results. At the same time, methodology is improving and a few very interesting studies have been done in recent years, among them the following three studies.

1. *Materials Damages Studies* · One effort is reported in *Investigation to Determine the Possible Need for a Regulation on Organic Emissions from Stationary Sources in the San Francisco*

Bay Area by the Bay Area Air Pollution Control District. This report is impressive for its detailed discussion of photochemical smog effects. It presents estimates of damage to agriculture, fabrics, rubber, electrical contact points, and paint. This is one of the very few instances where efforts at damage costs evaluation were even attempted in assessing the desirability of a control program, and the effort is certainly laudable. But it must be said that after detailed and technical discussion of the physical and chemical processes involved, the cost estimates usually turned out to be rather questionable. The estimate of damage to paint may be used as an illustration. It is noted that a pollution report made in England estimated per capita losses from paint damage at $1.70 per year. Because of the cleaner fuel burned in the Bay area, it is assumed that an estimate of half that amount would be appropriate. Multiplied by the Bay area population, the total cost is about $3 million.[2] As in many damage studies, no effort is made to relate damages to alternative levels of control.

An economist who has studied the matter closely, Ridker, suggests that what is needed for economic studies are experimental data derived from observations on economic objects in conditions corresponding closely to actual use and measurements on these objects of either the direct loss in economic function or the loss incurred to avoid or offset such direct losses.[3] Scale models might be useful in this activity. If we are to have more than the crudest estimates of the cost of materials damage, this kind of approach should be tried.

Another technique entirely is to ask persons in different pollution situations how much they spend or would be willing to spend for various activities related to materials damage and soiling. Such a study was recently reported. It compared results of questionnaires concerning pollution-related expenditures for Steubenville, Ohio (relatively polluted), and Uniontown, Pennsylvania (relatively clean).[4] The study found that there was indeed a claimed cost difference of $84 per capita per year between Steu-

2. H. C. Wohlers and M. Feldstein, "Corrosion Aspects of Air Pollution in the San Francisco Bay Area: Exterior Paint," Bay Area Air Pollution Control District (mimeo).

3. R. Ridker, *Economic Costs of Air Pollution: Studies in Measurement* (New York: Praeger, 1967).

4. I. Michelson and B. Tourin, "Comparative Method for Studying Costs of Air Pollution," *Public Health Reports* 81, no. 6 (June 1966), 505.

benville and Uniontown. It was also found that income level greatly influenced pollution-related expenditures. The authors view their undertaking as a pilot study. In fact, it is a long way from providing information on economic losses as a function of type and concentration of pollution. But questionnaire interview studies have demonstrated their ability to obtain information on perception of air pollution and attitudes toward it, and they merit additional trials as a means of obtaining economic information.

2. *Property Value Studies* · Of course, none of the studies so far discussed take into account the aesthetic losses due to letting materials deteriorate and allowing the environment to become soiled and undesirable. Reasoning about rational economic behavior as well as observation tells us that individuals will not fully counteract the effects of air pollution through cleaning, maintenance, air filtration, etc. Nevertheless we know that the residual effects represent losses of welfare to those suffering them, and after all, human welfare is the fundamental concern of economics.

These considerations plus the fact that data are often relatively easy to obtain make it attractive to try to measure the impact of air pollution on property values. Property values can be a surrogate for all the various direct and indirect impacts of an adverse environmental change. This has been explained as follows: "So far as air pollution is concerned, there is one market that is more likely than others to reflect the majority of effects. This is the land, or real estate, market. If the land market were to work perfectly, the price of a plot of land would equal the sum of the present discounted stream of benefits and costs derivable from it. If some of its costs rise (e.g., additional maintenance and cleaning costs are required) or some of its benefits fall (e.g., one cannot see the mountains from the terrace), the property will be discounted in the market to reflect people's evaluation of these changes. Since air pollution is specific to locations and the supply of locations is fixed, there is less likelihood that the negative effects of pollution can be significantly shifted onto other markets. We should, therefore, expect to find the majority of effects reflected in this market, and can measure them by observing associated changes in property value." [5]

5. Ridker, "Strategies for Measuring the Cost of Air Pollution," in *The Economics of Air Pollution*, H. Wolozin, ed. (New York: Norton, 1966).

This idea sounds simple; putting it to use is far from simple. Great statistical ingenuity is needed to isolate the effect of one element—air pollution—bearing upon property values from all other determinants. Nevertheless, recent analysis by economists has now made clear that impacts on land values, and therefore upon all the human values that attach to particular sites, can be substantial. A study in St. Louis found that property values are linearly related to mean annual sulfation rates. When sulfation levels were divided into eight equal zones of rising intensity, values appeared to decline about $250 per lot per zone, other things remaining constant.[6] This would appear to be enough to justify even a costly control effort, but it also seems that the disbenefit that people attach to air pollution is finite and possibly fairly measurable. It does not suggest that total prohibitions on use of the air's assimilative capacity is usually the right answer. The problem, rather, is one of determining costs and gains.

A property value study of a more limited range of affected interests in connection with a pollution problem in Polk County, Florida, has also produced significant results. Variables, including one representing the frequency of fluoride pollution fumigation of property supporting citrus groves, were correlated with the sale price of citrus properties. This variable was found to be significantly related to the sale prices of the properties. In general, the results indicated that a substantial portion of the Polk County citrus industry suffered moderate damages from atmospheric fluoride emissions during the years (1956–62, approximately) in which these emissions were at their historical maximum.

The results of these studies are very encouraging and differ from those of all other studies I have seen in that they take us at least a step toward defining a functional relationship between air quality and economic loss—a benefit function which might be weighed against a cost function.

3. *Health Costs* · Although our knowledge of the costs of ill health associated with air pollution is in an even worse state than in regard to other costs, something must be said about the matter. This is because, as contrasted with certain other environmental problems such as water pollution, air pollution appears heavily implicated as a major public health problem. While

6. Ridker, *ibid.*, 1966.

property value relationships could, in principle, incorporate persons' evaluations of the health costs of residing in certain locations affected by air pollution, in practice neither the layman nor the expert knows enough about the relationship of air pollution to health to make such rational calculation possible in choosing sites.

Trying to provide useful information about the cost associated with disease has been a major problem for economics. However, estimates of some economic impacts of a number of diseases have now been made, and there is considerable literature discussing the pros and cons of particular methods of measurement. The growing consensus is that the most useful measure so far devised is the present or capitalized value of the gross production lost. No economist presents these measures as a full evaluation of the costs, including the psychic costs, of illness and death, and they are perhaps more useful for comparative purposes than for measuring absolute values.

Even the absolute measures may be of some utility in that they can indicate the minimal cost that society can attach to disease, and this may suggest whether expenditures for research and control are far out of line. It is clear that the cost of even some of the less virulent diseases is very high. For example, the following total annual costs have been computed for diseases possibly associated with air pollution.[7]

Disease	$ in millions
Cancer of the respiratory system	680.0
Chronic bronchitis	159.7
Acute bronchitis	6.2
Common cold	331.0
Pneumonia	490.0
Emphysema	64.0
Asthma	259.0
TOTAL	1,989.9

This adds up to a truly impressive loss, but, of course, not all of this is attributable to air pollution. On the other hand, these estimates relate only to possible respiratory impacts and some

7. Ridker, *Economic Costs of Air Pollution*. These include four categories of cost: those due to premature death, morbidity, treatment, and prevention. They are capitalized for the year 1958 at a 5 percent interest rate.

pollutants, such as lead, which may be potentially dangerous to health and do not attack the respiratory system at all.

If we wished to use economic loss calculations in a systematic way for decision making, we would need to know not only what portion of existing disease costs is due to air pollution but also how the various categories of cost vary when concentrations and lengths of exposure change. Unfortunately, this is an area in which the capacity of medical science to forecast physiological effects falls short even of our ability to predict economic impacts. I know of no medical scientist willing to define any quantitative relationship between the unwanted ingestion or inhalation of chemical residuals at levels existing in our current environment and the rates and intensities of disease. Until this is possible, economic and other research that could assist decision-making with respect to health impacts will be stymied.

DEMAND FOR WATER QUALITY

In recent years there have been several attempts to measure the willingness to pay for improved water quality. First, I will briefly review results, many of them tentative, from studies of the costs of water quality deterioration to industrial and municipal users. Then I will present a more extended discussion of the recreational demand for water quality.

Industrial and Municipal • Several industry studies by RFF staff members or grantees seek to assess the net damage industries suffer when they have to use low quality water. Since a variety of adjustments are possible, the problem becomes complex. Several studies have been models of ingenuity in using limited data and modeling or simulating effects on industrial processes. Some results are available for the pulp and paper, petroleum refining, canning, thermal power, and beet sugar industries.

In all these instances, industrial costs turn out to be surprisingly insensitive to water quality within comparatively wide ranges, especially in regard to aspects of quality usually influenced by prior uses and discharge of effluents. Sensitivity is greater to pollutants that in most cases are of natural origin, such as chlorides and magnesium. One important reason for the comparative insensitivity is that the vast proportion of industrial water use is for purposes that can readily accommodate low quality—cooling, for instance. A second reason is that the really sensitive processes, such as high pressure boilers, ordinarily need water of such quality that extensive treatment is necessary if *any* kind of river water is used; water of distinctly low quality can be used with only minor incremental costs. High pressure boiler feed water must be distilled, and the cost of distillation is not particularly sensitive to the quality of intake water. The moral of this is that not much pollution control can be justified by benefits to industrial users.

The situation is surprisingly similar for municipal water supplies. Much of what has been said about the need for high quality water supplies as a basis for preparation of potable water is more the product of emotion than of logic. The water of the much discussed Hudson River, which allegedly should not be used for municipal supply because of its poor quality, is actually similar to that at the Torresdale intake of Philadelphia. This water has for many years, using very well-understood technology, been prepared for acceptable drinking water, albeit at the expense of some extra chemical applications. Moreover, a water treatment plant at Düsseldorf, Germany, using activated carbon and ozone, makes aesthetically pleasing drinking water from the Rhine, which is in far worse shape than either the Delaware or the Hudson. Poor water quality does impose extra costs for municipal water treatment, but, except in cases of extremely toxic or evil-tasting substances, it ordinarily cannot justify very high levels of waste effluent treatment.

But to go back to Gaffney's statement, quoted earlier, direct effects on people's satisfactions are the most straightforwardly "economic" of all, and it is in them that we must seek the major justification for high water quality in streams, if indeed such a justification exists.

There is, of course, clear evidence of a close relationship between water quality and human satisfactions. It does not seem to arise from a feeling that health is really endangered to any great extent or that the cost of manufactured goods has been substantially increased because manufacturers have had to provide costly treatment to the water they use. Rather, it is seen in the reactions of the fisherman who has experienced aesthetically displeasing water (perhaps with dead fish in it) and of the person who just prefers to see a clear stream and might even be willing to sacrifice something else (pay higher local taxes or higher prices for manufactured goods) to get it. Politicians have been sensitive to these feelings that have permitted, if not induced, progressively stronger federal legislation in recent years.

But politically expressed discontent is a highly generalized phenomenon. It does not say much about whether action is justified in a particular instance and, if so, how much. What standard for a water body will balance costs and gains in a particular instance? Clearly it depends on circumstances. How much does it cost to improve quality? What present and future uses does the water have? What alternatives are there? Economic analysis of benefits must help to answer all these questions.

Recreational · I propose to linger somewhat over the recreation benefits question. There are three reasons: (1) outdoor recreation activities are growing at a tremendous rate, and the satisfaction people get from these is likely to be sensitive to a variety of environmental insults; (2) some encouraging progress can be reported on the recreation evaluation front; and (3) recreation well illustrates some of the intricacies that benefit evaluation encounters.

For background, and as an example of what I feel is encouraging progress, permit me to recount a personal experience.

Over the last two years I have been engaged as a consultant by the Texas Water Development Board to assist in the preparation of a comprehensive water development plan for that state. Texas is mostly an arid state with few interesting natural features. For this reason one would suppose that the recreation benefit from artificial bodies of water, which provide opportunities for swimming and boating and relief from an otherwise tedious landscape, might be very valuable. Moreover, there was reason to believe that impounding reservoirs could yield substantial benefits for municipal and industrial water supply, irrigation, and water quality improvement. But there was no well-tried and justifiable method for recreation evaluation at hand. The federal agency methods have grave defects. They are based on market prices of doubtful applicability and fail to take account of many relevant circumstances for particular sites—most important in this case are such factors as size of the reservoir, nearness to potential markets (centers of population), and availability of closely substitutable recreation opportunities.

With some outside consulting help, the Texas Water Development Board staff applied a method of evaluation developed by Marion Clawson and Jack Knetsch,[8] which imputes willingness to pay on the basis of actual outlays to achieve access to correlative opportunities. Since outdoor recreation is usually not priced, this ordinarily means travel cost. One does not use the travel cost as such as the appropriate value, but rather infers how much use would drop off if travel costs were augmented by fees at various levels. In this way one obtains an estimate of the willingness to pay for the recreation opportunity as such.

Interviews were conducted and visitor counts were made at existing reservoirs. These provided information on the character of the recreation and on a variety of social and economic variables regarding the users. Using this information, estimates were made of the benefits of potential new reservoirs by means of estimating equations based on multiple regression analysis. Factors such as income, population, distance from the lake, lake size, and proximity of alternative lakes turned out to be significant explanations of benefits. By projecting these variables and using the projected values in the estimating equations, streams of benefit were calculated and these converted to present worths that could be compared with costs. Because of direct interdependencies between the lakes, this was done for different combinations and sequences of development. Such calculations were executed for more than 50 potential lakes.[9]

For the first time, recreation value estimates were made that are in concept equivalent to those routinely produced for, say, power and irrigation, and which took explicit account of salient characteristics of sites and of various spatial and temporal interdependencies. I would be the last to argue that these estimates could not be improved. There are still apparent deficiencies of concept and data. But unquestionably they are an immense im-

8. J. L. Knetsch, "Economics of Including Recreation as a Purpose of Water Resources Projects," *Journal of Farm Economics*, December 1964.

9. H. W. Grubb and J. T. Goodwin, "Economic Evaluation of Water-Oriented Recreation in the Texas Water Plan," Texas Water Development Board, August 1966 (mimeo).

provement over methods based on market prices for largely non-comparable recreation opportunities.

One thing these estimates definitely did not take appropriate account of is quality attributes of the various potential reservoirs. Appearance of shorelines and drawdown characteristics as well as quality characteristics of the water undoubtedly influence the quality of the recreation experience. I believe the methodology used can accommodate these questions, and progress on them is urgently needed.

To return once more to the matter with which we started off this discussion of recreation—pollution—some progress can also be reported on this front. At least two careful efforts have been made to evaluate recreation benefits from improved water quality. One of these, the study of the Delaware estuary, is still under way.

Along the shores of the Delaware estuary is perhaps the greatest urban industrial complex in the United States. The estuary experiences low, even zero, dissolved oxygen almost every year during low-flow periods. To raise the DO is an extremely expensive proposition. To achieve a target of 2 ppm, a least-cost program would cost about $100 million, and a similar program for 4 ppm would cost around $300 million. Imposing as these costs are, an econometric study of potential increases in participation rates shows that these higher oxygen levels might be justified on recreational grounds alone.

These preliminary results suggest that placing a value on increased boating of about $2.50 a day might justify maintaining 3 ppm of DO even if no other benefits were considered. At today's levels of discretionary income, $2.50 a day does not seem a ridiculously high figure to attach to a day of boating. Note that this is a different method than the Clawson-Knetsch technique used in Texas. Here an effort is made to project the increase in participation rates that might occur with an improvement in quality, and then one asks what the minimum per-person willingness to pay would have to be to justify the increase. The work done on other nonrecreational benefits of quality improvement in the Delaware estuary suggests that they are modest when compared with the massive costs of improvement. The decision of whether to achieve high levels of quality will probably turn almost entirely on recreational values.

The only other systematic study of recreational values associated with water quality that I know about was conducted at the other end of the country by some researchers at Oregon State University.[10] This Public Health Service–sponsored study focused on Yaquina Bay on the Oregon coast. The bay lies on a beautiful, but comparatively undeveloped, part of the coastline. The population is light, and there are many alternative recreational opportunities available. The bay is potentially threatened by paper mill waste, which might reduce its biological productivity. A function was envisaged between the input of angling efforts and the output or yield of fish taken. Angling success per unit of effort was taken to represent the quality of the recreational experience. Demand equations based on the so-called Clawson method were estimated for three estuarial fisheries. Among the statistical explanations of demand was a variable representing success per unit of effort. Shifts in the demand for angling in Yaquina Bay were then obtained by means of various assumed reductions in angling success.

The direct recreational losses were identified as the total net willingness to pay, which would result from reduction in the quality of the fishing resource. Examples of the results are as follows: If waste disposal resulted in a total loss of the sports fisheries, the annual value of this loss would equal $22,747. Another way of putting this is that if the entire Yaquina sport fishery were destroyed, the present worth loss involved would be about one half million dollars if discounted at 6 percent. This is less than the capital cost of a basic sewage treatment plant for a comparatively small city.

A more realistic occurrence might be one that resulted in less than total destruction of the fishery. It would be much more common if waste disposal resulted in incremental reductions in water quality, fish life, and recreational values. Accordingly, the direct benefits of avoiding the losses associated with more normal waste disposal conditions would be even less. The authors of the Oregon State study were very careful to point out that many assumptions were involved in their analysis, and that it did not incorporate the whole complex of goals and criteria

10. This research is reported in a paper by J. B. Stevens, "Recreation Benefits from Water Pollution Control," *Water Resources Research*, vol. 2 (Second Quarter 1966).

appropriate for natural resources decision-making. Also it assumed a steady-state condition, i.e., it did not account for the extremely rapid rise in recreation demand.

Nevertheless, I think comparison of the Delaware and the Yaquina Bay studies is instructive. Anyone evaluating the quality of the recreational resource represented by Yaquina Bay and the Delaware estuary on the basis of purely physical criteria would surely rate the bay much higher. Yaquina Bay combines interesting shoreline with mountains and forests and an altogether natural environment. While the Delaware estuary has some handsome stretches, the shoreline is flat and uninteresting for the most part and dominated by the artifacts of an industrial society. But, the total value that must be attached to recreational resources is a function of the number of people who have access to it and the availability of alternatives as well as some inherent natural qualities of the site.

I think economic studies can go a long way toward helping to illuminate the factors determining the value of water quality for recreation and can potentially provide usable values for economic optimization analysis. But they are still in a primitive state. I think improvement of our ability to measure the recreational benefits associated with water quality improvement is perhaps the most urgent task confronting water quality management.

Since I believe that our limited ability to evaluate the recreational losses associated with poor quality water, or, conversely, the benefits of water improvement, is an extremely important barrier to rational water quality management, I will devote the final section of my paper to pointing out a few components of this problem that I feel are critically in need of research. They may also serve to illustrate more generally the complexities that benefit-estimation concerning aspects of environmental quality tends to encounter.

The first of these is the relationship between the level of various water quality parameters and the recreational attractiveness of the water resource. This relationship can be viewed as being composed of two linkages: a natural one and a human one. I think these are both about equally ill understood. It is my impression, gained from being associated with research and consulting endeavors at a number of locations, that the biological sciences are almost never able to tell us specifically what difference a change in measured parameters of water quality will make in those biological characteristics of the water that contribute to its recreational value. I personally have encountered this inability in such diverse places as the Delaware, the Potomac, Yaquina Bay, and the Texas Gulf Coast bays and estuaries. Perhaps the undeveloped state of forecasting is a result of the fact that biologists have seldom been confronted with the case, our ability to forecast these effects must be radically improved if all efforts to evaluate the recreational benefits of quality improvement are not to flounder.

There is also a human linkage that is ill understood. What quality characteristics of water do human beings find attractive for recreation? This is still largely an area of ignorance, although some small progress can be reported. A good example is the work at Oregon State. Statistical analysis of angler behavior was used to forecast the fishermen's response to success per unit of effort expended. Further work along these lines could be highly instructive.

I would like to turn to a more general problem in the estimation of recreation demand, a problem not unique or specific to water quality. This is what might be called the "learning-by-doing" relationship. If water recreational facilities are either unavailable or not easily accessible, many people will not engage in these activities at all. Once they are exposed to the opportunity, however, the demand may go through a dynamic adjustment process. Some activities require special skills. If facilities are not readily available, the skills are not developed and there is little desire to participate. However, as skills are acquired and accessory investments, such as boats, motors, diving equipment, etc., are required, demand will increase, and participation will tend to become more frequent in time.

An extension of this, if we are thinking of truly long-term investments such as are often involved in quality control, is that the more of the present generation introduced to water recreational activities, the more the future population will demand and enjoy these activities. Thus, the "learning-by-doing" phenomenon suggests there is an interaction between present and future demand functions, and to understand the impact of a major change, such as a distinct improvement in the quality of an entire river, this dynamic adjustment process must be understood. Until now, it has not received systematic attention in studies of recreational demand, but I am pleased to report that the "learning-by-doing" relationship is now being studied by economists.

CONCLUSION

Measurement of the demand for environmental quality is still in a primitive state, but encouraging progress can be reported in a few instances. It is of the highest importance that efforts to improve methodology and provide empirical results be pressed.

As some of the grosser environmental insults are dealt with, the question of "how much more improvement" will become central. Virtually every known technique for reducing environmental contamination displays rapidly rising incremental costs. One might even claim that while removing gross ugliness may not be too costly, achieving genuine beauty will require high levels of skill and resource commitment. In a world that demands high military budgets, space programs, wars on poverty, greatly improved standards of education, grand-scale resources development, and environmental improvement, massive demands are made on public budgets from all directions. Amid our affluence we face a demanding resources allocation problem. It is essential that we achieve a better understanding of costs and returns even, or perhaps especially, in fields where measurement is difficult. I think this is certainly one of the most important tasks confronting environmental science.

Air Pollution and Human Health

LESTER B. LAVE and EUGENE P. SESKIN

*Lester B. Lave is professor and head of the Department of Eco-
nomics, and Eugene P. Seskin is Research Associate in Economics
at the Graduate School of Industrial Administration, Carnegie-
Mellon University. This article was published in* Science *in August
1970. This condensed version of the article was prepared with the
assistance of the authors.*

AIR POLLUTION is a problem of growing importance; public interest seems to have risen faster than the level of pollution in
recent years. Presidential messages and news stories have reflected the opinion of scientists and civic leaders that pollution
must be abated. This concern has manifested itself in tightened
local ordinances (and, more importantly, in increased enforcement of existing ordinances), in federal legislation, and in extensive research to find ways of controlling the emission of
pollutants from automobiles and smokestacks. Pollutants are natural constituents of the air. Even without man and his technology, plants, animals, and natural activity would cause some
pollution. For example, animals vent carbon dioxide, volcanic
action produces sulfur oxides, and wind movement insures that
there will be suspended particulates; there is no possibility of
removing all pollution from the air. Instead, the problem is one
of balancing the need of polluters to vent residuals against the
damage suffered by society as a result of the increased pollution.
To find an optimum level, we must know the marginal costs and
marginal benefits associated with abatement. This article is focused on measuring one aspect of the benefit of pollution abatement.

Polluted air affects the health of human beings and of all
animals and plants. It soils and deteriorates property, impairs
various production processes (for example, the widespread use
of "clean rooms" is an attempt to reduce contamination from
the air), raises the rate of automobile and airline accidents, and

generally makes living things less comfortable and less happy. Some of these effects are quite definite and measurable, but most are ill defined and difficult to measure, even conceptually. Thus, scientists still disagree on the quantitative effect of pollution on animals, plants, and materials. Some estimates of the cost of the soiling and deterioration of property have been made, but the estimates are only a step beyond guesses. We conjecture that the major benefit of pollution abatement will be found in a general increase in human happiness or improvement in the "quality of life," rather than in one of the specific, more easily measurable categories. Nonetheless, the "hard" costs are real and at least theoretically measurable.

In this article we report an investigation of the effect of air pollution on human health; we characterize the problem of isolating health effects; we derive quantitative estimates of the effect of air pollution on various diseases and point out reasons for viewing some earlier estimates with caution; we discuss the economic costs of ill health; and we estimate the costs of effects attributed to air pollution.

THE EFFECT OF AIR POLLUTION ON HUMAN HEALTH

In no area of the world is the mean annual level of air pollution high enough to cause continuous acute health problems. Emitted pollutants are diluted in the atmosphere and swept away by winds, except during an inversion; then, for a period that varies from a few hours to a week or more, pollutants are trapped and the dilution process is impeded. When an inversion persists for a week or more, pollution increases substantially, and there is an accompanying increase in the death rate.

Much time has been spent in investigating short-term episodes of air pollution. We are more concerned with the long-term effects of growing up in, and living in, a polluted atmosphere. Few scientists would be surprised to find that air pollution is associated with respiratory diseases of many sorts, including lung cancer and emphysema. A number of studies have established a qualitative link between air pollution and ill health.

A qualitative link, however, is of little use. To estimate the benefit of pollution abatement, we must know how the incidence of a disease varies with the level of pollution. The number of studies that allow one to infer a quantitative association is much smaller.

Quantifying the Relation · Our objective is to determine the amount of morbidity and mortality for specific diseases that can be ascribed to air pollution. The state of one's health depends on factors (both present and past) such as inherited characteristics (that cause a predisposition to certain diseases), personal habits such as smoking and exercise, general physical condition, diet (including the amount of pollutants ingested with food), living conditions, urban and occupational air pollution, and water pollution. Health is a complex matter, and it is exceedingly difficult to sort out the contributions of the various factors. In trying to determine the contribution of any single factor one must be careful neither to include spurious effects nor to conclude on the basis of a single insignificant correlation that there is no association. Laboratory experimentation is of little help in the sorting process. . . .

Epidemiological Studies · Epidemiological data are the kind of health data best adapted to the estimation of air pollution effects. These data are in the form of mortality (or morbidity) rates for a particular group, generally defined geographically. For example, an analyst may try to account for variations in the mortality rate among the various census tracts in a city. While these vital statistics are tabulated by the government and so are easily available, there are problems with the accuracy of the classification of the cause of death (since few diagnoses are verified by autopsy and not all physicians take equal care in finding the cause of death). Other problems stem from unmeasured variables such as smoking habits, occupations, occupational exposure to air pollution, and genetic health factors. Whenever a variable is unmeasured, the analyst is implicitly assuming either that it is constant across groups or else that it varies randomly with respect to the level of air pollution. Since there are many unmeasured variables, one should not be surprised to discover that some studies fail to find a significant relationship or that others find a spurious one. For the same reason, one should not expect the quantitative effect to be identical across various groups, even when the relationship in each group is statistically significant. Whatever the source of data, the investigators must rest their cases by concluding that the associations which they find are so strong that it is extremely unlikely that omitted variables could have given rise to observed correlations; they cannot account for all possible variables.

Episodic Relationships · Another method of investigating the effects of pollution involves an attempt to relate daily or weekly mortality (or morbidity) rates to indices of air pollution during the interval in question. The conclusions of these studies are of limited interest, for two reasons. First, someone who is killed by an increase in air pollution is likely to be gravely ill. Air pollution is a rather subtle irritant, and it is unlikely that a healthy twenty-five-year-old will succumb to a rise in pollution levels. Our interest should be focused on the initial cause of illness rather than on the factor that is the immediate determinant of death. Thus, morbidity data are more useful than mortality data. Second (and more important for the morbidity studies), there are many factors that affect the daily morbidity rate or daily rate of employee absences. Absence rates tend to be high on Mondays and Fridays for reasons that have nothing to do with air pollution or illness. One would expect little change in these absence rates if air pollution were reduced. Other factors, such as absence around holidays, give rise to spurious variation; this can be handled by ignoring the periods in question or by gathering enough data so that this spurious variation is averaged away. Some of these factors (such as high absence rates on Fridays and seasonal absence rates) may be correlated with variations in air pollution and no amount of data or of averaging will separate the effects. We have chosen to disregard the results of these episodic studies, with a few exceptions, cited below.

It is difficult to isolate the pollutants that have the most important effects on health on the basis of the studies we survey here. Measurement techniques have been crude, and there has been a tendency to base concentration figures on a single measurement for a large area. A more important problem is the fact that in most of these studies only a single pollutant was reported. Discovering which pollutants are most harmful is an important area, where further exploration is necessary. We have tried, nevertheless, to differentiate among pollutants in the survey that follows. The problem is complicated, since pollution has increased over time, and since lifetime exposure might bear little relation to currently measured levels. These problems are discussed elsewhere.[1]

[Lave and Seskin's study consists of two phases. In the first phase they reviewed the results of a large number of studies by others, and where possible applied statistical techniques to the published data in an attempt to find an association between mortality and morbidity and air pollution indices. Some of their conclusions were stated as follows:]

These studies indicate a strong relationship between bronchitis mortality and a number of indices of air pollution. We conclude that bronchitis mortality could be reduced by from 25 to 50 percent depending on the particular location and deposit index, by reducing pollution to the lowest level currently prevailing in these regions. . . .

The results of our reworking of the data for lung cancer mortality for England and Wales (there is no control for smoking) imply that, if the quality of air of all boroughs were improved to that of the borough with the best air, the rate of death from lung cancer would fall by as much as 44 percent (of the six regressions run, two suggested no relationship). . . .

On the basis of these studies we conclude that a substantial abatement of air pollution would lead to 10 to 15 percent reduction in the mortality and morbidity rates for heart disease. We caution the reader that the evidence relating cardiovascular disease to air pollution is less comprehensive than that linking bronchitis and lung cancer to air pollution.[2]

1. L. B. Lave, "Air Pollution Damage," in *Environmental Quality Analysis: Theory and Method in the Social Sciences*, A. V. Kneese and B. T. Bower, eds. (Baltimore: Johns Hopkins Press, 1972).

2. [In the second phase of their study, Lave and Seskin used multiple regression analysis on data from 114 Standard Metropolitan Statistical Areas (SMSA) in the United States in an attempt to explain the observed variation in mortality rates among SMSAs by differences in observed air pollution levels and socioeconomic characteristics. They report as follows:

In a study just being completed, we have collected data for 114 Standard Metropolitan Statistical Areas in the United States and have attempted to relate total death rates and infant mortality rates to air pollution and other factors. Socioeconomic data, death rates, and air pollution data were taken from U.S. Government publications.

TABLE 1. *Relationships Between Mortality and Air Pollution*

Measure of Air Pollution	Air Pollution Coefficient (a_1)	Population Density (a_2)	% Non-white (a_3)	% Over 65 (a_4)	% Poor (a_5)	Coefficient of Determination R^2
Total death rate						
1. Particulates[a]	.102	.001	.032	.682	.013*	.804
2. Sulfates[b]	.085	.001	.033	.652	.006*	.813
Infants less than one year						
3. Particulates	.393	—	.190	—	.150	.545
4. Sulfates	.150	—	.200	—	.123	.522
Infants less than 28 days old						
5. Particulates	.273	—	.089	—	.063*	.260
6. Sulfates	.170	—	.097	—	.047*	.263
Fetal death rate						
7. Particulates	.274	.004	.171	—	.106	.434
8. Sulfates	.171	.004	.181	—	.085	.434

* Not significantly different from zero at the .05 level.
[a] Suspended particulates in micrograms per cubic meter, minimum biweekly reading.
[b] Total sulfates in micrograms per cubic meter ($\times 10$), minimum biweekly reading.

Regression 1 (Table 1) shows how the total death rate in 1960 varies with air pollution levels and with socioeconomic factors. As the (biweekly) minimum level of suspended particulates increases, the death rate rises significantly. Moreover, the death rate increases with (1) the density of population of the area, (2) the proportion of nonwhites, (3) the proportion of people over age 65, and (4) the proportion of poor families. Eighty percent of the variation in the death rate across these 114 statistical areas is explained by the regression.

We fit the following equation to the data:
$$MR_i = a_0 + a_1 AP_i + a_2 P/M^2_i + a_3 \%N\text{--}W_i + a_4 \%{>}65_i + a_5 \% \text{Poor}_i + e_i$$
where MR_i is the mortality rate for a particular disease in $SMSA_i$, AP_i is a measure of air pollution in that SMSA, P/M^2_i is the population per square mile in the SMSA, $\%N\text{--}W_i$ is the percentage of nonwhites in the population ($\times 10$), $\%{>}65_i$ is the percentage of people over 65 years of age ($\times 10$), $\%\text{Poor}_i$ is the percentage of families with incomes under $3,000 ($\times 10$), and e_i is an error term with a mean of zero. *Editors.*]

Regression 3 shows how the 1960 infant death rate (age less than 1 year) varies. A smaller proportion (55 percent) of the variation in the death rate is explained by the regression, although the minimum air-pollution level, the percentage of nonwhites, and the proportion of poor families continue to be significant explanatory variables. Regression 5 is an attempt to explain variation in the neonatal death rate. The results are quite similar to those of regression 3. The fetal death rate is examined in regression 7. Here the minimum air-pollution level, population density, the percentage of nonwhites, and the percentage of poor families are all significant explanatory variables.

Regressions 2, 4, 6, and 8 are an attempt to relate these death rates to the atmospheric concentrations of sulfates for the 114 statistical areas of the study. Regression 2 shows that the total death rate is significantly related to the minimum level of sulfate pollution, to population density, and to the percentage of people over age 65; 81 percent of the variation is explained. Regressions 4, 6, and 8 show that the minimum atmospheric concentration of sulfates is a significant explanatory variable in three categories of infant death rates.

One might put these results in perspective by noting estimates on how small decreases in the air-pollution level affect the various death rates. A 10 percent decrease in the minimum concentration of measured particulates would decrease the total death rate by 0.5 percent, the infant death rate by 0.7 percent, the neonatal death rate by 0.6 percent, and the fetal death rate by 0.9 percent. Note that a 10 percent decrease in the percentage of poor families would decrease the total death rate by 0.2 percent and the fetal death rate by 2 percent. A 10 percent decrease in the minimum concentration of sulfates would decrease the total death rate by 0.4 percent, the infant mortality rate by 0.3 percent, the neonatal death rate by 0.4 percent, and the fetal death rate by 0.5 percent.[3]

3. [These relationships in percentage terms are derived from the relationships in Table 1, and they are valid for variations around the mean values of the variables provided in the original article.

For example, the mean total death rate in the population studied is 91.5 per 10,000. The mean of the minimum biweekly reading for suspended particulates is 45.2 micrograms per cubic meter. Thus, a 10 percent reduction in the minimum concentration of suspended particulates would amount

SOME CAVEATS

In preceding sections we have described a number of studies which quantify the relationship between air pollution and both morbidity and mortality. Is the evidence conclusive? Is it possible for a reasonable man still to object that there is no evidence of a substantial quantitative association? We believe that there is conclusive evidence of such association.

In the studies discussed, a number of countries are considered, and differences in morbidity and mortality rates among different geographical areas, among people within an occupational group, and among children are examined. Various methods are used, ranging from individual medical examinations and interviews to questionnaires and tabulations of existing data. While individual studies may be attacked on the grounds that none manages to provide controls for all causes of ill health, the number of studies and the variety of approaches are persuasive. It is difficult to imagine how factors such as general habits, inherited characteristics, and lifetime exercise patterns could be taken into account.

To discredit the results, a critic would have to argue that the relationships found by the investigators are spurious because the level of air pollution is correlated with a third factor, which is the "real" cause of ill health. For example, many studies do not take into account smoking habits, occupational exposure, and the general pace of life. Perhaps city dwellers smoke more, get less exercise, tend to be more overweight, and generally live a more strained, tense life than rural dwellers. If so, morbidity and mortality rates would be higher for city dwellers, yet air pollution would be irrelevant. This explanation cannot account for the relationships found. . . .

THE ECONOMIC COSTS OF DISEASE

Having found a quantitative association between air pollution and both morbidity and mortality, the next question is that of

---

to 4.52 micrograms per cubic meter. According to Regression 1, such a reduction would decrease the total death rate by .102 times 4.52 or .461 deaths per 10,000 population. This is a 0.5 percent (i.e., .461 divided by 91.5) reduction in the death rate. It would mean, for example, 461 fewer deaths annually in a city with a population of 10 million. *Editors.*]

translating the increased sickness and death into dollar units. The relevant question is, how much is society willing to spend to improve health (to lower the incidence of disease)? In other words, how much is it worth to society to relieve painful symptoms, increase the level of comfort of sufferers, prevent disability, and prolong life? It has become common practice to estimate what society is willing to pay by totaling the amount that is spent on medical care and the value of earnings "forgone" as a result of the disability or death. This cost seems a vast underestimate for the United States in the late 1960s. Society seems willing to spend substantial sums to prolong life or relieve pain. For example, someone with kidney failure can be kept alive by renal dialysis at a cost of $15,000 to $25,000 per year; this sum is substantially in excess of forgone earnings, but today many kidney patients receive this treatment. Another example is leukemia in children; enormous sums are spent to prolong life for a few months, with no economic benefit to society. If ways could be found to keep patients with chronic bronchitis alive and active longer, it seems likely that people would be willing to spend sums substantially greater than the forgone earnings of those helped. So far as preventing disease is concerned, society is willing to spend considerable sums for public health programs such as chest X-rays, inoculation, fluoridation, pure water, and garbage disposal and for private health care programs such as annual physical check-ups.

While we believe that the value of earnings forgone as a result of morbidity and mortality provides a gross underestimate of the amount society is willing to pay to lessen pain and premature death caused by disease, we have no other way of deriving numerical estimates of the dollar value of air-pollution abatement. Thus, we proceed with a conventional benefit calculation, using these forgone earnings despite our reservations.

Direct and Indirect Costs · Our figures for the cost of disease are based on *Estimating the Cost of Illness*, by Dorothy P. Rice.[4] Rice defines direct disease costs as including expenditures for hospital and nursing home care and for services of physicians, dentists, and members of other health professions.

4. D. P. Rice, *Estimating the Cost of Illness*, Public Health Service Publication No. 947–6, 1966.

Estimating indirect cost is an attempt to measure the losses to the nation's economy caused by illness, disability, and premature death. We would argue that such a calculation gives a lower bound for the amount people would be willing to pay to lower the morbidity and mortality rates. These costs are calculated in terms of the earnings forgone by those who are sick, disabled, or prematurely dead.

THE HEALTH COST OF AIR POLLUTION

The studies cited earlier in this article show a close association between air pollution and ill health. The evidence is extremely good for some diseases (such as bronchitis and lung cancer) and only suggestive for others (such as cardiovascular disease and nonrespiratory-tract cancers). Not all factors have been taken into account, but we argue that an unbiased observer would have to concede the association. More effort can and should be spent on refining the estimates. However, the point of this exercise is to estimate the health cost of air pollution. We believe that the evidence is sufficiently complete to allow us to infer, roughly, the quantitative associations. We do so with caution, and proceed to translate the effects into dollars. We have attempted to choose our point estimates from the conservative end of the range.

We interpret the studies cited as indicating that mortality from bronchitis would be reduced by about 50 percent if air pollution were lowered to levels currently prevailing in urban areas with relatively clean air. We therefore make the assumption that there would be a 25 to 50 percent reduction in morbidity and mortality due to bronchitis if air pollution in the major urban areas were abated by about 50 percent. Since the cost of bronchitis (in terms of forgone income and current medical expenditures) is $930 million per year, we conclude that from $250 million to $500 million per year would be saved by a 50 percent abatement of air pollution in the major urban areas.

Approximately 25 percent of mortality from lung cancer can be saved by a 50 percent reduction in air pollution, according to the studies cited above. This amounts to an annual cost of about 33 million.

The studies document a strong relationship between all respiratory disease and air pollution. It seems likely that 25 percent of all morbidity and mortality due to respiratory disease could be saved by a 50 percent abatement in air pollution levels. Since the annual cost of respiratory disease is $4,887 million, the amount saved by a 50 percent reduction in air pollution in major urban areas would be $1,222 million.

There is evidence that over 20 percent of cardiovascular morbidity and about 20 percent of cardiovascular mortality could be saved if air pollution were reduced by 50 percent. We have chosen to put this saving at only 10 percent—that is, $468 million per year.

Finally, there is a good deal of evidence connecting all mortality from cancer with air pollution. It is difficult to arrive at a single figure, but we have estimated that 15 percent of the cost of cancer would be saved by a 50 percent reduction in air pollution—a total of $390 million per year.

Not all of these cost estimates are equally certain. The connection between bronchitis or lung cancer and air pollution is much better documented than the connection between all cancers or all cardiovascular disease and air pollution. The reader may aggregate the costs as he chooses. We estimate the total annual cost that would be saved by a 50 percent reduction in air-pollution levels in major urban areas, in terms of decreased morbidity and mortality, to be $2,080 million. A more relevant indication of the cost would be the estimate that 4.5 percent of all economic costs associated with morbidity and mortality would be saved by a 50 percent reduction in air pollution in major urban areas. This percentage estimate is a robust figure; it is not sensitive to the exact figures chosen for calculating the economic cost of ill health.

A final point is that these dollar figures are surely underestimates of the relevant costs. The relevant measure is what people would be willing to pay to reduce morbidity and mortality (for example, to reduce lung cancer by 25 percent). It seems evident that the value used for forgone earnings is a gross underestimate of the actual amount. An additional argument is that many health effects have not been considered in arriving at these costs. For example, relatively low levels of carbon monoxide can affect the central nervous system sufficiently to reduce work efficiency and increase the accident rate. Psychological and esthetic effects are likely to be important, and additional costs associated with the effect of air pollution on vegetation, cleanliness, and the deterioration of materials have not been included in these estimates.

Income Distribution and Environmental Quality

A. MYRICK FREEMAN III

A. Myrick Freeman III is in the Department of Economics at Bowdoin College. This paper is based on research which was supported by Resources for the Future, Inc., and was reported more completely in Allen V. Kneese and Blair T. Bower, eds. Environmental Quality Analysis: Theory and Method in the Social Sciences, *published by the Johns Hopkins Press.*

ALTHOUGH THE BULK of economic analysis has been directed at the question of the efficient allocation of resources, there has always been a continuing concern with the ways in which the fruits of economic activity are distributed among the members of the society. In other words economics is concerned with the way the economic pie is shared as well as how big a pie is produced.

These twin concerns can be identified in the area of environmental economics as well. Market failures and spillover effects lead to inefficiency in the use of environmental resources. There is too much environmental pollution and not enough environmental quality. The over-all economic pie can be made larger by controlling pollution as long as the marginal benefits of pollution control exceed the marginal costs.

But in addition to questions of economic efficiency and the size of the pie, we are concerned with the way in which the damages of environmental pollution are distributed among different groups in the society, and the ways in which we might share the burdens of the costs of achieving pollution control. Specifically we are concerned with two kinds of questions with respect to income distribution and environmental quality. The first is: How are the damages of pollution distributed within the society? Is environmental pollution purely a middle- and upper-class concern, as some have alleged? Or does pollution hit rich and poor alike? Is pollution the great leveler? The other side of this coin is: Who will reap the benefits of pollution control? The second set of questions concerns who will bear the costs of pollution control, and what kinds of policies we can adopt to spread this burden more equitably among the members of the society.

POLLUTION DAMAGES AND POLLUTION CONTROL BENEFITS

One of the advantages of wealth is that it enables its possessors to buy protection from environmental insults such as air and water pollution. Take the case of air pollution. Most cities are characterized by high levels of air pollution in the central city and surrounding heavily industrialized areas, and low air pollution levels (high air quality) in the suburbs. If people perceive differences in air quality—for example, odor, haze, soot, and eye irritation—they will prefer to live in the areas of high air quality. Those who can will bid up the price of land in the areas of high air quality until they ration the limited supply of good land among those with the means and willingness to pay for it. If the best air quality is in the suburbs, and if the suburbs are preferred for other reasons as well, the result will be that high-income people will tend to live in the suburbs, and that low-income people will be forced by economic circumstances to live in those parts of the city with the highest air pollution.

Table 1 shows the results of this sorting out for Kansas City, St. Louis, and Washington, D.C.

In all three cities, low-income people live in areas which expose them to significantly higher levels of suspended particulates and sulfur oxides. Furthermore, as Table 2 shows, residential segregation by race reinforces the devastating effect of segregation by income. In all three cities, the average nonwhite, irrespective of income, endured higher levels of air pollution than did the average 0–$3,000-per-year low-income person, black or white.

How will the benefits of air pollution control be distributed? Pollution control efforts are likely to have their largest impacts on those areas with the lowest air quality, and therefore would most directly affect the poor and blacks. But the ultimate economic impact is less certain. If the central city areas now become relatively more desirable as residences by virtue of cleaner air, there may tend to be a movement of people back toward the city center. This would tend to bid up the price of

TABLE 1. *Air Pollution Exposure by Income Size Class*

Income Size Class	Suspended Particulates	Sulfation
(dollars)	Micrograms per Cubic Meter	Milligrams of Sulfur Trioxide per 100 Square Centimeters per Day
Kansas City		
0– 2,999	76.7	0.22
3,000– 4,999	72.4	0.20
5,000– 6,999	66.5	0.18
7,000– 9,999	63.5	0.17
10,000–14,999	60.1	0.15
15,000–24,999	57.6	0.14
25,000–over	58.1	0.12
St. Louis		
0– 2,999	91.3	0.97
3,000– 4,999	85.3	0.88
5,000– 6,999	79.2	0.78
7,000– 9,999	75.4	0.72
10,000–14,999	73.0	0.68
15,000–24,999	68.8	0.60
25,000–over	64.9	0.52
Washington, D.C.		
0– 2,999	64.6	0.82
3,000– 4,999	61.7	0.82
5,000– 6,999	53.9	0.75
7,000– 9,999	49.7	0.69
10,000–14,999	45.5	0.64
15,000–24,999	43.2	0.58
25,000–over	42.0	0.53

SOURCE: See A. M. Freeman III, "The Distribution of Environmental Quality," in *Environmental Quality Analysis: Theory and Method in the Social Sciences*, A. V. Kneese and B. T. Bower, eds. (Baltimore: Johns Hopkins Press, 1972), p. 265.

urban land and ultimately raise the rents that all would have to pay. If the urban poor and blacks tend to rent their dwellings rather than own them (which is true), then to the extent that cleaning up the urban air brings people back to the city, the benefits of pollution control will be captured by the landlord–property owner. But if urban land-use patterns are relatively rigid, and determined primarily by factors other than air quality, and to the extent that the observed correlation between air quality and income is a more or less accidental consequence of

TABLE 2. *Air Pollution Exposure by Race*

	Suspended Particulates	Sulfation
	Micrograms per Cubic Meter	Milligrams of Sulfur Trioxide per 100 Square Centimeters per Day
Kansas City		
White	64.3	.17
Nonwhite	83.3	.24
St. Louis		
White	78.2	.80
Nonwhite	102.6	1.22
Washington, D.C.		
White	42.8	.66
Nonwhite	78.4	.95

SOURCE: Same as Table 1.

these patterns, air pollution control will benefit primarily the urban poor and blacks.

The primary effect of water pollution is to reduce the opportunities of people for water-based recreation such as fishing, boating, and swimming. Several studies have shown that participation in these water-based recreation activities is positively correlated with income. And this is easily explained. Boating and fishing, for example, require investments in complementary equipment—boats and fishing gear. Furthermore there are associated travel costs to and from recreation sites and operation expenses for bait, gasoline, guides, etc. It would appear that water quality improvements would tend to benefit disproportionately the upper-income groups. However, to the extent that water pollution control efforts increased water-based recreation opportunities close to the urban centers, they would tend to spread a larger share of their benefits to lower-income urban residents as well.

COSTS

Pollution control costs are opportunity costs. Pollution control efforts absorb labor, land, and capital in recycling and recovering materials rather than discharging them to the environment, in intercepting wastes flows and treating them or rendering them harmless before discharge, and in altering production processes to make them more efficient. The resources absorbed in these activities could have been used to produce something else, and that forgone production is the cost of pollution control.

Who will bear these costs? The firms and producing units must pay for these resources to bid them away from their alternative uses. In the long run and in a world of mobile resources, the higher cost of production induced by pollution control efforts will largely be passed on to consumers in the form of higher prices for goods and services. Or where public agencies undertake pollution control activity, the resource costs are passed on to the taxpayer.

How are these costs likely to be spread among individuals of different income levels? Those costs passed on as higher prices are likely to have a regressive incidence on balance—like a sales or excise tax. This is because lower-income people spend a higher proportion of their income on goods and services.

However, there is one significant exception to this generalization. Since federal policy for controlling the emissions and air pollutants from automobiles is directed solely at new model cars, the costs of automotive air pollution control are reflected in higher prices of new model automobiles relative to used cars. And since low-income people tend to buy used cars rather than new cars, the costs of automotive air pollution control are weighing most heavily on middle-income groups, i.e., those who earn five to ten thousand dollars per year.

For those pollution control costs incurred by public agencies, the incidence depends on what form of tax is used to raise the revenues. Local governments building and operating sewage treatment plants and solid-waste disposal systems are more likely to raise revenues by regressive sales and property taxes.

If the burden of pollution control tends to be regressive, is it possible to shift these pollution control costs in the interests of greater equity? Several kinds of direct and indirect grants and subsidies can be designed to shift these costs from consumers as a group to taxpayers as a group, and within the group of taxpayers from lower-income to higher-income taxpayers. Direct and indirect cost subsidies can be used to shift the cost from consumers to taxpayers. Indirect cost subsidies involve no actual cash outlays on the part of government, but are created by changes in the tax rules which provide more favorable tax treatment in certain situations. For example, the cost to a firm of installing pollution control equipment can be reduced by permitting accelerated depreciation or by exempting the equipment from sales taxes or real property taxes. Direct subsidies can take the form of cash payments to public agencies and companies to reimburse them for some part of their pollution control costs.

Do these subsidies really result in a more equal distribution of income? Take the case of federal grants to help pay for local sewage treatment. If the federal tax system is more progressive than the local taxes used to finance municipal pollution control, then this form of cost subsidy benefits lower-income groups relative to higher-income groups. If direct or indirect cost subsidies are made available to firms, and if they result in lower product prices, then the net effect is to favor lower-income groups relative to upper-income groups.

However, there are two important qualifications to this line of reasoning. First, although cost subsidies can shift the distribution of burden from poor to rich, they also increase the total burden, i.e., the total cost of pollution control, by reducing the incentives to dischargers to find the least-cost solution to their pollution problems. If companies were relieved of all financial responsibility for treatment of their waste, they would have no economic incentive to control the volume of wastes being produced. The total of waste to be treated would be too high and the total cost of a given level of pollution control would be much higher than necessary. Conceivably everybody could be made worse off by efforts to redistribute the costs of pollution control from poor to rich by the vehicle of cost subsidy.

As for the second qualification, where cost subsidies go to aid industrial pollution control efforts there is some question whether these benefits will always be passed on to the consumer in the form of lower prices. Where markets are less than perfectly competitive, one can conceive of a variety of situations in which some or all of the cost subsidy could be absorbed by the firm as profit.

The two qualifications suggested here would seem to argue against any widespread use of cost subsidies to shift the burden of pollution control costs. However, there is one situation in which some efforts to shift pollution control costs might be appropriate, if not highly desirable. Suppose that stringent pollution control requirements have been imposed. High-pollution industries would be faced with rising costs, rising relative prices for their products, and shrinking markets. Some firms will be forced to contract output and there may be short-run losses. More important, some firms may have to reduce their levels of employment or shut down entirely. Labor and capital would be at least temporarily unemployed. Where the firms were significant parts of the local economy and where resources, especially labor, were not highly mobile, the result could be severe and prolonged unemployment and fiscal crises for municipal governments. In this situation an application of the concept of adjustment assistance might be appropriate.

Adjustment assistance consists of direct payments to labor and capital for the purpose of shifting the burden of pollution control and facilitating adjustment to newly imposed environmental standards where these new standards result in unemployment and economic losses. Although such payments are not at present part of any state or federal environmental policy, I believe that they should be. Where pollution control actions have resulted in idle facilities, lack of profits, or unemployment, firms should be able to obtain technical assistance in developing new products or lowering costs and low-interest loans or loan guarantees for new equipment or conversion to a new activity where market conditions are better. More important, workers should be able to obtain unemployment compensation and relocation allowances for moving to areas where the prospects of employment are better. Also workers should be eligible for retraining programs and grants to support them while they·learn new skills.

In addition to adjustment assistance for labor and capital, a well-conceived pollution control adjustment-assistance program should make provision for financial aid to those towns that lose tax revenues because of the loss of industry. There is a very delicate problem in defining the conditions of eligibility and in providing for an appropriate body to judge that eligibility. The challenge is to write regulations which are neither so strict as to defeat the intent of the program nor so liberal as to turn the program into a general subsidy for business and labor.

Standard-Setting

J. CLARENCE DAVIES III

J. Clarence Davies III is a political scientist who has taught at Princeton and is now on the staff of the U.S. Council on Environmental Quality. This paper is taken from his book The Politics of Pollution.

THE ESTABLISHMENT of standards is a crucial step in any pollution control program. Standards not only state the goals of the program, they also provide a measuring stick to determine the program's progress and a basis for determining what actions should be-taken by the program. In a very real sense, standards are the "marching orders" for a pollution control agency. Together with compliance, they are the core of the pollution control process.

To understand the standard-setting process it is necessary to distinguish between three kinds of standards, all of which are necessary for pollution control. First, there are the community *goals,* which state the objectives of the program in qualitative, nonnumerical terms. "Water suitable for swimming" or "Air which will not produce disease in healthy members of the population" are examples of goals. Second, there are *water quality or ambient air standards.* These translate the goals into specific numerical levels of quality to be applied to a body of water or to the air circulating in a community. Thus, "No more than X parts of suspended solids in River Y," or "No more than X parts per million of sulfur dioxide for any 8-hour period in city Y," are water quality or ambient air standards. The third kind of standards are *emission or effluent standards.* Emission standards prescribe how much of what kind of pollution is to be allowed from any given source, for example, "No industrial plant can discharge effluent containing more than X parts of suspended solids into River Y," or "No power plant can use fuel containing more than X percent of sulfur in city Y."

The establishment of goals is basically a political question.

The balance which must be struck in the political arena has been well described by the federal body responsible for setting radiation protection standards. "The use of radiation results in numerous benefits to man in medicine, industry, commerce, and research," states the Federal Radiation Council. "If those beneficial uses were fully exploited without regard to radiation protection, the resulting biological risk might well be considered too great. Reducing the risk to zero would virtually eliminate any radiation use, and result in the loss of all possible benefits. It is therefore necessary to strike some balance between maximum use and zero risk. In establishing radiation protection standards, the balancing of risk and benefit is a decision involving medical, social, economic, political, and other factors. Such a balance cannot be made on the basis of a precise mathematical formula but must be a matter of informed judgment."[1]

A community's designation of goals implies some kind of cost-benefit calculation, even though the calculation in most cases is intuitive or even unconscious. A community which decides that it wants to eliminate pollution in a given river to the extent that people can swim there is implicitly deciding that the benefits of being able to swim in the river are greater than the costs of eliminating the pollution. However, techniques are not now available, and probably never will be, to reduce the cost-benefit calculation to any kind of mathematical precision. The value which one community attaches to being able to swim may very well be different from that placed on swimming by the next community.

If there were complete knowledge of the effects of all pollutants, the transition from goals to quality standards would be almost automatic. Once it had been determined that River Y should be suitable for swimming, the scientists would be able to provide a listing of what level of control for each kind of pollutant was necessary to permit safe swimming. However, as we indicated above, such knowledge of effects is far from complete. In air pollution it is so imcomplete that the distinction between goals and quality standards tends to become lost, and contro-

1. "Background Material for the Development of Radiation Protection Standards," staff report of the Federal Radiation Council, May 13, 1960, reprinted May 1965 by HEW, p. 24. For a cogent argument along the same lines, see B. Commoner, *Science and Survival* (New York: Viking, 1967), pp. 90–102.

versy often rages over numerical quality standards without any consideration of what the quality standards represent in terms of substantive goals. Without knowledge of the effects of particular pollutants, communities do not know what they are "buying" for the costs of establishing particular quality standards.

The development of emission standards, despite the fact that they represent the "teeth" in any control program, has generally been considered the domain of the technicians. Community controversy usually takes place over goals and quality standards but only rarely over emission standards. It is presumed that once the quality standards have been established the emission standards can be mathematically calculated, although in fact the transition from quality to emission standards involves a number of assumptions which are by no means mathematical or automatic.

In many cases emission standards are not directly tied to quality standards, but rather are based on some standard of "good practice." Thus, a community may simply determine that all industries within its jurisdiction shall install the best control devices currently available. The guidelines issued by the Department of the Interior for water quality standards state that municipalities are expected to provide secondary treatment for wastes. These kinds of emission standards are arbitrary in that they are not related to the achievement of goals or quality standards. The application of secondary treatment to all municipal wastes flowing into a particular river may make the river cleaner than it has to be or may leave it in a condition completely inadequate for the desired use, depending on the proportion of pollution contributed by municipalities, the size of the municipalities along the river, the amount of water flowing in the river, and a number of other factors.

In cases where emission standards are based on quality standards, the process of deriving the former from the latter is usually complex. The basic step is generally to calculate the percentage reduction necessary to get from existing levels to the quality standards and then to apply this same percentage reduction to existing emissions. To take an actual example, HEW's recommended sulfur standard for New York City was derived as follows: The desirable level of quality for ambient air was set at an annual mean concentration of sulfur dioxide no greater than 0.02 parts per million. This was the lowest level associated with increased respiratory disease death rates in man, with significant corrosion of metals, and with injury to perennial vegetation. It was determined that in New York the existing concentration of sulfur dioxide in the air needed to be reduced by 83 percent to achieve the desired level. The total amount of sulfur dioxide emitted annually into the New York atmosphere (1,600,000 tons) was then divided by the total heat content of all coal and oil burned annually in the city (1,600 trillion British thermal units [BTU]), resulting in the figure of 2 pounds of sulfur dioxide per 1 million BTU. If an 83 percent reduction was to be achieved, then only 17 percent of the existing emissions could be allowed to continue. Seventeen percent of 2 pounds of sulfur dioxide per 1 million BTU is 0.34 pounds of sulfur dioxide per 1 million BTU which, with slight rounding, was the emission standard announced for the New York area.[2]

The kind of straightforward approach to calculating emission standards which calls simply for an equal percentage reduction from all pollution sources involves a number of assumptions which are open to question. It ignores the question of costs, although in many cases it would probably be much less expensive to have certain polluters reduce their emissions by 95 percent and others reduce their emissions by only 75 percent, rather than both sources reducing emissions by 85 percent. A simulation study by HEW revealed that for certain types of air pollution control objectives, the uniform reduction approach may cost seven times as much as an approach which utilizes variations in emission standards.[3] Thus the across-the-board standard may be the most equitable or the simplest to administer, but it is often not the least-cost solution.

The uniform reduction approach also does not take into account the location of the emission sources, meteorological condi-

2. To translate this emission standard into a limitation on the sulfur content of coal, it is only necessary to know that 1 pound of sulfur will produce 2 pounds of sulfur dioxide and that an average pound of coal contains 13,000 BTU. By multiplying the emission standard times 13,000 and then dividing by 2, one can translate the limit of 0.34 pounds of sulfur dioxide per million BTU into a limitation of 0.2 percent on the sulfur content of coal.

3. HEW, Office of the Assistant Secretary for Planning and Evaluation, "An Economic Analysis of the Control of Sulphur Oxides Air Pollution" (December 1967), p. V–1.

tions (in the case of air pollution), and other factors which influence the dispersion of the pollution. It does not consider changes in the amount of pollution which will occur in future years because of industrial expansion, plant relocation, or other factors. Alternatives to emission reduction, such as stream re-aeration in the case of water pollution or relocation of power plants in the case of air pollution, are usually not taken into account. In short, a number of simplifying assumptions are made, and if any of these assumptions were changed a different standard would probably result.

The Delaware Estuary Study: Effluent Charges, Least-Cost Treatment, and Efficiency

ALLEN V. KNEESE AND BLAIR T. BOWER

Allen Kneese and Blair Bower are director and associate director, respectively, of the Quality of the Environment Program at Resources for the Future, Inc. This paper was adapted from their book Managing Water Quality: Economics, Technology, and Institutions.

THE DELAWARE RIVER BASIN, though small by the standards of the great American river basins and draining an area of only 12,765 square miles, holds a population of over six million. Portions of the basin are among the most highly industrialized and densely populated regions in the world, and it is in these areas that the main water quality problems are encountered. The Delaware Estuary, an 86-mile reach of the Delaware River from Trenton, New Jersey, to Liston Point, Delaware, is most important in terms of the quantity of water affected, the area involved, the extent of industrial activity, and the number of people involved.

Despite early industrial and municipal development in the basin, water quality problems were neglected until the last few decades. The Interstate Commission on the Delaware River Basin (INCODEL) was formed in 1936, and under its auspices the states in the basin signed a reciprocal agreement on water quality control. This provided the legal basis for construction of treatment plants by municipalities after World War II. The standards of treatment achieved were not particularly high (on the average, not much more than removal of the grosser solids), and the residual waste load from the plants, together with industrial discharges, continued to place very heavy oxygen demands on the estuary. Especially during the warm summer months dissolved oxygen falls to low levels or becomes exhausted in a few portions of the reach of the estuary from Philadelphia to the Pennsylvania-Delaware state line.

In 1957–58, at the request of the Corps of Engineers, the U.S. Public Health Service made a preliminary study of water quality in the Delaware Estuary. The data it produced regarding the quality of the estuary led state and interstate agencies concerned with water quality to request a comprehensive study of the estuary under the provisions of the Federal Water Pollution Control Act. The study was begun in 1961 by the Water Supply and Pollution Control Division of the Public Health Service, and in the summer of 1966 a report was issued by the Federal Water Pollution Control Administration—*Delaware Estuary Comprehensive Study: Preliminary Report and Findings*. The study made an effort to measure external costs as well as costs of control and provided an outstanding analysis of effluent charges as a means of controlling discharge at low social cost when decentralized treatment at individual points of discharge is the means considered.

Among the other notable contributions of the estuary study was the development and application of a rigorous mathematical representation of the causal relationships defining the waste assimilative and transport characteristics of the estuary. The model permits estimating the effects of increases or decreases in the waste load discharged in a particular section on all other sections throughout the estuary area. A model of this character is an essential element in a systematic analysis for regional water quality management, whether or not an estuary is involved. This model, which characterizes physical, biological, and chemical relationships in the estuary, was wedded to an economic optimization (linear programming) model. This permitted the identification of cost-minimizing solutions which could then be compared with other solutions more characteristic of conventional administrative modes of water quality control.

The model was first used to analyze the total and incremental costs of achieving five "objective sets," each representing a different package and spatial distribution of water quality characteristics, with the level of quality increasing from set 5 (representing 1964 water quality) to set 1. An effort was then made to measure benefits associated with the improvement in water quality indicated by the successive objective sets. At the same time, limited analysis was made of collective measures which might substitute efficiently for waste treatment over certain ranges.

These included the dredging of bottom deposits that exert an oxygen demand, reoxygenation of the estuary, and diversion of wastes from the estuary. Finally the computer simulation model was used to calculate the costs of achieving given levels of water quality under the alternative strategies of effluent charges and uniform treatment regulations and to compare them with the least-cost solution found by the linear programming model.

COSTS OF ALTERNATIVE OBJECTIVES

The five alternative objective levels can be summarized as follows:

Objective Set 1 · This is the highest objective set. It makes provision for large increases in water-contact recreation in the estuary. It also makes special provision for 6.5 ppm levels of dissolved oxygen to provide safe passage for anadromous (migratory) fish during the spring and fall migration periods. Thus this objective set should produce conditions in which water quality is basically no obstacle to the migration of shad and other anadromous fishes.

Objective Set 2 · Under this objective set the area available for water-contact recreation is constricted somewhat. Some reduction in sport and commercial fishing would also be expected because of the somewhat lower dissolved oxygen objective. This set, like objective set 1, makes special provision for high dissolved oxygen during periods of anadromous fish passage.

Objective Set 3 · This set is similar to set 2. Although there is no specific provision for raising dissolved oxygen during periods of anadromus fish migrations, there is comparatively little difference in the survival probability under objective sets 2 and 3. Under the waste-loading conditions envisioned for objective 3, the estimated survival twenty-four out of twenty-five years would be at least 80 percent—compared with 90 percent for set 2.

Objective Set 4 · This provides for a slight increase over 1964 levels in water-contact recreation and fishing in the lower sections of the estuary. Generally, water quality is improved slightly over 1964 conditions and the probability of anaerobic conditions occurring is greatly reduced.

Objective Set 5 • This would maintain 1964 conditions in the estuary. It would provide for no more than a prevention of further water quality deterioration.

The costs of achieving objective sets 1 through 4 by various combinations of waste discharge reduction at particular outfalls for the waste-load conditions expected to prevail in 1975–80 are shown in Table 1 below.

BENEFITS OF IMPROVED WATER QUALITY

The *Delaware Estuary Comprehensive Study* pioneered by broadening the range of benefits considered in the water quality planning process and by introducing quantitative estimates of recreation benefits (reduced external costs) into the process. While the benefit figures were necessarily rather rough, they appear to be sufficiently accurate to comprise a general guide to the decision-making process.

Three general categories of recreation benefits were considered: (1) swimming, (2) boating, (3) sport fishing. Analyses conducted at the University of Pennsylvania, and based on a highly simplified model of recreation participation, indicated a large latent recreation demand in the estuary region. Another study, separately sponsored, tended to confirm the order of magnitude of the estimates.[1] In computing the monetary values associated with recreation demand under each objective set, a number of factors were considered—including recreation-bearing capacity of the estuary as influenced by improved quality. A range of benefits was calculated by the application of alternative monetary unit values to the total use projected for the estuary. The analyses indicated that the increase in the present value of direct quantifiable recreation benefits for set 1 would

1. P. Davidson, F. G. Adams, and J. Seneca, "The Social Value of Water Recreational Facilities Resulting from an Improvement in Water Quality: The Delaware Estuary," in *Water Research*, A. V. Kneese and S. C. Smith, eds. (Baltimore: Johns Hopkins Press, 1966).

range between $160 million and $350 million, for set 2 between $140 million and $320 million, for set 3 between $130 million and $310 million, and for set 4 between $120 million and $280 million. Since municipal and industrial benefits were deemed to be small and to some extent canceled by negative features in regard to industrial water use, these ranges were taken to be rough estimates of the total benefits from improved water quality in the estuary.

A comparison of the recreation benefits with the cost estimates (Table 1) shows that objective set 4 appears to be justified, even when the lowest estimate of benefit is compared with the highest estimate of cost. The incremental costs of going from set 4 to set 3 suggests that the justifiability of set 3 is marginal. On the assumption that some of the more widely distributed benefits of water quality improvement may not have been appropriately taken into account, it can probably be justified. Clearly, however, the incremental benefits of going to sets 2 and 1 are vastly outweighed by the incremental costs.

COLLECTIVE MEASURES FOR WATER QUALITY IMPROVEMENT

Some attention was given to the possibility of achieving improved water quality by means of collective measures such as

TABLE 1. *Costs and Benefits of Water Quality Improvement in the Delaware Estuary Area* [1]
(million dollars)

Objective Set	Estimated Total Cost	Estimated Recreation Benefits	Estimated Incremental Cost		Estimated Incremental Benefits	
			Minimum[2]	Maximum[3]	Minimum[2]	Maximum[3]
1	460	160–350				
			245	145	20	30
2	215–315	140–320				
			130	160	10	10
3	85–155	130–310				
			20	25	10	30
4	65–130	120–280				

[1] All costs and benefits are present values calculated with 3 percent discount rate and 20-year time horizon.

[2] Difference between adjacent minima.

[3] Difference between adjacent maxima.

dredging the estuary to reduce oxygen demand from sludge deposits, collecting wastes for treatment in regional treatment plants, diverting wastes from critical reaches of the estuary to Delaware Bay or to the Atlantic Ocean, and providing mechanical reoxygenation of the estuary. Some of these measures looked quite promising on the basis of preliminary reconnaissance, but they received very little emphasis in the study. For example, it appeared that even the great cost of collecting certain industrial wastes and piping them from the estuary to the Atlantic Ocean would reduce the over-all costs of achieving at least the higher objective sets, but this result is not stated in the report proper.

Rough estimates of the total cost of reaching various dissolved oxygen objectives by mechanical reoxygenation produced perhaps the most spectacular results. These are shown below, the costs being present values calculated with 3 percent discount rate and 20-year time horizon.[2]

Objective Set	Cost (millions)
1	$70
2	$40
3	$12
4	$10

The dissolved oxygen conditions of objective set 2—namely, 4 ppm of dissolved oxygen in the critical reaches during the summer and 6.5 ppm during anadromous fish passage—could be reached through reoxygenation at not much greater cost than simply maintaining present conditions with even the least-cost waste treatment alternative. However, as reoxygenation would meet only the dissolved oxygen objective, and the additional costs of meeting other water quality objectives were not presented, it is impossible to tell how reoxygenation might enter into the efficient achievement of the various objectives sets.

It is unfortunate that these collective measures were not adequately explored. Enough was done, however, to suggest that such measures should enter into a strategy for dealing with the water quality problems of the estuary.

2. The use of the 3 percent interest rate overstates the real costs of reaeration. Use of a more appropriate rate of discount would yield substantially reduced cost figures.

EFFLUENT CHARGES ON THE DELAWARE ESTUARY

Following the planning study described in the previous sections, another important study was undertaken using the same models and data. This was a study of the possible use of effluent taxes or charges as an economic incentive for controlling waste discharge.[3] Assuming that direct controls would be effective and that waste dischargers would respond rationally to economic incentives, the study analyzed four programs for achieving alternative dissolved oxygen objectives in the estuary.

The first, and in a sense a standard of comparison for the others, is the Least-Cost Linear Programming Solution (LC). This solution uses a mathematical programming technique to obtain the minimum cost distribution of waste removals. To implement this program as a control policy would require precise information on waste treatment costs at all outfalls and direct controls on all waste discharges. It would result in radically different levels of treatment and treatment costs at different outfalls. The reason is simply that it would concentrate treatment at those points where treatment is least expensive and has the greatest impact on water quality in the critical reaches.

The second is the Uniform Treatment Solution (UT). In this solution each waste discharger is required to remove a given percentage of the wastes previously discharged before discharging the remainder to the stream. The percentage is the minimum needed to achieve the dissolved oxygen standard in the stream and is the same at each point of discharge. This solution may be considered typical of the conventional administrative effluent standards approach to the problem of achieving a stream quality standard.

The third is the Single Effluent Charge Solution (SECH). This solution involves charging each waste discharger in the estuary the same price per unit of waste discharge. The solution examines responses of individual waste dischargers and identifies the minimum single charge which will induce sufficient reduction in waste discharge to achieve the standard. Unfortunately, only treatment was permitted as a response to the charge in this study. Had process changes and by-product recovery been investigated,

3. See E. Johnson, "A Study in the Economics of Water Quality Management," *Water Resources Research* 3, no. 2 (1967).

the calculated costs of obtaining the objective would have been reduced. Still, there is no reason to think that the relative costs of the alternative strategies would be changed much.

The fourth is the Zone Effluent Charge Solution (ZECH), which used a uniform effluent charge in each of three zones instead of a uniform charge over all reaches of the estuary.

In none of these cases is there an explicit measurement of damages resulting from water quality degradation. Rather, the stream standard is used as a surrogate for damages. The problem then becomes one of achieving these standards while meeting efficiency (least-cost) and equity (cost-distribution) criteria.

Before turning to a discussion of specific results in relation to the first criterion, we will state the general conclusions which the Federal Water Pollution Control Administration (FWPCA) staff drew from this study.

1. Effluent charges should be seriously considered as a method for attaining water quality improvement.

2. Costs of waste treatment induced by an effluent charge will approach the least costly treatment plan.

3. A charge level of 8 to 10 cents per pound of BOD [4] discharged appears to produce relatively large increases in critical dissolved oxygen levels.

4. Major regional economic readjustments from a charge of that level are not anticipated to occur in the study area.[5]

5. Administrative costs and difficulties of managing an effluent charge method are greater than conventional methods of water quality improvement. However, the problems are not insurmountable and are not sufficiently great to negate the advantages of the charge method.

6. Compared to a conventional method of improving water quality, the charge method attains the same goal at lower costs

4. [BOD, or biochemical oxygen demand, is a commonly used measure of the quantity of polluting substances in an effluent. It is defined as the number of pounds of oxygen required to decompose the organic matter contained in the effluent. *Editors.*]

5. In all but a few cases, the total cost (cost of treatment plus effluent charge) was less than 1 percent of the value of output. In most cases, it was a small fraction of 1 percent. See Johnson, *op. cit.*, Table 8. Another study shows roughly similar results with costs of waste treatment averaging approximately 1 percent of value added in several industries. D. F. Bramhall and E. S. Mills, *Future Water Supply and Demand*, Maryland State Planning Department, April 1965.

of treatment, with a more equitable impact on waste discharg-ers.[6] Also, the charge provides a continuing incentive on the discharger to reduce his waste discharge and provides a guide to public investment decisions.

Table 2 indicates the economic costs associated with the pro-gram for two levels of water quality. The 3–4 ppm standard was considered the practical maximum attainable in the estuary by the FWPCA staff.

TABLE 2. *Cost of Treatment under Alternative Programs*

D.O. Objective (ppm)	Program			
	LC	UT	SECH	ZECH
	(million dollars per year)			
2	1.6	5.0	2.4	2.4
3–4	7.0	20.0	12.0	8.6

The analysis indicates that the effluent charges system would produce the specified quality levels at about one-half the cost of the uniform treatment method. Especially at the higher qual-ity level, the cost-saving is of a highly significant magnitude. The present value of the cost stream saved is on the order of $150 million.

The least-cost system is capable of reducing costs somewhat further since it programs waste discharges at each point specifi-cally in relation to the cost of improving quality in the critical reach, but this comes at the cost of detailed information on treatment costs at each point and a distribution of costs such that some waste dischargers experience heavy costs and others virtually none. The least-cost system is closely approached by ZECH at the higher quality level. In effect, this zone charge procedure "credits" waste dischargers at locations remote from the critical point with degradation of their wastes in the inter-vening reach of a stream before they arrive at the critical reach. This is a necessary condition for full efficiency when effluent charges are used to achieve a standard at a critical reach in a stream. The reason that ZECH does not achieve quite the same efficiency as LC is that the "credit" is not specific to the in-

6. The FWPCA staff did not state what criteria of equity they were using, but presumably they regarded a charge proportioned to the use of assimila-tive capacity by a waste discharger as equitable.

dividual waste discharger but is awarded in blocks—three in this case.

At an effluent charge of 10 cents per pound of BOD, which the staff estimated would be needed for the zoned effluent charge program, the funds collected by the administrative agency would amount to about $7 million per year. Nevertheless, for the 3–4 ppm dissolved oxygen objective, the total cost to industry and municipalities as a whole—effluent charge plus cost of treatment —is about the same as the cost of treatment only under the uniform treatment program. About half of this outlay does not represent an actual resources cost but if deemed desirable could be redistributed back to waste dischargers on the basis of equity criteria, used for general governmental purposes, or devoted to collective measures for improving water quality.

It should be noted that an important efficiency advantage of the effluent charges programs as contrasted with the LC program is their relatively lesser demand for information and analytical refinement. A study of the type already performed for the Delaware Estuary could serve as the basis for an effluent charge scheme. An order of magnitude estimate of the required charge is provided and changes could be made if necessary as responses to the charge reveal themselves. Actually, since the costs do not take account of the possibility of process change, the charge of 10 cents per pound of BOD is probably too high and could be adjusted downward at a later point. Also, the charge provides a continuing incentive for the discharger to reduce his waste load by placing him under the continuing pressure of monetary penalties. He is induced to develop new technology and as it develops to implement it. As new technology develops, the effluent charge could be gradually reduced while the stream standard is maintained, or the standard could be allowed to rise if this is deemed desirable.

The direct control measures implicit in the LC program, on the other hand (as well as the effluent standard of the uniform treatment program), provide only a limited incentive to improved technology. Moreover, the minimum cost program would require not only detailed information on current cost levels at each individual outfall, but also information on changes in cost with changing technology in regard to industrial processes, product mix, treatment cost, and so on.

Clean Rhetoric and Dirty Water

A. MYRICK FREEMAN III AND ROBERT H. HAVEMAN

A. Myrick Freeman III teaches economics at Bowdoin College and Robert H. Haveman is on the faculty at the University of Wisconsin and the director of its Institute for Research on Poverty. This article was published in The Public Interest.

FOR NEARLY TWO DECADES now, the United States has been passing new legislation to improve the quality of the environment. Numerous laws with environmental implications have been passed, and rivers of rhetoric have flowed from members of Congress and executive agencies. We have seen the Water Pollution Control Act of 1956, the Water Quality Act of 1965, the Clean Water Restoration Act of 1966, and the Environmental Quality Improvement Act of 1970, among others. In 1965, we heard President Johnson say, as he signed the Water Quality Act, "Today, we begin to be master of our environment"; and in 1971, President Nixon stated, "The battle for a better environment can be won and we are winning it."

Unfortunately, the facts of environmental quality do not jibe with the rhetoric. Indices of environmental quality show that the waste loads imposed on environmental resources have been growing continuously, and rising waste loads mean deteriorating environmental quality. The recent report of the Council on Environmental Quality, for example, indicates that emissions of all the major air pollutants have increased at an overall rate of over 3 percent per year and that, in recent years, "the overall quality of the nation's waters probably has deteriorated because of accelerated eutrophication, increased discharges of toxic materials, greater loads of sediment, and other factors." The legislation of the past decades has, in fact, failed to deliver on its promises.

Existing legislation is based essentially on a regulatory strategy, with an added carrot of federal subsidy enabling the budget to reflect "environmental priorities." This rule-making, enforcement strategy pits the power of public agencies against polluters in a context in which the rules of the struggle and the information available to each party are biased against the government. Not surprisingly, this effort at regulation has failed to induce private sector behavior leading to achievement of the objectives of the legislation. Even more serious, this strategy fails to recognize the basic economic nature of the problem. Use of the services of scarce environmental resources continues to be free, and as a result there is no cost to a person who overuses, misuses, or abuses them. Moreover, no effective institutional mechanisms, with clearly spelled out functions and operating procedures, have been established to manage the utilization of environmental resources or to guide them into their most productive uses.

EXISTING LEGISLATION

Present federal water pollution control policy has two main elements. The first is a program of federal subsidies to cities for the construction of waste treatment plants. The second is a procedure for establishing regulations to limit discharges and for enforcing these rules through the police power of the state and, ultimately, the courts.

The Water Pollution Control Act of 1956 established the first federal subsidy for treatment plant construction. This subsidy takes the form of federal grants to municipalities which cover up to 55 percent of the cost of plant construction. As an added incentive, some states have augmented the grants to the point where cities are responsible for only 15 percent of total construction costs. Since 1956, this program has grown rapidly, and today nearly $1 billion per year is being spent by the federal government for such construction. This money is allocated among states on the basis of a formula which assigns the first $100 million according to population and inversely according to per capita income, and the rest according to population alone. To be eligible for such grants, a state must have adopted a plan for achieving water quality standards acceptable to the Environmental Protection Agency (EPA). Present regulations stipulate that such plans must require a minimum of secondary treatment (85 percent removal of organic wastes) or its equivalent.

This program encourages cities to provide at least secondary treatment to the wastes of all dischargers who use municipal sewer systems. These dischargers include the bulk of the nation's households and commercial enterprises, but the majority of the nation's *industrial* wastes are discharged directly into rivers and streams. To encourage waste treatment activities by these dischargers, the Tax Reform Act of 1969 allows accelerated depreciation of waste treatment plant investments for tax purposes. The objective of this $120 million annual "tax expenditure" is to stimulate more spending on pollution control by reducing the after-tax cost of such investments.

In addition to these subsidy programs, federal policy provides for regulations governing the disposal of wastes into rivers and mechanisms to enforce these rules. The first provision for federal enforcement actions against water polluters was contained in the 1956 Water Pollution Control Act, which relied primarily on voluntary compliance stemming from abatement conferences attended by polluters and government officials. Under this provision it usually proved impossible to get beyond the conference stage, and only one case ever got to court.

The Water Quality Act of 1965 assigns primary responsibility for implementing pollution control plans to the states. It requires states to establish water quality standards and to develop a program for attaining them. This program was envisioned as a bench mark for judging the progress of a state in attaining its water quality standards and for assisting federal officials in determining when and where to undertake federal enforcement actions. In implementing this program, state agencies must first determine the maximum amount of discharges consistent with their water quality standards. Then they issue licenses limiting dischargers in aggregate to this maximum. To enforce these license provisions, states must monitor dischargers and initiate judicial or quasi-judicial proceedings when violations occur.

The 1965 law also authorizes federal enforcement actions whenever it is found that state water quality standards are being violated. (A governor or state agency can also request EPA to initiate enforcement efforts to deal with an interstate pollution problem.) EPA can initiate court actions 180 days after notifying violators. This provision of federal law was not used at all until August 1969, and as of the end of 1971, EPA had issued only 27 notices.

The decision to proceed to litigation ultimately rests with the administrator of EPA. Because of the lack of guidelines for deciding when a pollution problem is sufficiently serious to warrant legal action, this decision becomes a political matter. Thus enforcement at the federal level is, in practice, far from comprehensive or uniform. While the large municipality or firm may confront a probability of ultimate legal action, the small polluter is virtually immune.

In practice, federal and state pollution control efforts have been limited in scope and coverage in two respects. First, they have been aimed primarily at organic pollutants and have given relatively little attention to nonorganic pollutants such as plant nutrients, heavy metals (e.g., mercury), toxic materials, and heat. This is less the result of any limitations in either federal or state law than of the fact that organic pollution is the most noticeable in its effects and is relatively easy to deal with, given present technology. In the second place, pollution control efforts to date have been limited to discharges from point sources (i.e., factories and sewer pipes) and have ignored pollution arising from erosion and siltation, agricultural fertilizer, irrigation water, pesticide run-offs, and other non-point sources. This is an area where neither technology nor policy is well developed. Yet as point sources are brought under better control, pollution from non-point sources will loom as a larger problem—both relatively and absolutely.

THE RECORD OF FAILURE

If its objective is the improvement of the quality of the nation's rivers, as it surely must be, then existing federal water pollution policy has been a dismal failure. In 1969, a General Accounting Office (GAO) study of several rivers concluded that even though $5.4 billion had been spent at all levels of government for waste treatment plant construction during the previous 12 years, the nation's rivers were in worse shape than ever before.

This record of failure is attributable to both the subsidy and the enforcement aspects of current policy. Consider, for example, the waste treatment grant program. Because of the structure and administration of that program, much was spent but little achieved. Five of the chief reasons for this result are:

1. By subsidizing only conventional "end-of-the-pipe" treatment systems, the grant program induces planners to overlook what in some cases may be less costly or more effective alternatives, such as the storage (ponding) of wastes during critical periods of low stream flow and the augmentation of the assimilative capacity of the stream through instream aeration and other devices.

2. Current regulations require secondary waste treatment for *all* municipalities along a watercourse. An optimal basin-wide plan would relate the degree of desired municipal treatment to streamflow conditions and downstream uses (among other variables). In this optimal plan, some municipalities may require tertiary treatment while others may require only primary treatment. The drive for uniform secondary treatment results in excessive treatment costs at some outfalls and insufficient treatment costs at others.

3. States have failed to target federal funds on the municipalities with the most harmful discharges. More than one town situated downstream from major industrial locations has used federal funds to build treatment plants with the result that *its treated effluent is of higher quality than the river into which it is discharged.* Also, federal funds have been concentrated on smaller, largely suburban communities rather than the larger cities with the most pollution. For example, nearly 40 percent of the federal grant money has gone to towns with populations of less than 10,000, which contain less than 16 percent of the U. S. urban population. The largest cities, containing 25 percent of the total urban population, have received only 6 percent of the total federal grant money.

4. *Construction* of treatment facilities does not guarantee their effective *operation.* In fact, the structure of the recent program creates incentives which work in the opposite direction. A second study by the GAO has confirmed the widely held belief that municipal plants are often operated inefficiently. Over one-half of the plants surveyed were providing inadequate treatment, due to overzealous efforts to reduce plant operating costs, the difficulty and expense of hiring trained personnel to operate the plants, and the failure of cities to maintain and repair equipment. By subsidizing only one part of the cost of effective waste treatment—plant construction costs—the federal government has

induced resources into construction activity but has provided no similar inducement for efficient plant operation.

5. Federal grants for municipal waste treatment plant construction provide an indirect subsidy to industrial and commercial waste dischargers. By subsidizing the capital costs of municipal treatment facilities, the existing policy tends to reduce the sewer charges imposed on industrial, commercial, and domestic waste dischargers connected to the sewerage system. Because approximately 50 percent of the wastes handled by municipal treatment plants are from industrial sources, the size of the subsidy to business is substantial. The effect of this subsidy is to weaken the incentives for waste dischargers to seek such alternatives to the public treatment of their waste flows as production process changes, recycling, and materials recovery. There are many such alternatives, and these are often less costly. Yet because they do not receive federal subsidies, firms overlook them. The tax subsidies have a similar distorting effect on the decisions made by firms as to the techniques they choose to reduce their discharges.

Thus, through federal grants for municipal waste treatment facilities, as well as through tax subsidies for industrial pollution-control equipment, current policy is, in effect, allowing polluters to generate and dispose large quantities of wastes without bearing the full cost of their dischargers—and then using taxpayers' money to clean up after them. With little effective constraint on the generation of industrial wastes and with rapid economic growth, the burden on the environment will skyrocket in the coming decades. One recent study showed that the *annual* costs of applying secondary treatment to an unconstrained flow of wastes would be $18 billion in 1973, $27 billion in 1980, and $55 billion by the year 2000. The continued spending of taxpayers' money to clean up after polluters—along the lines of the current strategy—is going to be an enormously expensive and relatively fruitless venture.

WHY "ENFORCEMENT" DOESN'T WORK

In regard to the regulatory/enforcement aspects of present policy, it is widely agreed that enforcement has not been effective so far, both at the federal level and at the state level, where the primary responsibility now lies. The question is whether the regulatory/enforcement strategy can be made to work by tightening up the laws and increasing our efforts, or whether failure is inherent in the enforcement process. We incline to the latter view and believe that both history and a clear understanding of the nature of the regulatory process support our position.

It is in the American tradition to create regulatory agencies to deal with problems caused by malfunctions in the economic system. The existence of agencies such as the Interstate Commerce Commission, the Federal Power Commission, and the Federal Drug Administration is sufficient to convince most people that the problems for which these agencies were created are being dealt with successfully. But a careful analysis of the evidence shows that this is rarely the case.

The naive view of the regulatory process is that the agency establishes rules and regulations to govern the behavior of the regulated and to further the public interest. The threat of sanctions is thought to be sufficient to deter violations; but if any occur, it is assumed that violators are quickly brought to justice. The reality is quite different. Regulatory agencies have substantial discretionary power concerning the interpretation and application of their rule-making and enforcement powers. As a consequence, regulation/enforcement becomes essentially a political process entailing bargaining between parties of unequal power. In this process the real issues are camouflaged in technical jargon, and the regulators are largely isolated from political accountability for their actions. The regulatory agency and the interests they regulate bargain over the regulations to be set. They bargain over whether violations have occurred and, if so, who was responsible. They bargain over what steps shall be taken to correct infractions. And in the rare instances where the bargaining process breaks down and the conflict moves to the courts for resolution, the judicial system seeks an "acceptable solution" or a "reasonable compromise." Only rarely is it forced by the flow of events into making either/or choices. At every stage of this multi-level bargaining process those being regulated have a lot at stake, while the public interest is diffuse, poorly organized, and poorly represented. Predictably, the bargains struck favor those being regulated.

The regulatory/enforcement strategy pits the power of pollution control authorities against the power of the polluter in an unending sequence of skirmishes and battles over licensing and the enforcement of regulations. As a consequence, the enforcement process is long and drawn out and often inconclusive. Industrial polluters get higher returns from hiring lawyers to fight enforcement than from money spent on pollution control.

The inherent difficulties with the regulation/enforcement process are nowhere more apparent than in the recent attempts to make the 1899 Refuse Act work. This law prohibits the discharge of "any refuse matter of any kind or description whatever" into any waters unless the discharger has obtained a permit from the U.S. Army Corps of Engineers. Virtually none of the present estimated 40,000 industrial dischargers hold a valid permit. This all but forgotten law made headlines beginning in 1969 when charges were brought against several firms as a consequence of individuals' initiatives. Some convictions were obtained, fines levied, and rewards paid to vigilant citizens, as the law provides. But in June 1970, as the number of cases began to increase, the Justice Department issued guidelines to its attorneys instructing them not to bring charges against firms for which residuals discharge was a part of normal plant operations, or against firms holding a permit issued by a state or local government. With this action, the Justice Department, in effect, established a policy of selective non-enforcement of one of the nation's laws. This policy was reinforced in December 1970, when the Administration announced that, while permits were required of all dischargers (including those "exempted" by the earlier Justice Department policy), no prosecutions would take place so long as an application had been filed by July 1, 1971, and not subsequently rejected by the government. The effect of this is to grant firms an immunity from prosecution which is likely to last for several years while the government works its way through the backlog of unprocessed permit applications. And since all permit applications are forwarded to the relevant state for certification that the discharge is consistent with the state's pollution control plan, the new policy has contributed nothing to the establishment of a more effective pollution control effort. It has, however, generated a flood of new permit applications to burden the work load of federal and state officials while, in effect, repealing the one potentially effective federal law against pollution.

THE MUSKIE BILL

Although there is growing disenchantment with federal water pollution control policies, the recent legislative response has been more of the same. Both the Senate and the House have passed bills in 1971–72 which are based on a legislative finding that past efforts have failed. Quantum jumps in regulatory controls and subsidies are contained in both bills. But if past experience is any guide, these efforts will at best be patch jobs on an already sieve-like structure.

The clearest example of the "let's hitch our belts one notch tighter and forge ahead" philosophy implicit in these efforts is the so-called Muskie bill, which passed the Senate by an 86–0 vote late in 1971.[1] That bill essentially ends the use of water quality standards as the measuring rod for performance and substitutes standards or regulations regarding effluent control and treatment. The bill requires that industry apply the "best practicable" waste treatment technology available by 1976 and completely eliminate discharges of pollutants by 1981 if it can be done at "reasonable cost." If zero discharge cannot be attained at reasonable cost, industry must install the "best available treatment" facilities, "taking into account the cost." A date of 1985 is set as a target for zero discharge.

The basic weakness of the bill is its reliance on precisely that sort of discretion which has vitiated numerous other rule enforcement efforts. Who is going to define "reasonable," "best available," and "best practicable," and who is going to "take into account the cost"? All of these terms are open to widely divergent interpretations, and none has a precise legal meaning. Perhaps more important, this bill implicitly requires federal surveillance and enforcement action on a case-by-case basis on each of 40,000 industrial pollution sources to police the ill-defined discharge standards.

Aside from these enormous administrative difficulties, there is

1. [A modified version of this bill was passed over President Nixon's veto in October 1972. *Editors.*]

the further consideration that, should the rules actually be enforced, the cost would be enormous. Given existing technology and its foreseeable developments, attainment of either the best available technology or the zero-discharge goals will be prohibitively expensive. Because costs rise swiftly at very high treatment levels, the total cost of meeting these objectives could be several times that required to meet current quality standards and far in excess of any benefits resulting from elimination of the last few units of residual discharge. As the Report of a Panel of Experts to the Director of the Office of Science and Technology stated:

The . . . costs in achieving or even approaching such a goal would be very great and would almost certainly in every instance constitute a misallocation of the nation's resources. Removing the last few per cent of the common pollutants from water is usually extremely costly, yet the added benefits due to the extra treatment in that regard are extremely questionable in all cases.

The subsidy component of the present strategy is also reaffirmed and extended in this bill. Appropriations of $20 billion are authorized through fiscal year 1975, and a minimum of secondary waste treatment is required for all municipalities by 1976. The share of municipal waste treatment construction costs to be covered by federal grants is also enlarged.

PAYING BY THE POUND

If our appraisal of the effectiveness of both the current strategy and recent legislation is correct, a major restructuring of water pollution control policy is required if we are to improve water quality. This restructuring, to be successful, must recognize the basic economic nature of the pollution problem and the economic incentives governing the behavior of polluters. It must force waste dischargers to bear the costs which their actions generate. If these costs can be imposed on dischargers, incentives will be present to constrain the waste generation proclivities of industrial and municipal polluters and to keep valuable environmental resources from being diverted to low-valued uses. The necessary incentives can be created by imposing user or effluent charges on waste dischargers such that the size of the charge is related to the volume of harmful substances which is released into the environment. In effect, waste dischargers should be required to "pay by the pound."

Numerous arguments can be offered in support of this user-charge strategy. The most cogent argument is that it will succeed in reducing waste discharges—not just retarding their growth. The recorded response of waste dischargers to the imposition of municipal sewerage charges provides strong evidence. For example, after putting a relatively small user charge into effect, the city of Cincinnati reported that industrial waste was reduced nearly 40 percent in one year. Another city found discharges cut to one-third of the former level.

That user charges have induced such dramatic reductions in waste discharges is not surprising. When a price is placed on wastes discharged into watercourses, a number of actions that previously looked unattractive to dischargers become appealing alternatives. These include changes in production procedures within the plant to reduce waste generation, as well as the installation of waste treatment facilities at the plant site. Moreover, such charges would stimulate research and development efforts aimed at developing new technologies for reducing waste generation or recycling wastes. Finally, if environmental services are priced, those commodities whose production imposes large environmental damages will experience price increases relative to commodities whose production imposes minor environmental costs. Because higher prices mean smaller demand, production and consumption would tend to be shifted away from those commodities with the most damaging environmental effects.

In addition to providing incentives for reductions in waste generation, a comprehensive national effluent-charge policy would have a second important effect. It would end the system of bargaining and negotiating between agencies and individual producers—a system which rewards delaying tactics—and replace it with a system which rewards compliance and effective and continuing controls on waste discharges.

Finally, while the current strategy has placed substantial demands on a tight federal budget, a user-charge strategy would actually *generate* revenues. These revenues could be used to finance environmental measures that municipalities and firms cannot be expected to undertake, such as basic research and development, establishment of regional or river basin authorities to manage the use of regional environmental resources, and construction of installations to artificially reaerate streams or to increase stream flows during low-flow periods.

In evaluating the merits of an economic—i.e., user-charge—approach to environmental policy, it must be emphasized that an effluent charge will, by itself, be inadequate to insure the efficient use of environmental resources. For one thing, it cannot cope with non-point sources of pollution such as agricultural fertilizer and pesticide run-off. But this is also true of the subsidy/enforcement strategy. Comprehensive environmental management requires the establishment of regional authorities whose responsibilities would include planning for the optimal use and augmentation of environmental resources; undertaking collective investments; setting water and air quality standards and charge levels designed to meet these standards; monitoring discharge levels into both water and air resources; and regulating patterns of regional land use. To be effective in managing the environment consistently with regional preferences, these authorities should be governed by directly elected rather than appointed officials. The sad history of the appointive regulatory commissions and their capture by those interests which they were supposed to regulate should be a powerful lesson.

THE CONVENTIONAL OBJECTIONS

Proposals for an economic-incentives approach to pollution control have not been enthusiastically received by waste dischargers—especially industrial polluters. Indeed, powerful corporate interests have objected strenuously to the effluent-charge strategy. Industry, it is claimed, is already spending as much as possible on pollution control efforts. As H. C. Lumb, vice-president of Republic Steel Corporation, stated before a congressional committee: "Taking money away from industrial companies in the name of a tax on pollution . . . would harm the cause of pollution control." The vacuousness of this position should be apparent. By implication, it denies that economic incentives—prices and costs—influence business decisions and behavior, a contention that is contradicted by daily observation. For example, when firms purchase labor-saving capital equipment in response to rising wages, they are demonstrating not only their responsiveness to economic incentives but their ability to finance cost-saving investment. The purpose of an effluent-charge policy is to provide a similar economic incentive. The financial resources for responding can be found. Industry expects to spend $4.9 billion on pollution control in 1972. But this figure is only 5.3 percent of all planned capital expenditures. A doubling in the level of spending for pollution control could be accommodated with only a 5.6 percent reduction in other capital spending. It is not financial resources that are lacking but the incentive to use more of these resources for pollution control.

A second objection which has been raised to an effluent-charge policy is that it will be too complex to administer and that, as a consequence, its effectiveness will be eroded by powerful interests. This objection, we would argue, sees the real situation in reverse. In our view, the effluent-charge strategy will be more straightforward to administer and far more effective than the current regulatory strategy.

Once environmental quality standards have been set, a single charge would be levied on each unit of the prominent harmful substances found in effluents or emissions. Each discharger would be responsible for monitoring his discharge, reporting its composition and quantity to the public authority, and making the appropriate payments. There is an obvious comparison with the system of reporting and paying income taxes. As in the case of the income tax, rules and standards of accuracy for measurement would have to be specified, and audits for compliance would have to be undertaken. Dischargers would be required to install and maintain the required monitoring equipment, subject to audit and calibration for accuracy by the authorities. Information on dischargers and payments would be recorded and made available for public scrutiny.

With such a system there is little room for administrative discretion and bargaining. The primary decision is the level of the charge to be imposed, and this decision is a significant and highly visible one. There is also a clear performance criterion by which to judge the correctness of the decision on the level of the charge. If water quality standards are being met, the rate is high enough—if not, the rate should be raised. Moreover, while the zeal and effectiveness of regulatory agencies diminish over time, the effect of an effluent charge is durable. It remains in place unless there is an explicit political decision to remove it. It is clear, then, that an effluent-charge system poses no unique or particularly difficult administrative problems. In fact, it is an administratively simple strategy which avoids many of the pitfalls of the regulatory/enforcement approach, and which leaves little room for powerful interests to gain special advantages through low-visibility negotiations with the regulatory agency.

A PROBLEM OF PLURALISM

When one compares the failure of existing policy with the widely acknowledged potency of an economic-incentives strategy, a natural question arises: If improved water quality is a national objective, then why the reluctance to modify policy and incorporate the advantages of a promising alternative strategy? The answer is to be found in the nature and dynamics of a pluralistic representative democracy.

The political system is in large part a mechanism for reconciling conflicting interests. With respect to the pollution issue, the conflict is over how much cleaning up of pollution is actually going to be done and who is going to pay for it.

Now, policy-makers, like other decision-makers, act in their own self-interest. Elected officials behave so as to assure their own reelection; bureaucrats behave so as to be promoted, not to alienate the legislature, or to assure themselves of a lucrative position in private industry at a later date. If a policy-maker supports a policy which takes something away from a part of his constituency, he alienates that group. As a consequence, he would tend to support any policy only if the losers were small in number or without influence and if the beneficiaries were large in number or influential. Thus, policy-makers search for policies whose costs are hidden or can be shifted to less influential or less organized elements of their constituencies. Policy-makers also try to postpone decisions (since every decision has a cost) and to avoid the costs of a decision by shifting the responsibility for making it to another place in the political system.

In a system with full information on the part of both policy-makers and voters and with no basic structural imperfections, a decision-maker would be accountable to all groups affected by his decisions, and all of these groups would have access to him. Such perfection, however, does not characterize our political system. Certain institutional arrangements, such as the congressional seniority system and loose compaign-finance regulations (which enable economic power to be readily transformed into political power), undermine both accountability and accessibility. And when such structural imperfections persist, policy-makers gain the leeway which they desire to avoid those decisions likely to alienate major sources of their support. They have the latitude to choose those strategies which shift costs to unwary sectors of their constituencies, which shift responsibility for unpopular decisions to other parts of the political system, and which postpone those decisions likely to generate adverse political repercussions.

These few rough propositions about pluralistic democracies provide some insight into why the type of pollution control policy that has emerged from our political process is not surprising. Let us review some of the characteristics of existing policy:

• Through existing and pending legislation, federal legislators have consistently shifted the burden for making difficult decisions to the states (e.g., the setting of standards) or to decision-makers within the federal bureaucracy. Federal legislation typically passes the Congress with large majorities, sometimes —as with the Muskie bill—unanimously. One can only conclude that if all legislators are for the policy, they must have found some way to duck the real issues.

• Policy-makers have been willing to subsidize industrial dischargers wherever this could be hidden in tax depreciation formulas or municipal cost-sharing programs.

• Federal law fails to require states to hold public hearings on the setting of water quality standards. Obviously, there can be considerable public controversey surrounding the choice of standards. The failure to stipulate public hearings serves the interests of dischargers at the expense of the public, whose accessibility to the decision-making process is greatly diminished.

• Setting environmental quality standards is a meaningless exercise unless effective mechanisms are developed for achieving the standards. Without exception, states have placed primary reliance on some form of licensing of discharges (including discharge limits) accompanied by judicial enforcement of the license terms. As we have seen, this leads to multi-stage bargaining with minimal accessibility and accountability, and the consequence is delay or nonenforcement of the standard.

In short, the political response to the water pollution problem has been to shift the real decisions from the federal to the state level and from the legislature to the bureaucracy; to make decisions in arenas where there is less accountability and accessibility; and to avoid once-and-for-all resolutions of the political conflicts in favor of the piecemeal, fragmented decisions characterizing the enforcement process. These tendencies work against the public interest in pollution control and in favor of polluters.

The economic-incentives approach which we (along with many other economists) have suggested has heretofore had little political appeal. This is in part because it runs directly counter to the tendencies cited above. Establishment of a pollution-charge system in conjunction with environmental quality standards would resolve most of the political conflict over the environment. And it would do so in a highly visible way, so that those who would be hurt by such a policy could see what was happening. It is the openness and explicitness of such choices that policy-makers seek to avoid.

It is not entirely facetious to suggest that the reason an economic-incentives approach has not been tried in this country is that it would work. In the absence of effective pollution control policies, polluters are able to expropriate the environment for their own use by the act of discharging wastes. A system of pollution charges, on the other hand, would establish the principle that the environment is owned by the people as a whole and that the polluters must pay for the privilege of using part of the environment for waste disposal. Such massive transfers of "property rights" and the wealth they represent seldom occur without political upheaval. Viewed in this light, the most formidable barrier to controlling pollution is probably not technology, population, or public attitudes, but rather the politics of power in our pluralistic democracy.

A Criticism of the Effluent Charge

DAVID R. ZWICK

*While a student in the Harvard Law School, David Zwick was a
co-editor of the Ralph Nader Task Force Report on Water Pollution. He made this statement before Senator Proxmire's Joint Economic Committee hearings on efficiency in government.*

THE FEDERAL OFFICIALS concerned with the problem are hard
pressed to name a single major body of water where Federal
abatement action has improved the condition of the water, so
that it is once again suitable for human use, as drinking water
supply, fish habitats, and recreation spot.

Now, some economists have interpreted this failure to produce
cleanup as the signal that we should abandon the regulatory
approach to pollution abatement, setting standards and enforcing them, in favor of an economic incentive scheme, an alternative scheme, such as a national tax on effluents keyed to the
amount and strength of discharge. The regulatory approach, this
argument goes, has been tried and it has failed.

I would disagree. The regulatory approach has never really
been tried. With the exception of the recently "rediscovered"
Refuse Act of 1899, which went almost completely unenforced
up until its 70th birthday, the Federal laws on water pollution
barely deserve to be called a regulatory scheme at all. The Federal Water Pollution Control Act contains no penalties, it imposes crippling jurisdictional restrictions on the Administrator of
EPA, and it frustrates the abatement process with time-con-
suming mandatory delays. Some Federal officials have estimated
it takes somewhere around 58 months to get an injunction under the Federal Water Pollution Control Act.

The Refuse Act at least has fines for polluting, but they are
too small—a maximum of $2,500—to deter a large company's vio-
lation. And because citizens apparently have no way under the
law to compel the Attorney General to use and enforce the
Refuse Act, if he chooses not to do it, polluters have been spared

even that small inconvenience in the vast majority of cases. I would for those reasons consider the development of a strong workable Federal enforcement scheme of paramount importance in restoring our waters.

A national effluent tax scheme could not and should not take the place of Federal standard setting and enforcement, for several reasons. In the first place, none of the administrative problems of the regulatory approach can be avoided by imposing an effluent charge. The Government would still have to monitor polluters' discharges, to make sure they weren't cheating on their "tax returns." And when Federal effluent tax inspectors discovered a "false" return, a penalty should obviously be imposed, just as it should be under any pollution enforcement scheme when a violation is discovered.

More important, however, a flat national effluent tax would, in all probability, simply not work to do what it would ostensibly be intended to do. It would not restore our waters to usable quality. That is because each place along each body of water has its own unique characteristic—its own unique size and current. A level of taxation which would work to eliminate pollution in one place—the Mississippi River, for example—would leave another place, say the Brandywine Creek, inundated with effluent.

The Federal Government could not conceivably begin to attempt to compute the different tax rates that would be necessary to protect the water along every bend in every river and stream, considering the different industries involved. Were local agencies to be given the option of adding to the flat national tax for a given pollutant, there is no guarantee that they would do it at all, or do it well.

The cost of making a mistake in computing the proper level, based on complex and inaccurate data, might be the loss of a species of aquatic life, or a serious health hazard in a swimming area. To even begin attempting to insure that the water quality in each spot was the water quality desired, the level of taxation would not only have to be changed by some public agency each time a trial revealed an error, but, in addition, each time a new industry, or a different industry, came to the area, creating new opportunities for error in economic predictions and calculations.

Such a system would serve only to create thousands of new jobs for economists, without solving the water pollution problem.

An unfortunate side effect would be that industrial planning and spending would be disrupted with each administrative change in the tax rate. One way to avoid all these problems, of course, would be to set a flat national tax so high that for every industry, in even the smallest creeks, for many years to come, the condition of the water would fulfill our most optimistic expectations. Following this tack, however, would eliminate what is touted as the principal advantage of the effluent tax—economic efficiency.

In summary, I believe that an effluent tax is not, by itself, a workable strategy for eliminating water pollution. We simply cannot afford to do away with the concept—heretofore unrealized, of course—of setting limits on the amount of gunk that can be dropped into a given stream by a given polluter and enforcing those limits by imposing severe penalties for infractions. . . .

Water Wasteland: Conclusions and Recommendations

DAVID R. ZWICK and MARCY BENSTOCK

Marcy Benstock is a member of the graduate faculty of economics at the New School for Social Research. With David Zwick, she was a co-editor of the Ralph Nader Task Force Report on Water Pollution. This paper is taken from the summary and conclusions of that report.

THE MAJOR PROBLEM in pollution control is the vast economic and political power of large polluters. Water pollution exists, in large part, because polluters have more influence over government than do those they "pollute." As long as this disproportionate influence persists, so will the pollution. It is a mistake to suppose that new laws with higher cleanup requirements and tougher penalties will ultimately succeed in eliminating environmental contamination; unless new laws also tip the scales of influence over government in favor of the public, the requirements they set will be consistently violated and the penalties rarely used.

As an essential first step toward making the nation's pollution control effort less vulnerable to political sabotage, pollution control officials must be deprived of the discretion to enforce or not, as they choose. Discretion invites pressure from polluters to see that it is exercised in their favor. Federal officials in the field must be charged with a mandatory legal duty to investigate and issue abatement orders immediately upon receiving notice of a violation, to impose civil sanctions, and to seek criminal sanctions from the courts.

Removing governmental discretion would itself provide people with a right they do not now have—the right to go to court to compel pollution control officials to carry out their assigned duties. To make the removal of discretion fully effective, the people should have additional power at their disposal. Public authorities who knowingly acquiesce in pollution should be subject to more than court command to do their job. By violating their public trust they become co-conspirators in environmental crime. Officials should be subject to the same penalties for conscious nonfeasance as the polluters are for pollution. . . .

Summarized below are the Task Force's conclusions and policy recommendations in the key areas we investigated.

STANDARD-SETTING AND ENFORCEMENT

What little there has been of the federal enforcement effort has produced more tangible motion in the right direction than any other federal program dealing with water pollution. It has not, however, cleaned up the country's water. The irony of the government's position is to be found in the following fact: Federal enforcement is needed because the states are often too weak to stand up to their large polluters; yet Washington's pollution control laws, particularly the ones enacted in the last fifteen years, are far weaker than the laws that many of the states have to work with. Metaphysical jurisdictional restrictions, lack of information-gathering authority, mandatory waiting periods, and debilitating instructions to the court (e.g., consider the "economic feasibility" of abatement) have so hamstrung abatement efforts under the Federal Water Pollution Control Act that they have merely slowed the pace of continuing deterioration of our lakes and rivers. The Refuse Act of 1899 is the best law the government has to work with against industrial polluters. (It is not applicable to municipal sewage.) It has been given only minimal use so far, however, because, like the later laws, it gives federal officials excessive discretion not to enforce it. (Any discretion at all has proved to be excessive.)

Some 70 years late, pollution control should now be brought into the twentieth century. As a starter, Congress should not only eliminate the discretion in the Federal Water Pollution Control Act but eliminate its other obvious defects as well by incorporating into the newer regulatory scheme all the powers the federal government now has with respect to industry under the Refuse Act. The President should reconsider the announced Administration policy, under its forthcoming permit system, of acquiescing to moribund state pollution control standards on intrastate waters. Unless the Administration changes its mind on this crucial point, the Refuse Act permit system will provide industries on the majority of the nation's waterways with federal "licenses to pollute."

Beyond that, the law should no longer require the government to go to court to seek a civil fine against polluters. The Administrator should be given the authority—indeed, the duty—to assess fines himself. The burden of proving pollution should be shifted so that the government does not have to prove each separate day of a continuing violation in order to award a penalty for each day. Once an illegal discharge has been shown, the polluter should have the burden of demonstrating to the Administrator's satisfaction that he has come back into compliance. Until he does, the penalty fines would continue to be added on automatically each day.

In addition to penalty fines against polluting companies and municipalities, the government should be required to bring sanctions to bear against individuals knowingly responsible for violations. Sanctions which attach to the individual are especially needed because of the oligopolistic (i.e., dominated by a few large noncompetitive firms) structure of most heavily polluting industries (e.g., steel, oil, etc.). When a company is not in active price competition with other companies in the industry, it can much more easily pass on a fine to the consumer in the form of higher prices rather than absorbing it as a loss out of profits. Under such circumstances, companies may even use pollution penalties as an excuse to raise prices by more than the added cost, thereby actually increasing profits. This is because noncompetitive firms know that they can often count on other firms in the industry to match a price increase by one firm with price increases of their own. The best way to guard against this phenomenon is to impose penalties that cannot be passed on. Company executives who are guilty of repeated violations of pollution laws should be barred from working in the same capacity for any company and in the same industry for, say, three years. (There is precedent for such a penalty in several laws, including Landrum-Griffin, which mandates removal from union office of labor officials found guilty of certain corrupt practices.) We should no more allow pollution-prone corporate officials to remain in office and endanger the public than we would permit a repeated and reckless motor vehicle law violator to retain his driver's license or a union official to continue to damage his union members.

As for the intricate water quality standards approach to setting effluent requirements, it should ultimately be made irrelevant (except as a check on our ability to prevent secret dumping and control runoff pollution) by instituting a "no dumping" policy everywhere. Land disposal of wastes and natural recycling based on ecological principles is already a feasible alternative for domestic wastes in many, if not all, locations, and for many, if not all, industries. As a short-term interim measure, the Task Force believes that the water quality standards approach to regulation can be made workable provided that unanswered scientific questions are resolved in favor of the public rather than in favor of the polluters. The Pollution Control Act should state clearly that polluters wishing to deposit a given material in the water have the burden of convincing the Administrator of EPA that their discharge will not damage present or possible future desired water uses or degrade the quality of the receiving waterbody. The Administrator of EPA should be empowered to designate certain waterbodies as deserving special protection—water of exceptionally high quality, for example, like Lake Superior or Lake Tahoe, and water whose degradation may become irreversible if it proceeds any further, like Lake Michigan. No dumping whatsoever should be permitted in these waters as an immediate policy, and the government should move toward implementing the zero discharge requirements on as rapid a timetable as is reasonably possible. . . .

Part Three Resources, Man, and the Environment

Resources and Man: A Study and Recommendations

THE COMMITTEE ON RESOURCES AND
MAN: NATIONAL ACADEMY OF SCIENCES
—NATIONAL RESEARCH COUNCIL

*This article summarizes the Committee's conclusions and recom-
mendations. It is adapted from the book-length report of the same
title.*

THIS STUDY is about problems that confront man in seeking a
durable accommodation with his natural resources. Concepts of
resources, to be sure, change from time to time and from place
to place, but the general notion is always of something necessary or useful, like food, clean air and water, and materials that
skilled hands and discerning minds can turn to the improvement
of the human lot.

The central question is: can man approach a kind of dynamic
equilibrium with his environment so as to avert destructive imbalances? Ultimately this question involves the entire globe
and the distant future. We have chosen, however, to concentrate on material resources other than air and water, and on
North America—although with global cognizance and in ecological context. As for time scale, we have tried to look well
beyond the year 2000, but to keep the shorter term in view.

In preliminary discussions we asked particularly what resources are vital to our well-being and economy now, which are
likely to be vital in the future, what substitutions and technological innovations might modify resource priorities, and what

limits are placed on population and material growth by resource availability. We also considered the consequences of limited supply of resources and of varying social and economic concepts that affect their use and adequacy.

A prime conclusion of ecology is that species whose populations exceed or approach too closely the carrying capacity of resources in the space occupied undergo reduction. Such reductions are often severe and may lead to extinction because of disease, pestilence, predation, or aggressive competitors. Although it is true that man has repeatedly succeeded in increasing both the space he occupies and its carrying capacity, and that he will continue to do so, it is also clear that both the occupiable space and its carrying capacity have finite limits which he can approach only at great peril.

It is essential, therefore, that we carefully assess and continually reassess these limits, and that we take steps to assure that future generations, as well as people now living, will have the resources necessary for a satisfying life. These resources, moreover, must be so distributed as to exclude catastrophe as a factor in limiting population density. Few species of animals ever really multiply to the absolute limit of their food supply under natural conditions; other controlling factors intervene, often of the sort that humans would call psychic or psychosomatic. Man also must adapt to his ecosystem—to his physical environment and its biological components. We cannot long operate as a force apart from it, for we are not. Above all, we must be wary of man's tendency to reduce the variety of components in his ecosystem, for this increases susceptibility to adverse change.

Many people outside the Atlantic community of nations are now threatened with poverty and famine as a result of population increases that locally exceed the carrying capacity of the land. To a greater or lesser degree the same potential danger threatens all people, as Malthus first clearly recognized in 1798. Wishful thinking does not banish the problem. Harrison Brown asked in 1954: [1] "Is betterment of the situation really within the realm of possibility? And if betterment is possible, at what level can the greatly increased numbers be supported? Lastly are the earth's resources sufficient to meet the enhanced demand?" The same questions haunt us with increasing intensity

1. *The Challenge of Man's Future* (New York: Viking, 1954), p. 61.

—an intensity as yet almost unrelieved by significant decreases in rates of population growth. By average American standards, two-thirds of the world's people are still ill-fed, ill-housed, and ill-clothed, including many in North America. What can we in North America do to aid our own underprivileged, to meet the population increases that will yet precede real population control, and to help the rest of the world?

The answer is that much can be done, given sufficient effort in resource management. But other dangers arise. The quality of life, which we equate with flexibility of choices and freedom of action, is threatened by the demands of an expanding economy and population. This happens in three principal ways: (1) through the restrictive and harmful effects of pollution; (2) through the increasing frequency and complexity of unconstructive but unavoidable human contacts; and (3) through the necessary increase of regulatory measures—all in consequence of increasing use of and competition for resources, space, recreation, transportation, housing, and even educational facilities.

Thus, in addition to energy, mineral, and food resources, the quantity and quality of the human resource itself are critical components of the equation. Man is not only a part of his ecosystem, he is the most powerful influence in it. He is simultaneously its potentially most precious resource and its most serious threat. The gains from technological development must always be balanced in as much detail as possible against its costs. Man's own best interests plead for a more generous attitude toward the rest of nature and for less materialistic measures of well-being and success—especially in the developed countries. Such changes in attitude would make it easier to bring about dynamically balanced relations between the need for materials and the quantity available on the one hand and the quality of life and quantity of consumers on the other.

The growing quantity of people is a key factor whose future dimensions we should like to be able to estimate. Only two things seem certain: there are going to be more people in the future and they will live in denser aggregates. The number of people to be accommodated by the end of the century, moreover, adds a new dimension to current crises. To accommodate these populations, the developed world will require, by the year 2000, additional urban facilities equivalent to all of those already in existence, and correspondingly more for the underdeveloped world. This calls for an entirely different view of our cities and their resource requirements than if we think only of ameliorating specific crises step by step as they arise. Complete urban renovation, the creation of new and better living clusters throughout the country, and better and more diversified use of suburban and rural space are a big order; but it is an order that is practicable, necessary, and urgent. There is no simple "best solution." A variety of solutions must be tried, and for all of them the resource component (including clean air and water) will be central.

Somehow we must manage by the year 2000 to support a population increase in the United States from the present 200 million people to between 300 million and 340 million, and an increase in world population from the now more than 3.5 billion people to between 6 billion and 7 billion—an increasing proportion of them in cities. Failure to support that population increase would have unacceptable consequences. Population control, essential in the long run, cannot come soon enough to eliminate the challenge. To stabilize populations requires that the birth rate not exceed 14 live births per year per thousand people at the 70-year life expectancy sought as a goal for all. Only Hungary, Japan, and Bulgaria currently have such a low birth rate. This shows that a stabilized population can be achieved, but as Kingsley Davis has emphasized,[2] the inadequate measures that now pass for population control at best eliminate only unwanted births. Birth rates over most of the world cannot be brought to control levels by presently accepted measures. Steps must be taken to realize a zero rate of population increase as the ultimate goal. In the meanwhile, the increasing number of people to be accommodated will severely tax the capacity of the human ecosystem.

Nutrition is the first essential; yet problems of distribution, of local failure to exploit potentialities, and with social customs that dictate what food is acceptable are more immediately urgent than the problem of quantity of food available or producible on a global scale. If present world food production could be evenly rationed, there would be enough to satisfy both energy

2. *Science* 158 (1967), p. 730.

(calories) and protein requirements for everyone—although with drastic reductions for the now affluent. All-out effort, including the provision of ample fertilizer, and genetic, ecological, and chemical research, could probably quadruple production from the lands and double production from the waters by the end of the century. If such increased production were evenly distributed, it could keep up with population growth expected during the same time and even permit some improvement of diet. But will such all-out effort be started and sustained?

The probable ultimate increase in production of food from the sea on a sustained basis is not likely to be much more than about two and one-half times the present annual production of 60 million metric tons of fish, containing 12 million tons of usable protein. An increase to as much as four times the present production is unlikely. Perhaps the most important thing to bear in mind about aquatic food products, however, is that although they are an excellent source of protein they are a poor source of calories. Only the land can supply calories in adequate quantity for the needs anticipated. An eventual increase of possibly eight times the present land production is foreseen. To attain this, however, will call for maximum increases in productivity of existing lands, cultivation of all potentially arable lands, new crops, the use of more vegetable and less animal protein, continued risky use of ever-new but hopefully degradable biocides, chemical or microbiological synthesis of foods, and other innovations.

Foreseeable increases in food supplies over the long term, therefore, are not likely to exceed about nine times the amount now available. That approaches a limit that seems to place the earth's ultimate carrying capacity at about 30 billion people, *at a level of chronic near-starvation for the great majority* (and with massive immigration to the now less densely populated lands)! A world population of 30 billion is only slightly more than three doublings from the present one, which is now increasing at a doubling time of about 35 years. At this rate, there could be 30 billion people by about 2075 in the absence of controls beyond those now in effect. Hopeful allowance for such controls suggests that populations *may* level off not far above 10 billion people by about 2050—and that is close to (if not above) the maximum that an *intensively managed* world might hope to support with some degree of comfort and individual choice, as we estimate such immeasurables. If, in fulfillment of their rising expectations, all people are to be more than merely adequately nourished, effort must be made to stabilize populations at a world total much lower than 10 billion. Indeed it is our judgment that a human population less than the present one would offer the best hope for comfortable living for our descendants, long duration for the species, and the preservation of environmental quality.

Man must also look with equal urgency to his nonrenewable resources—to mineral fuels, to metals, to chemicals, and to construction materials. These are the heritage of all mankind. Their overconsumption or waste for the temporary benefit of the few who currently possess the capability to exploit them cannot be tolerated.

The nonfuel mineral resources are very unequally distributed, both as to location and as to grade. No nation is self-sufficient in all of them, even in the short term. The ultimate resources of major industrial metals such as iron and aluminum, to be sure, are very large, for their availability depends mainly on improvements in recovery methods. But true shortages exist or threaten for many substances that are considered essential for current industrial society: mercury, tin, tungsten, and helium for example. Known and now-prospective reserves of these substances will be nearly exhausted by the end of this century or early in the next, and new sources or substitutes to satisfy even these relatively near-term needs will have to be found. Neither is abundant cheap energy a panacea for waning resources. Innovation of many kinds will be needed—in methods of finding ore, in mining, in extraction of metals, in substitution, in transportation, and in conservation and waste disposal. For all reusable materials in short supply, appropriate laws or codes restructuring economic incentives could facilitate conservative recovery, more efficient use, and reuse, thereby appreciably extending now foreseeable commodity lifetimes.

It is not certain whether, in the next century or two, further industrial development based on mineral resources will be foreclosed by limitations of supply. The biggest unknowns are population and rates of consumption. It is self-evident, however, that the exponential increases in demand that have long prevailed cannot be satisfied indefinitely. If population and demand level off at some reasonable plateau, and if resources are used wisely, industrial society can endure for centuries or perhaps millennia. But technological and economic brilliance alone cannot create the essential raw materials whose enhancement in value through beneficiation, fabrication, and exchange constitutes the basic material fabric of such a society.

The mineral and chemical resources of the sea will increasingly supplement those from the land—but only for a few of the many commodities we need. Information on which to base a durable assessment of such resources is not now available, but it can be expected to improve as research and exploration increase. Although ocean waters cover two-thirds of the earth, what little is known about the composition and probable history of the three-quarters of the sea bottom that lies beyond the continental rises does not support the popular belief that this region harbors great mineral wealth. Beneath a thin veneer of young sediments, the floor of the ocean basins appears to consist of young basaltic rocks, only sparsely metalliferous and in constant slow motion toward and beneath the continents. Much more promising are the potentialities of the submerged parts of the continents—of oil from the sediments of the continental shelves, slopes, and rises and of mineral placers near the coast. Seawater is also an important source of some useful elements and salts, but only for a few of those needed.

On the one hand, therefore, mineral and mineral-fuel production from the sea are certainly worth going after and will increasingly help to meet needs and shortages in certain commodities. On the other hand, there is little basis for assuming that many marine mineral and chemical resources are of large usable volume or feasible recoverability or that for many essential substances there are any marine resources at all. The roughly $4 billion 1964 world production of offshore mineral resources shows clearly that profits are to be had from the sea. Whether offshore minerals will provide an adequate supplement to the mineral resources of the lands in the needed variety of products is quite another matter.

Known or potential energy resources include power from flowing waters, tidal power, geothermal power, solar energy, and mineral fuels. Of these, conventional water power, if fully developed, would be about equal to that currently generated from fossil fuels. Important as they could be, however, especially in presently underdeveloped parts of the Southern Hemisphere, conventional sources of water power are erratically distributed, and reservoirs silt up. Tidal power and geothermal power are only locally available and neither represents a potential energy supply of more than about 2 percent of that available from water power. Solar energy, although daily renewable and enormous in amount, offers little promise as a major source of industrial power because of the difficulty of achieving the essential concentration and continuity of energy and because of the large quantities of metals and other materials that would be required for solar energy plants of significant capacity.

Sources of power for the future are to be sought among the mineral fuels, and above all in nuclear energy. It will take only another 50 years or so to use up the great bulk of the world's initial supply of recoverable petroleum liquids and natural gas! Recoverable liquid fuels from tar sands and oil shales, although their estimates are very uncertain, might supplement conventional petroleum fuels sufficiently to extend the total lifetime of the petroleum family of fuels as an important source of industrial energy to as much as a century from now. The remaining effective lifetime for coal, if used as the principal source of energy at expected increased demands, would be no more than two or three centuries (although the normal tapering-off in use of a diminishing resource will assure its continued production for perhaps another 500 years from the present). Moreover, we cannot simultaneously use the fossil fuels for fuels, petrochemicals, synthetic polymers, and bacterial conversion to food without going through them even more rapidly. A major side benefit from converting to nuclear energy as our main energy source, therefore, could be the adoption of measures to conserve the fossil fuels for other useful purposes and for *essential* liquid fuels.

Nuclear power from naturally fissionable uranium-235 and from fissionable isotopes obtained by neutron irradiation of uranium-238 and thorium-232 is potentially orders of magnitude larger than that obtainable from all the fossil fuels combined. The supply of uranium-235 from high-grade ores, however, is severely limited, and the production of nuclear power at a cost competitive with fossil fuels or water power, using the present light-water converter reactors and uranium-235 as the principal energy source, can be sustained for only a few decades.

If the potential of nuclear power based on the fission reaction is to be realized, therefore, this can be accomplished only by an early replacement of the present light-water reactors (which can use only about 1 percent of natural uranium) by fully breeding reactors capable of consuming the entire amount of natural uranium or thorium supplied to them.

Controlled fusion has not yet been achieved and may never be. Should it be, however, the energy obtainable from the deuterium contained in 30 cubic kilometers of seawater would be about equal to that of the earth's initial supply of fossil fuels!

On a long-term basis, an achievement no less essential than a practical nuclear-energy economy itself must be the development of an adequate system of safe disposal of nuclear-fission wastes. Much progress has been made within the last decade by the U.S. Atomic Energy Commission in the processing and safe underground disposal of low-volume, high-level wastes. Less satisfactory progress has been made in the handling of the voluminous low-level wastes and solid trash. In fact, for primarily economic reasons, practices are still prevalent at most Atomic Energy Commission installations with respect to these latter categories of waste that on the present scale of operations are barely tolerable, but which would become intolerable with much increase in the use of nuclear power.

To summarize: since resources are finite, then, as population increases, the ratio of resources to man must eventually fall to an unacceptable level. This is the crux of the Malthusian dilemma, often evaded but never invalidated. This study considers the possibility of a final evasion of this dilemma by population control and by increasing resources of food, minerals, and energy. The inescapable central conclusion is that both population control and better resource management are mandatory and should be effected with as little delay as possible.

We must add an elaboration, however. Studies of animal populations suggest that environmental factors other than simple limitation of material resources may act in unexpected ways to limit populations before theoretical maxima are reached. To consider whether the earth might support three more doublings of the human population is probably to consider a purely hypothetical situation. It seems more likely that further crowding, the necessary social and governmental restrictions that accompany dense settlement, and certain kinds of boredom resulting from isolation from nature in an immense, uniform, secular society may prove so depressing to the human spirit or so destructive of coherent social organization that no such population size will ever be reached. Current urban problems are perhaps premonitory of what can come in the absence of more effective attention to the broader problems of resources and man. In attempting to deal with such problems we would do well to consider the basic causes as well as the symptoms. To delay progress toward full self-regulation of population size is to play "Russian roulette" with the future of man.

Man and His Environment

Ansley J. Coale, an economist, is director of the Office of Popula-
tion Research at Princeton University. This paper was first pub-
lished in Science *in 1970.*

AN ECONOMIST'S REVIEW OF RESOURCE EXHAUSTION

ONE OF THE QUESTIONS most frequently raised about the environmental effects of modern life is the rapid and rising rate of
extraction of raw materials. Are we running out of resources?

I would first like to note that the distinction between renewable and nonrenewable resources is not a clear one. There are, of
course, instances of nonrenewable resources in the form of concentrated sources of energy, such as the fossil fuels. These are
reservoirs of reduced carbon embodying radiant energy from the
sun that accumulated over many thousands of years. When these
fuels are used, the energy that is released is to a large extent
radiated into space, and we have no way of reclaiming it. The
geological processes that are constantly renewing the fossil deposits of carbon are so slow compared to the rate at which we are
burning the fuels that the designation "nonrenewable" is appropriate.

On the other hand, when we think of our resources of such
useful materials as the metallic elements of iron, copper, nickel,
lead, and so forth, we should realize that spaceship Earth has
the same amount of each element as it had a million years
ago, and will have the same amount a million years from now.
All we do with these resources is to move them around. The
energy we use is lost, but the minerals we find useful are still
with us. It does not pay to recycle these minerals (that is, to
use them repeatedly by reclaiming scrap) because the deposits
of minerals in the ground or in the ocean are still such a cheap
source. It must be noted that the mining of fresh ore is cheaper
than the use of scrap in part because miners are not charged for
their "externalities." If harmful by-products of mining could not

be discharged into streams, if mine tailings were regulated, and erosion-producing or even unesthetic practices forbidden, minerals would be more expensive and recycling more attractive. In the production of any metallic element, the easier sources are exploited first. As mining gets more difficult, the ore gets more expensive, and recycling becomes more nearly competitive. It seems wholly probable that the technology of recycling will be improved.

The surprising fact is that raw materials are not at the moment very costly, and moreover their cost relative to the cost of finished goods has not been increasing. The gross national product in the United States is more than $4,500 per capita and the raw materials component per capita is less than $100. The price of raw materials relative to the price of finished goods is no higher now than at the beginning of the century, and if we were running out of raw materials, they would surely be rising in relative expensiveness. A prominent exception is saw lumber, which is substantially more expensive relative to the cost of finished wooden products than it used to be.

The reason that the future of our resource situation always seems so bleak and the past seems quite comfortable is that we can readily construct a plausible sounding estimate of the future demand for a particular raw material, but cannot form such a plausible picture of the future supply. To estimate the future demand, we need merely note the recent trends in the per capita consumption of whatever it is we are concerned about, utilize whatever plausible projection of population we are prepared to accept, multiply the two together, and project an astonishingly high rate of usage 50 years in the future. If this demand does not seem overwhelming, we need only make a projection 100 years in the future. What we cannot so readily foresee is the discovery of new sources and of new techniques of extraction, and, in particular, the substitution of other raw materials or the substitution of other industrial processes which change the demand away from the raw material we are considering. Hence it can always be made to appear that in the future we are going to run out of any given material, but that at present we never have.

It is possible to set plausible limits to the stores of fossil fuels that we are likely to discover, and with the very rapid rise in the use of these fuels they will surely become more expensive in some not too distant time. It should be noted, however, that we will not suddenly "run out" of fossil fuels. Long before the last drop of oil is used, oil will have become much more expensive. If gasoline were $5 or $10 a gallon, we would utilize it much more sparingly, with small economical automobile engines, or perhaps the substitution of some non-petroleum-based fuel altogether. In fact, the principal user of our petroleum deposits may be the petrochemical industries. I have given this special attention to fossil fuels because there is no substitute in prospect for such fuels in small mobile units such as automobiles. On the other hand, the supply of overall energy seems to pose no problem. There seems to be ample fissionable material to supply rising energy needs for many centuries, if breeding reactors are perfected. If fusion proves a practical source, the supply of energy can properly be considered limitless.

Another aspect of the relation of the United States economy to resources that is much publicized today is the fact that we are consuming such a large fraction of the current annual extraction of raw materials in the world. A much quoted figure is that 6 percent of the world's population is using 30 percent of the resources. It is concluded from figures such as these that we are robbing the low-income countries of the world of the basis of their future prosperity—that we are using up not only our resources, but theirs as well. Most economists would find this a very erroneous picture of the effect of our demand for the raw materials extracted in the less developed parts of the world. The spokesmen for the less developed countries themselves constantly complain about the adverse terms of trade that they face on world markets. The principal source of their concern is the low price of raw materials and the high price of finished goods. The most effective forms of assistance that the developed countries (including the United States) give to the less developed countries are the purchases they make from the less developed countries in international trade. A developing country needs receipts from exports in order to finance the purchase of the things they need for economic development. For example, in order to industrialize, a nonindustrialized country must for a long time purchase capital equipment from more advanced countries, and the funds for such purchases come from exports—

principally of raw materials. Economists in the developing countries feel that the demand for raw materials is inadequate. Perhaps the most important adverse effect of slowing down the growth of the gross national product in the United States would be that it would diminish the demand for primary products that we would otherwise import from the less developed countries. After all, if a developing country wants to retain its raw materials at home, it can always place an embargo on their export. However, it would be a policy very damaging to economic progress of that very country.

Note that the effect of our high demand for raw material is a different matter from the desirability of the domestic control of mineral resources within the developing countries. Selling oil on the world market provides immense economic advantages to a developing country. Whether foreign interests should be represented in the extraction of raw materials is another question.

POPULATION GROWTH IN THE UNITED STATES

I shall begin a discussion of population with a brief description of recent, current, and future population trends in the United States. Our population today is a little over 200 million, having increased by slightly more than 50 percent since 1940. I think it is likely to increase by nearly 50 percent again in the 30 years before the end of the century.

This rate of increase cannot continue long. If it endured throughout the next century, the population would reach a billion shortly before the year 2100. Within six or seven more centuries we would reach one person per square foot of land area in the United States, and after about 1,500 years our descendants would outweigh the earth if they continued to increase by 50 percent every 30 years. We can even calculate that, at that rate of increase, our descendants would, in a few thousand years, form a sphere of flesh whose radius would, neglecting relativity, expand at the velocity of light.

Every demographer knows that we cannot continue a positive rate of increase indefinitely. The inexorable arithmetic of compound interest leads us to absurd conditions within a calculable period of time. Logically we must, and in fact we will, have a rate of growth very close to zero in the long run.

The only questions about attaining a zero rate of increase for any population is when and how such a rate is attained. A zero rate of increase implies a balance between the average birth and death rates, so the choice of how to attain a zero rate of increase is a choice between low birth and death rates that are approximately equal. The average growth rate very near to zero during mankind's past history has been attained with high birth and death rates—with an average duration of life that until recently was no more than 30 or 35 years. I have no difficulty in deciding that I would prefer a zero rate of growth with low rather than high birth and death rates, or with an average duration of life in excess of 70 years, as has been achieved in all of the more advanced countries of the world, rather than the life that is "nasty, brutish, and short." The remaining question then is *when* should our population growth level off.

A popular answer today is "immediately." In fact a zero rate of increase in the United States starting immediately is not feasible and I believe not desirable. The reason is the age composition of the population that our past history of birth and death rates has left to us. We have an especially young population now because of the postwar baby boom. One consequence is that our death rate is much lower than it would be in a population that had long had low fertility. That is, because our population is young, a high proportion of it is concentrated in ages where the risk of mortality is small. Therefore, if we were to attain a zero growth rate immediately, it would be necessary to cut the birth rate about in half. For the next 15 or 20 years, women would have to bear children at a rate that would produce only a little over one child per completed family. At the end of that time we would have a very peculiar age distribution with a great shortage of young people. The attendant social and economic disruptions represent too large a cost to pay for the advantages that we might derive from reducing growth to zero right away.

In fact, a more reasonable goal would be to reduce fertility as soon as possible to a level where couples produced just enough children to insure that each generation exactly replaced itself. If this goal (early attainment of fertility at a replacement level) were reached immediately, our population would increase 35 to 40 percent before it stabilized. The reason that fertility at the

mere replacement level would produce such a large increase
in population is again the age distribution we have today. There
are many more people today under 20 than 20 to 40, and when
the relatively numerous children have moved into the childbearing ages, they will greatly outnumber the persons now at
those ages, and when the current population under age 20 moves
into the old ages, they will be far more numerous than the people
now at the old ages. Thus to move the population to replacement would be to insure approximately that the number of
children under 20 will be about the same as it is today, but
that the number above that age will be substantially higher.
The net effect is the increase of 35 to 40 percent mentioned just
above. It is the built-in growth in our age composition that led
me to state earlier that I think an increase in the order of 50
percent of the U.S. population is not unlikely.

A sensible choice in reducing our growth rate to zero then
is between early or late attainment of fertility at the replacement level. Is there any reason that we should not attempt to
attain a fertility at replacement as soon as possible? My own
opinion is that an early move in that direction is desirable, but
for the sake of completeness, I must point out that there is a non-
negligible cost associated with attaining a stationary population—
the population that will exist with fertility at replacement after
the age distribution left over from the past has worked out its
transitory consequences.

A stationary population with the mortality levels that we have
already attained has a much older age distribution than any the
United States has ever experienced. It has more people over
60 than under 15, and half the population would be over 37
rather than over 27, as is the case today. It would be an age
distribution much like that of a health resort.

Moreover, if we view the age pyramid in the conventional
way, with the number of males and females being drawn out
as in the branches of a Christmas tree (age representing alti-
tude of the tree), the pyramid for the stationary population is
virtually vertical until age 50 because of the small number of
deaths under the favorable mortality conditions we have attained. In contrast, the age distribution of the United States to
date has always tapered more or less sharply with increasing
age. The stationary population with its vertical sides would no

longer conform in age composition to the shape of the social structure—to the pyramid of privilege and responsibility. In a growing population, the age pyramid does conform, so there is a rough consonance of shape between diminishing numbers at higher ages and the smaller number of high positions relative to low positions. In a stationary population there would no longer be a reasonable expectation of advancement as a person moves through life. I have indicated that sooner or later we must have a stationary population, so that sooner or later we must adjust to such an age composition. I am pointing to this disadvantage to show that there is a choice between moving more gradually to a stationary population at the expense of a larger ultimate population size in order to continue to enjoy for a longer time the more desirable age distribution of a growing population.

CONNECTION BETWEEN POPULATION AND POLLUTION

The connection between the current growth in our population and the deterioration of our environment of which we have all become aware is largely an indirect one. The problem has arisen because we are permitting the production of bads (pollution, or negative externalities) along with goods. There seems little doubt that the rapid increase in the production of goods has been responsible for the rapid increase in the production of bads, since we have made no effective effort to prevent the latter from accompanying the former. But per capita increase in production has been more important than population growth. Population has increased by 50 percent since 1940, but per capita use of electricity has been multiplied several times. A similar statement can even be made about the crowding of our national parks. The population has increased by about 50 percent in the last 30 years—attendance in national parks has increased by more than 400 percent.

A wealthy industrial urban population of 100 million persons would have most of the pollution problems we do. In fact, Sydney, Australia, has problems of air and water pollution and of traffic jams, even though the total population of Australia is about 12 million in an area 80 percent as big as the United States. Australia is actually more urbanized than the United

States, in spite of its relatively small population and large over-all area.

If we have the will and intelligence to devise and apply proper policies, we can improve our environment and can do so either with the current population of 200 million, or with the population that we will probably have in another 50 years of 300 million. On the other hand, if we ignore environmental problems and continue to treat pure air and water and the disposal of trash as if they were free, and if we pay no attention to the effects of the techniques that we employ upon the balance of nature, we will be in trouble whether our population grows or not. There is no doubt that slower population growth would make it easier to improve our environment, but not much easier.

POLICIES THAT WOULD AFFECT THE GROWTH OF POPULATION

We must, at some time, achieve a zero rate of population, and the balance should surely be achieved at low birth and death rates rather than at high rates. If, as at present, only about 5 percent of women remain single at the end of the childbearing span, and if 96 percent of women survive to the mean age of childbearing, and if finally the sex ratio at birth remains about 105 males for every 100 females, married couples must have an average of about 2.25 children to replace themselves. What kinds of policies might be designed to assure such a level of fertility or, more generally, to produce the fertility level that is at the moment socially desirable?

I begin with a set of policies that are consistent with general democratic and humanitarian principles, although a minority of the population would oppose them on religious grounds. These are policies that would, through education and the provision of clincial services, try to make it possible for every conception to be the result of a deliberate choice, and for every choice to be an informed one, based on an adequate knowledge of the consequences of bearing different numbers of children at different times. A component of such a set of policies would be the development of more effective means of contraception to reduce the number of accidental pregnancies occurring to couples who are trying to avoid conception. These are policies that call for a substantial government role and I think that an effective government program in these areas is already overdue. I personally believe that education in the consequences of childbearing and in the techniques of avoiding pregnancy, combined with the provision of contraceptive services, should be supplemented by the provision of safe and skillful abortion upon request. It is clear that the public consensus in favor of abortion is not nearly as clear-cut as that in favor of contraception, and I know that the extent and the strength of the moral objection to induced abortion is much greater. Nevertheless, I am persuaded by experience in Japan and eastern Europe that the advantages of abortion provided under good medical auspices to cause the early termination of unwanted pregnancies are very important to the women affected, as is evident in the fact that when medically safe abortion has been made available at low cost, the number of abortions has initially been as great or greater than the number of live births. Later there is a typical tendency for women to resort to contraception rather than repeated abortions.

The reason I favor abortion is that such a high proportion of births that occur today are unwanted, and because a large number of desperate pregnant women (probably more than a half a million annually) resort to clandestine abortions today, with high rates of serious complications. In contrast, early abortion, under skilled medical auspices, is less dangerous than tonsillectomy, and substantially less dangerous than carrying a child to full term.

In recent years the number of births that were unwanted in the United States constituted about 20 percent of the total (an unwanted birth was defined as one in which the woman said that conception occurred either as a result of a failure of contraception or in the absence of contraception but without the intent to become pregnant as soon as possible, when at the time the conception occurred the husband or wife or both did not want another child then or later). The rate at which women are having children today would lead to a completed family size of slightly under three children.[1] If all unwanted births

1. [Since Professor Coale wrote this article, birth rates have continued to decline. In the first nine months of 1972 the birth rate was one which, if continued, would result in an average completed family size of 2.1 for those married women now in the childbearing years. *Editors.*]

were eliminated, the number of children born per married woman would be about 2.4 or 2.5 on average. This is very little above replacement, and when allowance is made for the likely possibility that women understated the proportion of births that were unwanted, it is probable that the elimination of unwanted births would bring a fertility at or below replacement.

If it is true that the elimination of unwanted pregnancies would reduce fertility very nearly to replacement, it must be conceded that this outcome is fortuitous. It is highly unlikely that over a substantial period of time the free choice by each couple of the number of children they want would lead exactly to the socially desirable level of fertility. The erratic behavior of fertility in America and in other advanced industrialized countries in the last 30 or 40 years is ample evidence that when fertility is voluntarily controlled, the level of fertility is subject to major fluctuations, and I see no logical reason to expect that on average people would voluntarily choose a number of children that would keep the long-run average a little above two per couple. In other words, we must acknowledge the probable necessity of instituting policies that would influence the number of children people want. However, there is no need for haste in formulating such policy, since, as I have indicated, improved contraceptive services combined with a liberal provision of abortion would probably move our fertility at present quite close to replacement, and a gradual increase in population during the next generation would not be a major addition to the problems we already face.

It is particularly difficult to frame acceptable policies influencing the number of children that people want. While it is still true that so many large families result from unwanted pregnancies, the unwanted child that is the most recent birth in a large family already faces many deprivations. The psychological disadvantages of the unwanted child cause some of our most serious social problems. In addition to these psychological disadvantages, the unwanted child in a large impoverished family faces an inadequate diet, much below average chances for schooling, and generally inferior opportunities. I hardly think it a wise or humane policy to handicap him further by imposing a financial burden on his parents as a result of his birth.

When unwanted births have become negligible in number, we

could imagine trying to design a policy in which the couple is asked to pay some part of the "externalities" that an additional birth imposes on society. In the meantime, I suggest as a desirable supplement to better contraception and free access to abortion the extension of more nearly equal opportunities in education and employment for women, so that activities outside of the home become a more powerful competitor to a larger family. We should start now devoting careful attention to formulation of policies in this area—policies that could increase fertility when it fell too low as well as policies to induce people to want fewer children.

Some aspects of the deterioration of our environment appear to be critical and call for prompt action. We need to start now to frame and apply actions that would arrest the careless destruction of the world in which we live. We also need policies to reduce promptly the incidence of unwanted births. In the long run we shall also need ways to influence the number of births people want. To design policies consistent with our most cherished social and political values will not be easy, and it is fortunate that there is no valid reason for hasty action.

Does Human Fertility Adjust to the Environment?

RICHARD A. EASTERLIN

Richard A. Easterlin is an economic historian at the University of Pennsylvania. This paper was published in the American Economic Review.

FROM MALTHUS TO PAUL EHRLICH, there have been those who see the growth in man's numbers driving him inexorably, like lemmings to the sea, toward misery and death. A basic premise of this view is that human reproductive behavior does not voluntarily respond to environmental conditions. Instead, man, following his natural instincts, will breed without restraint and population will grow until environmental limits force a halt through higher mortality.

Nowhere, I think, is this view called more into doubt than by American historical experience. Here, if anywhere, environmental constraints on population growth at the start of the nineteenth century appeared to be at a minimum. . . . American fertility was extremely high. According to Coale and Zelnik, the birth rate at the start of the nineteenth century "was markedly higher than that ever recorded for any European country."[1]

The astounding thing is that from about 1810 on, American fertility started to decline. And this, shortly after a vast expansion of natural resources had been accomplished through the Louisiana Purchase! While the data are not perfect, by 1860, for the white population, the ratio of children under five to women 20–44 years old (the fertility measure most generally

1. A. J. Coale and M. Zelnik, *New Estimates of Fertility and Population in the United States* (Princeton: Princeton University Press, 1963), p. 35. While source references in this paper have been kept to a minimum, a number are given in *American Economic Growth: An Economist's History of the United States*, L. E. Davis, R. A. Easterlin, and W. N. Parker, eds. (New York: Harper & Row, 1971), chap. 5, and R. A. Easterlin, *Population, Labor Force, and Long Swings in Economic Growth* (New York: Columbia University Press, 1968), part 2.

available) had fallen by a third from its 1810 level, and by 1910, by over a half. Put differently, in 1790 almost half of the free families contained five or more persons; by 1900, the proportion of families with five or more persons had fallen to less than a third.

How can one reconcile this dramatic reduction in fertility with the seemingly abundant state of natural resources throughout much of this period? In this paper, I shall suggest that, while our state of knowledge is far from adequate, a plausible case can be made that the secular decline in American fertility was a voluntary response to changing environmental conditions. For obvious reasons we need to know much more about the mechanisms involved, but if the line of reasoning here is correct, it refutes the analogy commonly drawn between human population growth and that of fruit flies in a jar.

THEORY

The analysis builds on the economic theory of fertility. In this theory, tastes, prices, and income determine the optimal number of children. The optimal number of children, together with infant and child mortality conditions, determines the optimal number of births. Finally, the extent to which actual births exceed optimal births depends on attitudes toward and extent of information about fertility control practices, and the supply conditions of such practices.

The population is subdivided into several component groups, each subject to rather different conditions. For the present discussion, attention is focused on a classification in terms of location—frontier areas, settled agricultural areas, new urban areas, and old urban areas. The argument is that the basic fertility determinants—in particular, the cost of children, fertility control practices, and factors other than income change influencing tastes —vary among these locations in such a way that fertility tends to be progressively lower as one moves from the first to the fourth of these situations. Since the course of American economic growth in fact involved a population shift in just this direction, the result was a continuing secular pressure toward fertility reduction.

To take up first the matter of tastes, two determinants directly bound up with economic and social development are the progress of education and the introduction and diffusion of new goods. Both tend to alter preferences for goods versus children in a manner adverse to fertility, because they create or strengthen consumption outlets competitive with children as a source of satisfaction. Education creates awareness of new modes of enjoyment and opens access to them. (For example, while children are a recognized source of satisfaction to all, it is usually only persons of higher educational status who consider foreign travel as a serious consumption alternative.) The progress of education during economic development means that a growing number of households experience a widening of consumption alternatives. Considering different locations at a given time, education was typically more advanced, and hence this influence stronger, in older rural areas than on the frontier, in urban areas than rural, and in older urban areas than in newer urban areas.

Much the same type of argument may be made regarding new goods. New products were more available in older rural areas than on the frontier, because the marketing system was more advanced: hence a wider range of items competed with children in the older areas. Similarly, people in urban areas were more exposed to new goods than people in rural areas by virtue of the greater market potential offered by the denser populations, residents of older urban areas being more exposed than those in newer.

As for costs of childbearing, both the outlays on and returns from children tended to create cost differentials among areas with an effect on fertility similar to that of tastes. On the frontier, with its demands for breaking and clearing new land, the potential labor contribution of children was greater than in established agricultural areas. Also, with land relatively abundant, the problem of establishing mature children on farms of their own was less serious. Nevertheless, in the established agricultural areas, the labor contribution of children on family farms was higher than in cities where work possibilities were more restricted. At the same time the costs of raising children were higher in the cities, since food and housing were typically more expensive there than in rural areas. Thus, taking account of both costs and returns, children were increasingly expensive as the situation changed from frontier to settled agriculture to an urban location.

Finally, consider the situation with regard to methods of fertility limitation. In general, knowledge and availability of a variety of fertility control practices were greater in urban areas than in rural. Similarly these conditions were better in settled agricultural areas than on the frontier, which was at the periphery of the communications network.

Putting together these influences—tastes, cost, and fertility control practices—leads one to expect the following ordering of areas from high to low fertility at any given time: frontier, settled agriculture, new urban areas, old urban areas. Also since frontier areas gradually become transformed into settled agriculture and new urban areas into old, one would expect that over time fertility would decline as new areas "age." Moreover, since "new" and "old" are matters of degree, not of kind, one might expect that even in settled agricultural areas and older urban areas, fertility would continue to decline, at least for some time, as "aging" continues.

In urban areas this process of aging is reinforced by the trend in the composition of the population by origin. Initially, the populations in urban areas are dominated by in-migrants from rural areas or abroad who bring with them a high fertility heritage. In the course of time, these first generation urbanites are gradually replaced by second and later generations born and raised in urban areas, and with consequently lower fertility "tastes." Even today fertility among new rural migrants to urban areas exceeds that of persons who originate in urban areas. Thus to the pattern of cross-section differences by location noted above, one can add an expectation of fertility declines through time in all four locations.

EVIDENCE

These expectations are supported by the available evidence, though much more work is needed. In Figure 1, the ratio of children under five to females aged 20–44 is shown for the rural white population in each geographic division from 1800 to 1960; Figure 2 presents similar data for the urban white population.

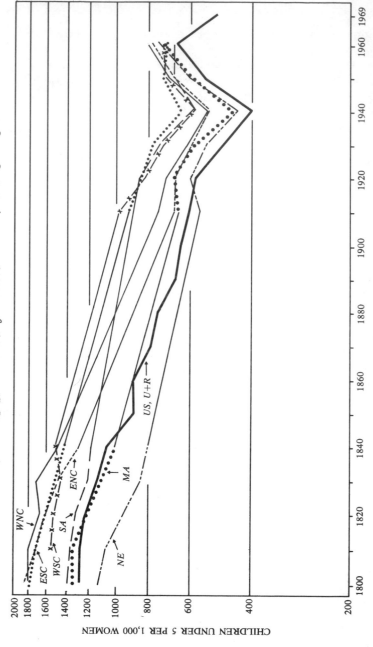

FIGURE 1. *Number of Children under 5 Years Old per 1,000 White Women 20 to 44, United States, 1800–1969, and Rural, by Division, 1800–1840 and 1910–1960*

SOURCE: U.S. Bureau of the Census, *Historical Statistics of the United States, Colonial Times to 1957* (Washington, D.C., 1960) and *Historical Statistics of the United States, Colonial Times to 1957; Continuation to 1962 and Revisions* (Washington, D.C., 1965) Series B39–B68. The 1969 U.S. figure was kindly supplied by Wilson H. Grabill of the Bureau of the Census. Urban and rural classified by 1010 Census rules.

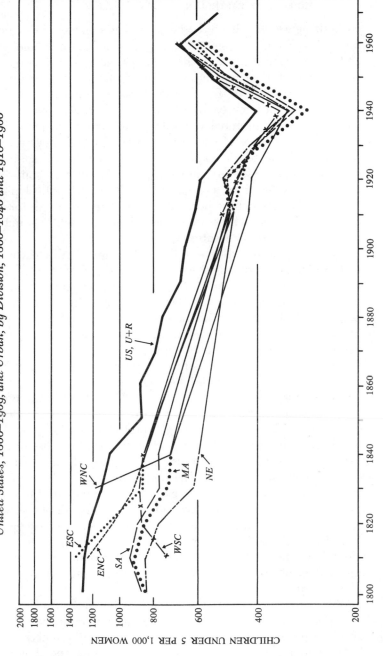

FIGURE 2. *Number of Children under 5 Years Old per 1,000 White Women 20 to 44, United States, 1800–1969, and Urban, by Division, 1800–1840 and 1910–1960*

SOURCE: Same as Figure 1.

172 RICHARD A. EASTERLIN

In both figures the United States ratio is depicted by a heavy line. This is the average for the population as a whole, rural and urban combined, and therefore provides a common reference point in the two figures. Unfortunately the rural-urban data are not available from 1850 to 1900; hence the 1840 and 1910 observations for each division are connected with a thin line. The Mountain and Pacific divisions have been omitted, because of the absence of data for the period when they were being settled. One would expect these divisions to be somewhat different from the others, however, because of the importance of mining rather than agriculture in their early development. Similarly, the nonwhite population has been omitted for lack of data. It is the white population, however, which predominantly accounts for the national patterns.

Consider first the differentials by location in the early part of the nineteenth century. As shown in Figure 1, among rural areas, fertility was lower in the older settled areas in the East than in those undergoing settlement, the areas west of the Appalachians. This differential between new and old areas existed in both the North and the South. Differences among areas in the age distribution of women of reproductive age, whether due to vital rates or migration, had little to do with this fertility differential. The same differential between newer and older regions holds also for urban areas (Figure 2). Thus it is the three older East Coast divisions which are grouped together at the bottom of Figure 2. Even the seemingly partial exception, the West South Central division, is not really an exception, because the figures are dominated by Louisiana, an area which was settled early. Finally, within every division, urban fertility is lower than rural fertility. This is quickly seen by comparison with the United States reference line in the two figures. Virtually all of the urban ratios are below the United States average, and except for New England, almost all rural ratios are above. Thus, there is a clear and consistent pattern of fertility in frontier areas exceeding that in older established areas, and of rural fertility generally exceeding urban.

With regard to trends, the United States ratio declines from 1810 on, and this is seen to occur in both rural and urban sections of all geographic divisions, though with some differences in timing. Frontier areas become progressively settled and new urban areas are transformed into old, while within the older rural and urban areas the process of aging continues. . . .

The question arises whether the growth of per capita income associated with economic development may have exerted a strong counter force tending to raise fertility. The answer to this, in my view, is that income growth is a two-edged sword. On the one hand, it tends to make for higher fertility by augmenting the resources available to a household. On the other, it tends to lower fertility through what might be described as an "intergeneration taste effect." The argument in its simplest form is that in a steadily growing economy successive generations are raised in increasingly affluent households and hence develop successively higher living aspirations in the course of their normal upbringing. Thus, while, on the one hand, each generation on reaching adulthood normally has more resources at its command, on the other, it has greater goods aspirations. If long-term growth is not steady, but fluctuating, temporary disparities can result between the growth of resources and that of aspirations with consequent swings in fertility, such as the United States has been experiencing in recent decades. Secularly, however, the two influences tend to cancel out in their effect on fertility. Whether they do so completely remains an open and important empirical question. It is clear, however, that if this view is adopted, then the presumption no longer holds that secular per capita income growth tends to raise fertility—the net effect could be positive, negative, or zero. . . .

It is worth noting that the fertility declines of the past were accomplished entirely by voluntary action on the part of the population. To some extent marriage was deferred. But also there were declines in fertility within marriage. These developments took place in a situation where not only was there no public policy to help those interested in fertility limitation, but attitudes, and even laws in many states, were hostile to the practice or even discussion of contraception or other fertility control practices. To emphasize the voluntary nature of this development, however, is not to suggest that there was no need for family planning policies then or, for that matter, that there is no need today. What historical experience shows is a voluntary decline in fertility, but this is not necessarily the optimal rate of decline from the point of view of social welfare. One can only conjecture how many households suffered from the miseries of unwanted children because of the hostile public environment. Today our evidence on this matter and on the need for intelligent public policy is straightforward.

In the literature on the demographic transition, the secular fertility decline is typically linked to the processes of urbanization and industrialization. But the American experience suggests an additional dimension associated with the transformation of a rural area from frontier to settled agriculture. Nor is this peculiar to the United States. Canada seems to show a similar pattern, while in Europe the association of high fertility and settlement has been noted with regard to parts of Scandinavia, Finland, and Russia in the nineteenth century. Thus, seen very broadly, the American fertility decline reflects not only the processes of urbanization and industrialization but that of settlement as well. This aspect is crucial, because of its implications for today's less developed countries. The traditional view of secular fertility decline has led to emphasis on industrialization in these areas as a prerequisite to a decline. The American experience raises the possibility that as population increasingly presses against land resources, fertility declines set in within the rural sector itself.

One may, of course, discount the possibility that American experience is relevant to today's less developed countries. This would carry the highly questionable implication that Americans are in some way a distinctive and exceptionally rational species of mankind. Moreover, the historical experience of Europe and Japan shows that elsewhere in the world, as similar pressures for reducing population growth have mounted, similar responses have taken place. It seems reasonable to suppose that history will, in time, record that the same was true of today's less developed nations as well. Indeed, fertility declines are already occurring in some of these areas.

CONCLUSION

The conclusion to which this discussion points is that both theory and the empirical research done so far on historical American fertility suggest that human fertility responds voluntarily to environmental conditions. If this is so—and it seems hard to ignore the evidence—then the nature of what is called "the population problem" takes on a radically different guise. The question is not one of human beings breeding themselves into growing misery. Rather, the problem is whether the voluntary response of fertility to environmental pressures results in a socially optimal adjustment. In thinking about this, it seems useful to distinguish between the potential for population adjustment and the actual degree of adjustment. The staggering change in American reproductive behavior over the past century and a half clearly demonstrates the immense potential for adjustment. Whether, currently, the degree of adjustment is socially optimal remains a matter for research. Such research requires clarification of the mechanisms through which environmental pressures influence reproductive behavior—a subject to which economic analysis can contribute much more than it has so far. One may add—though this lies outside the scope of the present paper—that further research also requires a deeper understanding of the wants and aspirations of individual families in regard to human welfare.

Ecological Armageddon

ROBERT HEILBRONER

Robert Heilbroner has written a number of popular books in economics, including The Worldly Philosophers. *He is on the graduate faculty of the New School for Social Research. This article first appeared in the* New York Review of Books *in 1970.*

ECOLOGY has become the Thing. There are ecological politics, ecological jokes, ecological bookstores, advertisements, seminars, teach-ins, buttons. The automobile, symbol of ecological abuse, has been tried, sentenced to death, and formally executed in at least two universities (replete with burial of one victim). Publishing companies are fattening on books on the sonic boom, poisons in the things we eat, perils loose in the garden, the dangers of breathing. The *Saturday Review* has appended a regular monthly Ecological Supplement. In short, the ecological issue has assumed the dimensions of a vast popular fad, for which one can predict with reasonable assurance the trajectory of all such fads—a period of intense general involvement, followed by growing boredom and gradual extinction, save for a die-hard remnant of the faithful.

This would be a tragedy, for I have slowly become convinced during the last twelve months that the ecological issue is not only of primary and lasting importance, but that it may indeed constitute the most dangerous and difficult challenge that humanity has ever faced. Since these are very large statements, let me attempt to substantiate them by drawing freely on the best single descriptive and analytic treatment of the subject that I have yet seen, *Population, Resources, Environment* by Paul and Anne Ehrlich of Stanford University. Rather than resort to the bothersome procedure of endlessly citing their arguments in quotation marks, I shall take the liberty of reproducing their case in a rather free paraphrase, as if it were my own, until we reach the end of the basic argument, after which I shall make clear some conclusions that I believe lie implicit in their work.

Ultimately, the ecological crisis represents our belated awakening to the fact that we live on what Kenneth Boulding has called, in the perfect phrase, our Spaceship Earth. As in all spaceships, sustained life requires that a meticulous balance be maintained between the capability of the vehicle to support life and the demands made by the inhabitants of the craft. Until quite recently, those demands have been well within the capability of the ship, in its ability both to supply the physical and chemical requirements for continued existence and to absorb the waste products of the voyagers.

It is only in our time that we are reaching the limit of earthly carrying capacity, not on a local but on a global basis. Indeed, as will soon become clear, we are well past that capacity, provided that the level of resource intake and waste output represented by the average American or European is taken as a standard to be achieved by all humanity. To put it bluntly, if we take as the price of a first-class ticket the resource requirements of those passengers who travel in the Northern Hemisphere of the Spaceship, we have now reached a point at which the steerage is condemned to live forever—or at least within the horizon of the technology presently visible—at a second-class level; or a point at which a considerable change in living habits must be imposed on first class if the ship is ever to be converted to a one-class cruise.

This strain on the carrying capacity of the vessel results from the contemporary confluence of three distinct developments, each of which places tremendous or even unmanageable strains on the life-carrying capability of the planet and all of which together simply overload it. The first of these is the enormous strain imposed by the sheer burgeoning of population. The statistics of population growth are by now very well known: the earth's passenger list is growing at a rate that will give us some four billion humans by 1975, and that threatens to give us eight billion by 2010. I say "threatens," since it is likely that the inability of the earth to carry so large a group will result in an actual population somewhat smaller than this, especially in the steerage, where the growth is most rapid and the available resources least plentiful.

We shall return to the population problem later. But meanwhile a second strain is placed on the earth by the simple cumulative effect of *existing* technology (combustion engines, the main industrial processes, present-day agricultural techniques, etc.). This strain is localized mainly in the first-class portions of the vessel where each new arrival on board is rapidly given a standard complement of capital equipment and where the rate of physical and chemical resource transformation per capita steadily mounts. The strain consists of the limited ability of the soil, the water, and the atmosphere of these favored regions to absorb the outpourings of these fast-growing industrial processes. . . . To raise the existing (not the anticipated) population of the earth to American standards would require the annual extraction of 75 times as much iron, 100 times as much copper, 200 times as much lead, and 250 times as much tin as we now take from the earth, with corresponding increases in throughput and waste discharges.

I will revert later to the consequences of this prospect. First, however, let us pay attention to the third source of overload, this one traceable to the special environment-destroying potential of newly developed technologies. Of these the most important —and if it should ever come to full-scale war, of course the most lethal—is the threat posed by nuclear radiation.

But the threats of new technology are by no means limited to the specter of nuclear devastation. There is, immediately at hand, the known devastation of the new chemical pesticides that have now entered more or less irreversibly into the living tissue of the world's population. Most mothers' milk in the United States today—I now quote the Ehrlichs verbatim—"contains so much DDT that it would be declared illegal in interstate commerce if it were sold as cow's milk"; and the DDT intake of infants around the world is twice the daily allowable maximum set by the World Health Organization. We are already, in other words, being exposed to heavy dosages of chemicals whose effects we know to be dangerous, with what ultimate results we shall have to wait nervously to discover. (There is food for thought in the archaeological evidence that one factor in the decline of Rome was the systematic poisoning of upper-class Romans from the lead with which they lined their wine containers.)

But the threat is not limited to pesticides. Barry Commoner

predicts an agricultural crisis in the United States within fifty years from the action of our fertilizers, which will either ultimately destroy soil fertility or lead to pollution of the national water supply. At another corner of the new technology, the SST threatens not only to shake us with its boom, but to affect the amount of cloud over (and climate) by its contrails. And I have not even mentioned the standard pollution problems of smoke, industrial effluents into lakes and rivers, or solid wastes. Suffice it to report that a 1968 UNESCO Conference concluded that man has only about twenty years to go before the planet starts to become uninhabitable because of air pollution alone. Of course "starts to" is imprecise; I am reminded of a cartoon of an industrialist looking at his billowing smokestacks, in front of which a forlorn figure is holding up a placard that says: "We have only 35 years to go." The caption reads, "Boy, that shook me up for a minute. I thought it said 3 to 5 years."

I have left until last the grimmest and gravest threat of all, speaking now on behalf of the steerage. This is the looming inability of the great green earth to bring forth sufficient food to maintain life, even at the miserable threshold of subsistence at which it is now endured by perhaps a third of the world's population. The problem here is the very strong likelihood that population growth will inexorably outpace whatever improvements in fertility and productivity we will be able to apply to the earth's mantle (including the watery fringes of the ocean where sea "farming" is at least technically imaginable).

Here the race is basically between two forces: on the one hand, those that give promise that the rate of population increase can be curbed (if not totally halted); and on the other, those that give promise of increasing the amount of sustenance we can wring from the soil.

Both these forces are subtly blended of technological and social factors. Take population growth. The great hope of every ecologist is that an effective birth control technique—cheap, requiring little or no medical supervision, devoid of taboos or religious hindrances—will rapidly and effectively lower the present fertility rates which are doubling world population every thirty-five years. No such device is currently available, although the Pill, the IUD, vasectomies, abortions, condoms, coitus interruptus, and other known techniques could, of course, do the job, if the requisite equipment, persuasion (or coercion), instruction, etc. could be brought to the 80 to 90 percent of the world's people who know next to nothing about birth control.

It seems a fair conclusion that no such world-wide campaign is apt to be successful for at least a decade and maybe a generation, although there is always the hope that a "spontaneous" change in attitudes, similar to that in Hungary or Japan, will bring about a rapid halt to population growth.

The other element in the race is our ability to match population growth with food supplies, at least for a generation or so, while birth control techniques and campaigns are being perfected. Here the problem is also partly technological, partly social. The technological part involves the so-called "Green Revolution"—the development of seeds that are capable, at their best, of improving yields per acre by a factor of 300 percent, sometimes even more. The problem, however, is that these new seeds generally require irrigation and fertilizer to bring their benefits.

There are as well other technical problems of an ecological nature associated with the Green Revolution, mainly the risk of introducing locally untried strains of plants that may be subject to epidemic disease. But putting those difficulties to the side, we must recognize as well the social obstacles that a successful Green Revolution must overcome. The new seeds can only be afforded by the upper level of peasantry—not merely because of their cost (and the cost of the required fertilizer), but because only a rich peasant can take the risk of having the crop turn out badly without himself suffering starvation. Hence the Green Revolution is likely to increase the strains of social stratification within the underdeveloped areas. Then too, even a successful local crop does not always shed its benefits evenly across a nation, but results all too often in local gluts that cannot be transported to starving areas because of transportation bottlenecks.

None of these discouraging remarks is intended in the slightest to disparage the Green Revolution, which represents the inspired work of dedicated men. Yet at best these improvements will only stave off the day of reckoning. Ultimately the problem posed by Malthus must be faced—that population tends to increase geometrically, by doubling; and that agriculture does not;

so that eventually population *must* face the limit of a food barrier.

The Malthusian prophecy has been so often "refuted," as economists have pointed to the astonishing rates of growth of food output in the advanced nations, that there is a danger of dismissing the warnings of the Ehrlichs as merely another premature alarm. To do so would be a fearful mistake. For unlike Malthus, who assumed that technology would remain constant, the Ehrlichs have made ample allowance for the growth of technological capability, and their approach to the impending catastrophe is not shrill. They merely point out that a mild version of the Malthusian solution is already upon us, for at least half a billion people are chronically hungry or outright starving, and another 1½ billion under or malnourished. Thus we do not have to wait for "gigantic inevitable famine"; it has already come.

What is more important is that the Ehrlichs see the matter in a fundamentally different perspective from Malthus, not as a problem involving supply and demand, but as one involving a total ecological equilibrium. The crisis, as the Ehrlichs see it, is thus both deeper and more complex than merely a shortage of food, although the latter is one of its more horrendous evidences. What threatens the Spaceship Earth is a profound imbalance between the totality of systems by which human life is maintained, and the totality of demands, industrial as well as agricultural, technological as well as demographic, to which that capacity to support life is subjected.

I have no doubt that one can fault bits and pieces of the Ehrlichs' analysis, and there is a note of determined pessimism in their work that leads me to suspect (or at least hope) that there is somewhat more time for adaptation than they suggest. Yet I do not see how their basic conclusion can be denied. Beginning within our lifetimes and rising rapidly to crisis proportions in our children's, humankind faces a challenge comparable to none in its history, with the possible exception of the forced migration of the Ice Age. It is with the responses to this crisis that I wish to end this essay, for telling and courageous as the Ehrlichs' analysis is, I do not believe that even they have fully faced up to the implications that their own findings present.

The first of these I have already stated: it is the clear conclusion that the underdeveloped countries can *never* hope to achieve parity with the developed countries. Given our present and prospective technology, there are simply not enough resources to permit a "Western" rate of industrial exploitation to be expanded to a population of four billion—much less eight billion —persons. It may well be that most of the population in the underdeveloped world has no ambition to reach Western standards—indeed, does not even know that such a thing as "development" is on the agenda. But the elites of these nations, for all their rhetorical rejection of Western (and especially American) styles of life, do tend to picture a Western standard as the ultimate end of their activities. As it becomes clear that such an objective is impossible, a profound reorientation of views must take place within the underdeveloped nations.

What such a reorientation will be it is impossible to say. For the near future, the outlook for the most population-oppressed areas will be a continuous battle against food shortages, coupled with the permanent impairment of the intelligence of much of the surviving population due to protein deficiencies in childhood. This pressure of population may lead to aggressive searches for *Lebensraum;* or, as I have frequently written, may culminate in revolutions of desperation.

In the long run, of course, there is the possibility of considerable growth (although nothing resembling the attainment of a Western standard of consumption). But no quick substantial improvement in their condition seems feasible within the next generation at least.

The implications of the ecological crisis for the advanced nations are not any less severe, although they are of a different kind. For it is clear that free industrial growth is just as disastrous for the Western nations as free population growth for those of the East and South.

The necessity to bring our economic activities into a sustainable relationship with the resource capabilities and waste absorption properties of the world will pose two problems for the West. On the simpler level, a whole series of technological problems must be met. Fume-free transportation must be developed on land and air. The cult of disposability must be replaced by that of reusability. Population stability must be attained through tax and other inducements, both to conserve resources and to preserve reasonable population densities. Many of these problems will tax our ingenuity, technical and socio-political, but the main problem they pose is not whether, but *how soon* they can be solved.

But there is another, deeper question that the developed nations face—at least those that have capitalist economies. This problem can be stated as a crucial test as to who was right— John Stuart Mill or Karl Marx. Mill maintained, in his famous *Principles of Economics,* that the terminus of capitalist evolution would be a stationary state, in which the return to capital had fallen to insignificance, and a redistributive tax system would be able to capture any flows of income to the holders of scarce resources, such as land. In effect, he prophesied the transformation of capitalism, in an environment of abundance, into a balanced economy, in which the capitalist, both as the generator of change and as the main claimant on the surplus generated by change, would in effect undergo a painless euthanasia.

The Marxian view is of course quite the opposite. The very essence of capitalism, according to Marx, is expansion—which is to say, the capitalist, as a historical "type," finds his *raison d'être* in the insatiable search for additional money-wealth gained through the constant growth of the economic system. The idea of a "stationary" capitalism is, in Marxian eyes, a contradiction in terms, on a logical par with a democratic aristocracy or an industrial feudalism.

Is the Millian or the Marxian view correct? I do not think that we can yet say. Some economic growth is certainly compatible with a stabilized rate of resource use and disposal, for growth could take the form of the expenditure of additional labor on the improvement (aesthetic or technical) of the national environment. Indeed, insofar as education or cultural activity are forms of national output that require little resource use and result in little waste product, national output could be indefinitely expanded through these and similar activities. But there is no doubt that the main avenue of traditional capitalist accumulation would have to be considerably constrained; that net investment in mining and manufacturing would effectively cease; that the rate and kind of technological change would need to be supervised and probably greatly reduced; and that as a consequence, the flow of profits would almost certainly fall.

Is this imaginable within a capitalist setting—that is, in a nation in which the business ideology permeates the views of nearly all groups and classes, and establishes the bounds of what is possible and natural, and what is not? Ordinarily I do not see how such a question could be answered in any way but negatively, for it is tantamount to asking a dominant class to acquiesce in the elimination of the very activities that sustain it. But this is an extraordinary challenge that may evoke an extraordinary response. Like the challenge posed by war, the ecological crisis affects all classes, and therefore may be sufficient to induce sociological changes that would be unthinkable in ordinary circumstances. The capitalist and managerial classes may see—perhaps even more clearly than the consuming masses—the nature and nearness of the ecological crisis, and may recognize that their only salvation (as human beings, let alone privileged human beings) is an occupational migration into governmental or other posts of power, or they may come to accept a smaller share of the national surplus supply simply because they recognize that there is no alternative. When the enemy is nature, in other words, rather than another social class, it is at least imaginable that adjustments could be made that would be impossible in ordinary circumstances.[1]

There is, however, one last possibility to which I must also call attention. It is the possibility that the ecological crisis will simply result in the decline or even destruction of Western civilization, and of the hegemony of the scientific-technological view that has achieved so much and cost us so dearly. Great challenges do not always bring great responses, especially when those responses must be sustained over long periods of time and require dramatic changes in life styles and attitudes. Even educated men today are able to deny the reality of the crisis they face: there is wild talk of farming the seas, of transporting men

1. Let me add a warning that it is not only capitalists who must make an unprecedented ideological adjustment. Socialists must also come to terms with the abandonment of the goal of industrial superabundance on which their vision of a transformed society rests. The stationary equilibrium imposed by the constraints of ecology requires at the very least a reformulation of the kind of economic society toward which socialism sets its course.

to the planets, of unspecified "miracles" of technology that will avert disaster. Can we really persuade the citizens of the Western world, who are just now entering the heady atmosphere of a high consumption way of life, that conservation, stability, frugality, and a deep concern for the distant future must now take priority over the personal indulgence for which they have been culturally prepared and which they are about to experience for the first time? Not the least danger of the ecological crisis, as I see it, is that tens and hundreds of millions will shrug their shoulders at the prospects ahead ("What has posterity ever done for us?"), and that the increasingly visible approach of ecological Armageddon will bring not repentance but Saturnalia.

Yet I cannot end this essay on such a note. For it seems to me that the ecological enthusiasts may be right when they speak of the deteriorating environment as providing the *possibility* for a new political rallying ground. If a new New Deal, capable of engaging both the efforts and the beliefs of this nation, is the last great hope to which we cling in the face of what seems otherwise to be an inevitable gradual worsening and coarsening of our style of life, it is possible that a determined effort to arrest the ecological decay might prove to be its underlying theme. Such an issue, immediate in the experience of all, carries an appeal that might allow vast improvements to be worked in the American environment, both urban and industrial. I cannot estimate the likelihood of such a political awakening, dependent as these matters are on the dice of personality and the outcome of events at home and abroad. But however slim the possibility of bringing such a change, it does at least make the ecological crisis, unquestionably the gravest long-run threat of our times, potentially the source of its greatest short-term promise.

Coming to Terms with Growth and the Environment

WALTER W. HELLER

Walter W. Heller is Regents' Professor of Economics at the University of Minnesota. He served as chairman of the Council of Economic Advisers for Presidents Kennedy and Johnson (1961–64). This article was prepared for a conference at Resources for the Future, Inc., and was published in Energy, Economic Growth, and the Environment, *edited by Sam Schurr.*

A CONFERENCE of ecologists and environmentalists, economists and technologists—convened to illuminate the complex interplay of energy, economic growth, and the environment—should open, not with a declaration of war or of conflicting faiths, but with a declaration of humility. Conceptually, to be sure, we know quite a lot about this interplay—about the *processes* of resource use and disposal that overload and degrade our natural environment; about the chilling *possibility* that untrammeled growth and uncontrolled technology could eventually destroy the ecosystem that sustains us; about the *methods*, both economic and technological, by which man can arrest or reverse the march to environmental ruin; and about the *directions of changes* in priorities and institutions needed to put these methods to work.

But empirically, we really know very little. In trying to determine the causal relationship, assess the trade-offs, and strike a reasoned cost-benefit balance between economic growth and environmental integrity, we constantly run into the unknown or unknowable (or even the unthinkable), into the unmeasured or unmeasurable (or even the infinite). Not surprisingly, then, much of what we "know," much of the evidence, is fragmentary and inconclusive. More disconcertingly, the findings are often contradictory. A case in point: qualified and concerned analysts of the energy-growth-environment linkage have arrived at radically different assessments of future shock to the environment —almost a "no-big-deal" versus a "crime-against-humanity" split on the projected impact of energy growth on the environment by the year 2000.

Humility should lead us, then, to acknowledge and define our collective ignorance, as well as our sparse knowlege, with two purposes in mind:

1. Identifying our joint research needs and priorities.

2. Shaping our responses to clear and present environmental dangers in light of that ignorance, i.e., pursuing courses of action that permit flexible and automatic adjustment to new information, new techniques, new values, and new resource parameters.

But humility in the context of this forum calls for more. It demands a sensitivity in one discipline to the concepts, concerns, and convictions in another. Let me set the framework for my further discussion in terms of the apparent differences in perception between ecologists and economists that have to be narrowed or reconciled if we are to make a productive joint attack on the growth-energy-environment problem.

First, in starkest terms, the ecologist lays down an environmental imperative that requires an end to economic growth— or sharp curtailment of it—as the price of biological survival.[1] The economist counters with a socioeconomic imperative that requires the continuation of growth as the price of social survival. Some ecologists see the arresting of growth as a necessary, though not sufficient, condition for saving the ecosystem. The economist sees growth as a necessary, though not sufficient, condition for social progress and stability. To focus differences even more sharply, the economist tends to regard the *structure* rather than the *fact* of growth as the root of environmental evil and indeed views growth itself as one of the prerequisites to success in restoring the environment.

Second, the ecologist counters that the Great God Growth has feet of clay. In his view, if we counted the full costs of water, air, land, visual, and noise pollution—i.e., the drawing down of our environmental capital—the advance of measured gross national product (GNP) in the past quarter-century might well turn out to be an illusion. In responding, the economist is at pains to make clear that he is anything but Mecca-nistic about GNP. He is under no illusion that GNP is an index of

---

1. I use the term "ecologist" here, not in the technical sense of a natural-systems biologist, but as a proxy for "noneconomist environmentalists."

social welfare (or, for that matter, that it is even feasible to construct a single index of welfare, or that greater material welfare is a guarantee of greater happiness). But he does believe that a careful reading of economic and social data yields persuasive evidence that real GNP per capita *has* advanced even after adjusting for increases in population, prices, and pollution; and that a rise in social welfare has accompanied the rise in output of goods and services.

Third, in a very real sense, the most vexing difference between ecologists and economists may not be in their conflicting interpretations of the evidence but in their divergent modes of thinking. At the risk of exaggerating a bit for emphasis, I perceive the dedicated environmentalist as thinking in terms of exponential rates of deterioration, thresholds, flash points, and of absolute limits to be dealt with by absolute bans. (And I confess to a bit of absolutism myself when it comes to roads in the North Cascades, oil exploration in Puget Sound, and 70,000 tons a day of taconite tailings dumped into Lake Superior.)

In basic approach, the economist could hardly agree less. He thinks in terms of marginalism, trade-offs, and a careful cost-benefit calculus—not marginalism in the sense of minor adjustments but in the sense of balancing costs and benefits at the margin. As he sees it, the right solution in striking a balance between nature and man, between environment and growth, and between technology and ecology, would be the one that pushes depollution to, but not beyond, the point where the costs—the forgone satisfactions of a greater supply of additional goods and services—just equal the benefits—the gained satisfactions of clear air, water, landscape, and sound waves. What the economist regards as rational is to seek, not total or *maximum* cleansing of the environment—prohibitions tend to be prohibitively expensive —but an *optimum* arising out of a careful matching of the "bads" that we overcome and the "goods" that we forgo in the process.

Fourth, when economists and ecologists turn to the search for solutions, they find a considerable area of agreement. They would agree, for example, that where the trade-off is between today's "goods" and tomorrow's "bads," government has to step in to enforce a rational calculus. Indeed, many environmental problems can be handled only by government prohibitions and regulations (mercury and DDT come to mind) and by public expenditures for collective sewage disposal, land reclamation, and environmental clean-up. They can also join in identifying the essentially costless changes that serve growth and the environment simultaneously, thus requiring no trade-offs. One thinks, for example, of technological advances that have substituted coal and oil for wood as energy sources (the per capita consumption of timber in the United States was no higher in 1968 than thirty years earlier) and have enabled us to reduce both costs and diesel engine pollution by moving oil and coal by pipeline rather than rail. And one looks forward to the day when thermal by-products of energy production can be converted from pollutants to a productive source of space heating and cooling for industrial, commercial, and apartment buildings.

But where hard choices will have to be made, the economist wants to put as much of the load on the price system as it can efficiently carry. His main device would be to put price tags —for example, in the form of effluent fees or pollution permits or refundable materials fees—on the now largely free use of air, water, and land areas as dumping grounds for industrial and commercial wastes. The environmentalist's instinct is to recoil against this "license to pollute." By the same reasoning, perhaps, he feels way down deep that to let mineral resources and fossil fuels be managed through the pricing system constitutes a "license to exploit" the biosphere, a license that should be revoked or subjected to tighter regulation. But the economist wants to spread the net of the pricing mechanism widely to capitalize on its automaticity in digesting information and responding to it, its ability to integrate a vast range of decisions, its stimulus to natural resource conservation, and its lowering of demands on the government bureaucracy. His goal, of course, is not to collect fees or taxes but to build enough economic incentives into the market system to bring pollution to bay.

THE ROLE OF ECONOMIC GROWTH

Turning to the first of these four issues, one should keep in mind that the growth-versus-environment contest is in one sense a mismatch: economic growth is a means, an instrumental goal, while environmental quality is an end in itself, an important component of the quality of existence. In assessing the instrumental goal of growth, we need to inquire:

1. Whether it is growth itself, or its particular forms, that lead to environmental trouble (and if the latter, how production and technology can be redirected into environmentally more tolerable channels).

2. What social costs the nation would incur in giving up growth.

3. Whether the war on pollution could, as a practical matter, be pressed and won without growth.

Can Growth Be Stopped? · To discuss the benefits of growth in the context of environmental quality implies, first, that a realistic option exists—one that is conceptually and institutionally possible—of stopping growth or slowing it to a crawl and, second, that there is a trade-off, an inverse relation, between the rate of economic growth and the quality of the natural environment.

Whether no-growth is a conceivable alternative depends first on the nature of the growth process and the sources of growth.[2] Growth of the U.S. economy in the basic sense of growth of output per capita is anchored in (1) increases in the stock of human capital through investments in education, training, and experience; (2) increases in the stock of nonhuman capital through investment in equipment, machinery, and plant; and (3) improvements in the state of U.S. scientific and managerial technology through investments in research and development, better management and organization, and more efficient production techniques. The deepest wellspring—the "major permissive source," as Simon Kuznets puts it—of modern economic growth is the advance of technology in its broadest economic sense, that is, the advance of knowledge.

Considering man's unquenchable thirst for understanding through better education and his enduring quest for increased knowledge and easier ways of doing things—through research and development, large-scale experimentation, and small-scale tinkering—one can only conclude that growth in output per man-hour cannot be stopped. Conceivably, total output could

2. For an authoritative and detailed examination of this subject, see E. F. Denison, *The Sources of Economic Growth in the United States and the Alternatives before Us* (Committee for Economic Development, 1962), and Denison's *Why Growth Rates Differ* (Brookings Institution, 1967).

be held in check by highly restrictive taxes and tight monetary policy or by direct controls. Since output per man-hour would continue to rise, stopping total growth would require a rapid decline in the average workweek—one calculation puts it at twenty-six hours by 1980—and a corresponding increase in leisure and nonmarket activity. (My secretary asks, "What's so bad about *that?*") This appraisal recognizes also that the labor force would continue to grow. Even with a zero population growth policy, it would take several decades to stabilize the population.

The point of a no-growth policy would be to check and reverse the erosion of the environment. But there is nothing inherent in a no-growth economy that would change our polluting ways. So one has to posit active and costly steps to restore and protect the environment. This would require an absolute reduction in material living standards, as conventionally measured, in exchange for a more livable natural environment.

Just to sketch this picture is to raise serious questions of its social, political, and economic feasibility. Short of a believable threat of human extinction, it is hard to imagine that the public would accept the tight controls, lowered material living standards, and large income transfers required to create and manage a stationary state. Whether the necessary shifts could be accomplished without vast unemployment and economic dislocation is another question. The shift to a no-growth state of being might even throw the fragile ecology of our economic system so out of kilter as to threaten its breakdown. Having said this, let me quickly add that if the human race were to discover that it would be committing suicide unless it reduced its standard of living (at least for its affluent people), I dare say it would develop ways of managing the economic system to accommodate this necessity. Short of dire threats, however, economic growth seems destined to continue. To cope with growing contamination of the environment, the United States is thus driven to a redirection of growth and technology and to a reordering of priorities in the uses of growth.

The Growth-Ecology Trade-Off • But this still does not resolve the question of whether national policymakers should continue to stimulate growth or should seek consciously to retard it. That depends not just on the benefits of growth, which I will discuss in a moment, but on its environmental costs, on the growth-ecology trade-off. To the question of how much growth may have to be given up to protect the natural environment and maintain a habitable planet, both ecologists and economists offer a wide range of answers.

Among those who focus on global environmental problems, the spectrum runs from those who are persuaded that global pollution puts life on this planet in jeopardy to those who conclude that no one knows enough to answer the question. In its significant but selective survey, the group for the Study of Critical Environmental Problems (SCEP) offered some reassurance on the climatic effects of growth in outout and fossil fuel energy but called for prompt counteraction to the ravages of toxic pesticides and heavy metals and excessive nutrient run-offs.[3]

Among economists there are those who accept the "spaceship earth" concept of finite limits to the assimilative capacity of the environment and who believe that growth will test those limits within relevant time horizons and must therefore be retarded. But a majority of the economics profession lean toward the findings of a recent econometric probe of this problem by William Nordhaus and James Tobin.

1. With respect to appropriable resources like minerals and fossil fuels, which the market already treats as economic goods, the Nordhaus-Tobin estimates show "little reason to worry about the exhaustion of resources." As in the past, rising prices of fossil

3. The SCEP group concluded, for example, that "the probability of direct climate change in this century resulting from CO_2 is small," though its long-term consequences might be large. With respect to particulate matter, SCEP found that "the area of greatest uncertainty in connection with the effects of particles on the heat balance of the atmosphere is our current lack of knowledge of their optical properties in scattering or absorbing radiation from the sun or the earth." On thermal pollution: "Although by the year 2000 global thermal power output may be as much as six times the present level, we do not expect it to affect global climate," but they noted that the problem of "heat islands" may become severe. They concluded that atmospheric oxygen is practically constant, having stood very close to 20.946 percent since 1910, and that "calculations show that depletion of oxygen by burning all the recoverable fossil fuels in the world would reduce it only to 20.800 percent." They recommended drastic curtailment of the use of DDT and mercury as well as the control of nutrient discharges, together with early development of technology to reclaim and recycle nutrients in areas of high concentration (*Man's Impact on the Global Environment: Assessment and Recommendations for Action*, Report of the Study of Critical Environmental Problems sponsored by the Massachusetts Institute of Technology [Cambridge, Mass.: MIT Press, 1970], pp. 12, 13, 19, 75, 136, 138, 149).

fuels are expected to provide strong incentives for conserving supplies and developing substitute materials and processes.

2. For nonappropriable resources, for "public goods" like air and water, they see the problem of abuse as much more serious. But the environmental disturbance and misdirection of resources that result from treating public natural resources as if they were free goods could, they believe, be corrected by charging for them. "The misdirection is due to a defect in the pricing system —a serious but by no means irreparable defect and one which would in any case be present in a stationary economy."

3. With respect to global ecological collapse, they appropriately conclude that "there is probably very little that economists can say." [4]

The issue is far from resolved. But the evidence to date supports the view that it is less the *fact* of growth than the *manner* of growth and the *uses* made of growth that lie at the bottom of U.S. environmental troubles. And elusive as a consensus on the basic growth-environment trade-offs may be, it appears that a consensus on the urgency of changing the forms and uses of growth is already materializing. As a consequence, the nation already is being confronted with hard choices and the need for painful institutional changes. I submit that both the hard choices and the painful changes required to restore the environment will come much easier in an atmosphere of growth than of stagnation.

Benefits of Growth · Turning to the benefits side of the picture, we are well advised, first of all, to take growth out of the one-dimensional context of the natural environment. In a broader context, the environmental claims against the bounties of growth must include shares not only for cleansing the physical environment of air, water, and land pollution and of urban congestion and sprawl, but also for:

1. Cleansing the social environment of the cancers of poverty, ignorance, malnutrition, and disease.

2. Cleansing the human environment of the degradation and blight of the urban ghetto and the rural slum.

4. W. D. Nordhaus and J. Tobin, "Is Growth Obsolete?" in *Economic Growth*, 50th Anniversary Colloquium–V, National Bureau of Economic Research, General Series No. 96 (New York: Columbia University Press, 1972).

3. Cleansing our personal environment of the fear of crime and violence.

Even with the aid of a rise of 55 percent in GNP and 34 percent in real per capita personal income from 1959 to 1969, we have found in the United States that our inroads on these problems have not kept pace with our rising expectations and aspirations. Imagine the tensions between rich and poor, between black and white, between blue-collar and white-collar workers, between old and young, if we had been forced to finance even the minimal demands of the disadvantaged out of a no-growth national income instead of a one-third increase in that income.

A specific example may be instructive. Between 1959 and 1969 the number of persons below the poverty line fell from 39 million to 24 million, from 22.4 percent to 12.2 percent of a rising population. The improvement came from a 3 percent increase in productivity per year, a drop in unemployment from 6 percent to 4 percent, shifts of the poor from lower to higher income occupations and regions, and an extraordinary growth in government cash transfers, from $26 billion in 1960 to over $50 billion in 1970. Every one of these factors was in some way the direct outgrowth of, or was associated with or facilitated by, per capita economic growth.[5] Given their huge stake in growth as a source of the wherewithal and much of the will to improve their lot, the poor could be pardoned for saying, "Damn the externalities, full speed ahead."

Looking ahead, the Council of Economic Advisers projected a rise in real GNP (in 1969 dollars) of roughly $325 billion, or 35 percent, from 1970 to 1976. In the face of claims on these increases that are already staked out or clearly in the making— claims that leave only a small net "fiscal dividend" by 1976— it will be hard enough to finance the wars on poverty, discrimination, and pollution even with vigorous economic growth. Consider the problem in a no-growth setting: to wrench resources away from one use to transplant them in another, to wrest incomes from one group for transfer to another, to redeploy federal revenues from current to new channels (even assuming that

5. Testimony of R. J. Lampman in *Economic Opportunity Amendments of 1971*, part 1, Hearings before the Subcommittee on Employment, Manpower, and Poverty of the Senate Committee on Labor and Public Welfare, 92nd Congress 1st session (March 23, 1971).

we could pry loose a substantial part of the $70 billion devoted annually to military expenditures)—and to do all this on a sufficient scale to meet the urgent social problems that face us— might well involve us in unbearable social and political tensions. In this context, one rightly views growth as a necessary condition for social advance, for improving the quality of the *total* environment.

Apart from the tangible bounties that growth can bestow, we should keep in mind some of its intangible dividends. Change, innovation, and risk thrive in an atmosphere of growth. It fosters a social mobility and opens up options that no stationary state can provide. This is not to deny that a no-growth economy, with its large rations of leisure, would appeal to those in the upcoming generation who lay less store by the work ethic and material goods than their forebears. But if they associate this with tranquillity—in the face of the intensified struggle for shares of a fixed income on the part of their more numerous and more competitive contemporaries—I believe they are mistaken.

Let me return now to the context of the natural environment, to the growing consensus that we have to stop and reverse the ugly and destructive waste disposal practices of our modern society. To accomplish this, the taxpayer must foot huge bills to overcome past neglect as well as to finance future collective waste treatment and preserve open space and wilderness. Producers and consumers will have to bear the brunt of outright bans on ecologically dangerous materials and to pay rent for the use of the environment's waste assimilation services that they have been enjoying largely free of charge.

A modest estimate of the demands on the federal budget for an adequate environmental program would raise the present outlay of $5 billion a year to about $15 billion, an increase of some $50 billion over the next five years. Without growth, and given the limits to the congressional will to tax, how could we hope to raise the required revenues?

Or take the case of agricultural and industrial pollution. Imagine the resistance of producers to the internalizing of external costs in a society without expansion and the profit opportunities that go with it. How could consumers be induced to accept the necessary price increases in a world of fixed incomes? Again, if the only alternative, if the ultimate cost, were biological self-destruction, the answers would be different. But in the absence of that fate, or because of its extreme remoteness, growth enters as a vital social lubricant and is the best bet for getting people to give up private "goods" to overcome public "bads."

GNP AND SOCIAL WELFARE

To some of what I just said, the ecologist may reply, "Not so fast, not so fast—when you count all the costs, especially when you subtract the costs of chewing up the environment, you'll find that what you call growth in outpout and income since World War II is really a case of living off our environmental capital." Or he may say, "The composition of production has changed in such a way that we are no better off than twenty-five years ago." True, he may say these things, but the evidence does not bear him out. But if he adds, "GNP is a mighty sorry index of welfare; you'll have to show me something better than that in rebuttal," the economist says, "Right on!"

Granting that rising GNP is a poor index of human betterment is not to deny that one is generally associated with the other. It should require no lengthy demonstration to show that, while a significant part of GNP is illusory in a welfare sense, wide differences and large advances in per capita GNP are associated with significant differences and advances in well-being. In a careful appraisal of the growth-welfare correlation, Robert Lampman found that a 26 percent gain in real GNP per capita from 1947 to 1962 brought with it a 26 percent gain in per capita private consumption, a distinct improvement in income security, and a significant reduction in poverty. He concluded: "All things considered, the pattern of growth in the United States in the post-war years yielded benefits to individuals far in excess of the costs it required of them. To that extent, our material progress has had humane content." [6]

A question that has more recently intrigued students of GNP is whether it is possible within the framework of a national accounts system to develop a better approximation of welfare.

6. R. J. Lampman, "Recent U.S. Economic Growth and the Gain in Human Welfare," in *Perspectives on Economic Growth*, W. W. Heller, ed. (New York: Random House, 1968), pp. 143–62.

Economists labor under no illusion that GNP is a satisfactory measure of welfare or that it can be turned into one. They would agree with J. Petit-Senn that "not what we have, but what we enjoy, constitutes our abundance." What makes people think that GNP has become the economist's Holy Grail is the indispensable role it plays in measuring the economy's output potential and its performance in using that potential. It is highly useful and constantly used by economists (1) as a guide to fiscal and monetary policy for management of aggregate demand, and (2) as a measure of the availability of output to meet changing national priorities.

For these purposes, the emphasis of the national accounts must be primarily on market, and secondarily on governmental, demand and output since these are central to national stabilization policies and priority-setting. And for these purposes, the national income and product accounts—with a bit of tinkering here and there—are generally respected and defended by economists.

But when the scene of battle moves to measurement of *social* performance, there is a sharp division of opinion over the possibility and advisability of modifying the GNP—or more properly, the net national product (NNP)—accounts to make them more useful in gauging social performance. Arthur Okun flatly rejected any such thought. And Edward Denison noted that to convert NNP into a welfare measure would require such unattainable measures as an index of real, rather than money, costs incurred in production; a measure of changes in needs that U.S. output must satisfy; measures of the quality of both the human and the physical environment; and a measure of the "goodness" of the size-distribution of income.[7]

Denison also weighed the possibility of getting a better measure of net gains from production by subtracting from the value of greater output the value of the environmental damage caused by producing it. But he concluded (1) that the impossibility of measuring the "goodness" of the environment and the portion of its deterioration traceable to production rules out such

7. See the comments contributed by A. M. Okun to the 50th Anniversary Edition of the Department of Commerce *Survey of Current Business,* January 1972, preprinted in *Brookings Bulletin,* vol. 8, no. 3 (Summer 1971); and E. F. Denison, "Welfare Measurement and the GNP," *Survey of Current Business,* January 1971.

an attempt; and (2) that to deduct, as a proxy for that deterioration, outlays made to improve the environment is totally undesirable, since it would mean that the more resources we diverted from other uses to improve the environment, the more we would reduce measured NNP.

But the Nordhaus-Tobin team take quite a different tack. They have boldly undertaken to appraise the rough quantitative significance of some of the deficiencies of GNP and, more particularly, of NNP as measures of economic welfare. The flavor of their pioneering probe is suggested by some of the adjustments they make in the NNP numbers (all in 1958 prices):

1. According to their estimates, putting dollar tags on the value of leisure and do-it-yourself work adds a huge $925 billion to the recorded NNP of $560 billion in 1965 (as against an add-on, for example, of $627 billion to the NNP of $292 billion in 1947).

2. They also add in almost $80 billion to represent the stream of services of private and public capital goods (against $37 billion in 1947).

3. Their subtractions from NNP include (a) $95 billion in 1965 (and $32 billion in 1947) representing "regrettables" like police services and national defense, that is, intermediate expenditures that are really costs, not enjoyments, of an advanced industrial society; (b) $91 billion of capital consumption allowances in 1965 (versus $51 billion in 1946) and $101 billion for the capital-widening requirements of growth in 1965 (and a negative $5 billion in 1947); and (c) an allowance of $31 billion in 1965 (as against $11 billion in 1947) for "disamenities" or "negative externalities" representing deterioration of the environment.

Having made these heroic adjustments, they concluded:

There is no evidence to support the claim that welfare has grown less rapidly than NNP. Rather, NNP seems to underestimate the gain in welfare, chiefly because of its omission of leisure from consumption. Subject to the limitations of the estimates, we conclude that the economic welfare of the average American has been growing at a rate that doubles every 30 years.[8]

8. Nordhaus and Tobin, "Is Growth Obsolete?"

DIVERGENT MODES OF THOUGHT

Part of the difficulty in achieving a meeting of the minds between economists and ecologists is that the economist tends to seek optimality by selecting the right procedures—for example, forcing the producer to bear the cost and the consumer to pay the price for waste-disposal access to the environment, thereby creating incentives to abate pollution—rather than prescribing the right outcome, namely, ending or drastically curtailing pollution. He is dedicated to that outcome but prefers to have the market system, rather than a government regulator, do as much of the work for him as possible. Whether a meeting of minds will evolve remains to be seen.

For his part, the ecologist will have to overcome his natural impatience with concepts of fine balancing of costs and benefits, an impatience that probably grows out of his feelings that cost-benefit analyses lack ethical content and moral inputs and that the more or less infinite benefits of environmental preservation make refined cost calculations more or less irrelevant.

For his part, the economist will have to break out of the web of marginal cost-benefit balance in cases where the relevant costs and benefits can't be captured in that web. Irreparable damage —whether to human health by arsenic, mercury, or lead poisoning, or to bald eagles by DDT, or to the Alaskan tundra by hot oil, or to the beauty of a canyon by a hydroelectric dam—cannot be handled by the fine tuning of marginalism. Nor is this approach applicable where the benefits are short-run and calculable while costs are long-run and incalculable. . . . The total or near-total ban is the only remedy. Whether mercury is a proxy for just a handful of cases or the forerunner of an exponential rise in contamination of the earth, land surface, air mass, and waterways, will determine in good part our relative reliance on total-ban versus marginal-adjustment approaches to environmental action.

The economist is inclined to doubt that such cases will multiply rapidly. Past demonstrations of the capacity of our economy, our technology, and our institutions to adapt and adjust to changing circumstances and shocks are impressive. We are still in the early stages of identifying, quantifying, and reacting to the multiple threats to our environment. It may be that we are too quick in accepting the concept of finite limits and closing physical frontiers implicit in the concept of spaceship earth. At least two previous episodes in U.S. history come to mind to suggest that we may yet escape (or push into the remote future) the ultimate biophysical limits, may yet be able to turn the ecological dials back from the "self-destruct" position without stopping growth in output, energy, technology, and living standards.

The first was the closing of America's geographical frontiers, which allegedly robbed this country of much of its mobility and dynamism. But other frontiers—scientific, technological, economic—soon opened up new vistas and opportunities, new frontiers that far surpassed any physical frontiers.

The second episode is much more recent. We do not need to stretch our memories very far to recall the great furor some twenty or twenty-five years ago about "running out of resources," especially energy, mineral, and other natural resources. We were being told by presidential commissions that we were about to exhaust our supplies of mineral resources and the productive potential of our agricultural land. But as we now know, intensive scientific research and technological development—responding partly to the alarums that were sounded but mostly to the signals sent out by the pricing system—resulted in the upgrading of old resources, the discovery of new ones, the development of substitutes, and the application of more efficient ways of utilizing available resources and adjusting to changes in relative availabilities.

Today, the problem is less one of limited resource availability and more one of growing threats to environmental quality and the metabolism of the biosphere. Concentrations of toxic and nondegradable wastes pose a mounting problem. But at this relatively early stage of our environmental experience and awareness, it seems premature to conclude that mounting problems are insurmountable. As our new knowledge and concern are translated into changes in our institutional arrangements and cost-price structure, strong incentives will be generated to redirect production and technology into less destructive channels. . . .

Much of the difference between economists and ecologists

on the speed and certainty of our descent into environmental hell rests in their divergent views on the role of technology. The ecologist sees pollution-intensive technology at the core of a mindless pursuit of economic growth. The economist points to the frequency of an inverse relationship between technological advance and pollution, as in materials-conserving and waste-recycling technology. And by institutional changes—such as creating property rights in, and charging for the use of, our collectively owned air, water, and landscape—he believes that technology will become ever more mindful of the environment.

What is important to note here is that the dichotomy runs much deeper than a disagreement on facts. For even if we accept Barry Commoner's verdict that the technology accompanying U.S. growth is the Frankenstein that is destroying our environment, there remains the critical operational question: Is this technology autonomous and out of control, an inevitable concomitant of growth? [9] Or does progress in science and technology respond to social and economic forces? If so, can it be bent to our will?

An affirmative answer to the last two questions is gaining support in recent investigations. The direction of technical changes in the private sector as well as the emphasis of research in the public sector are shown to respond to differences in the relative prices of resource endowments and other factors of production.[10] For decades the pattern of technical change has been biased in the direction of excessive production of residuals by zero-pricing or underpricing the use of the environment into which they are dumped. It follows that assessing the appropriate charges for waste disposal (and putting the right prices on resource amenities) will not only improve the pattern of production to the benefit of the environment but will also stimulate pollution-abat-

9. One economist who answers in the affirmative is E. J. Mishan, who says: "As a collective enterprise, science has no more social conscience than the problem-solving computers it employs. Indeed, like some ponderous multipurpose robot that is powered by its own insatiable curiosity, science lurches onward . . . " (*Technology and Growth: The Price We Pay* [New York: Praeger, 1970], p. 129).

10. See, for example, J. Schmookler, *Invention and Economic Growth* (Cambridge, Mass.: Harvard University Press, 1966), a searching study of inventive activity in which Schmookler concluded that the greater part of technical change in the United States has been a response to technical problems or opportunities perceived in economic terms.

ing technology. Indeed, as relative prices are changed to reflect real economic and social costs, the longer-run impact on the direction of technological effort may be considerably more important than the short-run resource allocation effects.

As the biases in the cost and pricing system that make pollution profitable are diminished or eliminated, we may well find more technical complementarities than our limited experience leads us to think. Making pollution abatement mandatory by regulation or making continued pollution painfully costly by waste disposal charges will create a sharp spur to pollution-abatement technology. The relevant technology will no longer be treated on a corrective, band-aid, and after-thought basis, an approach that is likely to be inefficient and costly. Instead, it will be done on a preventive, built-in, and advanced-planning basis. Heartening examples of making virtue out of necessity in the form of profitable recycling already abound. And as economic growth leads to the replacement of old processes, equipment, and plants with new ones, it will hasten the change to cleaner and healthier methods of production.

This brings me back to an earlier theme. In the past, the market mechanism (with some assistance from government inducements, incentives, and research and development investments) altered the technical coefficients for traditional natural resources like coal, iron, and oil in response to the signals sent out by the pricing mechanism. Those resources were conserved, while the ones that were largely left out of the pricing mechanism suffered. If prices are put on them now by internalizing the external costs of air, water, quiet, and landscape, it seems reasonable to assume that the market mechanism will cause new shifts in resource use and technology leading us to conserve *these* resources and let spaceship earth cruise on a good deal longer. . . .

CONCLUSION

Those who defend economic growth rest their case essentially on the following points:

1. For all the misallocations and mistakes, environmental and otherwise, that have been made in the process of growth, it is

still demonstrably true that growth in per capita GNP has been associated with rising levels of human well-being.

2. Much if not most of the environmental damage associated with growth is a function of the *way* we grow—of the nature of our technology and the forms of production. By prohibiting ecologically deadly or dangerous activities and forcing producers to absorb the cost of using air, water, and land areas for waste disposal, growth, technology, and production can be redirected into environmentally more tolerable channels.

3. To provide social and financial lubrication for this painful process as well as to repair the ravages of past neglect of the environment requires the resources, revenues, and the rising incomes that growth can put at our disposal.

4. Side by side with the problem of restoring our physical environment is the even greater problem of overcoming the ills of our human and social environment. Those ills seem to be cumulating even faster and to be even more stubbornly resistant to reversal than our environmental ills. How we could hope to cope with them and avoid unbearable sociopolitical tensions within the context of a stationary state is not apparent.

Coupled with a conviction that economic growth can more than atone for its sins is a belief that its environmental vices can be diminished and its virtues magnified by greater use of the pricing system, by putting appropriate price tags on use of the public environment for private gain. The economist readily recognizes that environmental quality is a highly subjective good on which it will be difficult to put those price tags. He also readily acknowledges that where damage to health, life, or the biosphere—either now or in the future—are severe or even infinite, the pricing system has neither the speed nor the capacity to deal with the problem.

But even recognizing such limits, the economist rightly asserts that across a large part of the pollution spectrum the pricing system *is* applicable. By charging producers—and ultimately consumers—for the full cost of waste disposal, their self-interest will be put to work in slowing or even reversing the march toward a degraded or exhausted environment.

To make economic growth not only compatible with, but a servant of, a high-quality environment won't be easy. Even after ecologists identify the source of the trouble, engineers identify solutions and develop monitoring devices, and economists identify appropriate taxing and pricing schemes, there remain crucial tests of public will and political skill. To get producers and consumers to pay the full cost of using the environment for waste disposal and to get the public to accept the reordered priorities and pay the higher taxes that will be needed to redirect growth and clean up past environmental mistakes will require great acts of both will and skill.

Is Growth Obsolete?

WILLIAM D. NORDHAUS and JAMES TOBIN

William D. Nordhaus teaches economics at Yale University. James Tobin is Sterling Professor of Political Economy at Yale. He was a member of the Council of Economic Advisers during the Kennedy administration, and was elected president of the American Economic Association in 1971. This paper appeared in Economic Growth, *which was recently published by the National Bureau of Economic Research.*

A LONG DECADE AGO economic growth was the reigning fashion of political economy. It was simultaneously the hottest subject of economic theory and research, a slogan eagerly claimed by politicians of all stripes, and a serious objective of the policies of governments. The climate of opinion has changed dramatically. Disillusioned critics indict both economic science and economic policy for blind obeisance to aggregate material "progress," and for neglect of its costly side effects. Growth, it is charged, distorts national priorities, worsens the distribution of income, and irreparably damages the environment.

Growth was in an important sense a discovery of economics after World War II. Of course economic development has always been the grand theme of historically minded scholars of large mind and bold concept, notably Marx, Schumpeter, and Kuznets. But the mainstream of economic analysis was not comfortable with phenomena of change and progress. The stationary state was the long-run equilibrium of classical and neoclassical theory, and comparison of alternative static equilibria its most powerful tool. . . .

By now modern neoclassical growth theory is well enough formulated to make its way into textbooks. It is a theory of the growth of potential output, or output at a uniform standard rate of utilization of capacity. The theory relates potential output to three determinants: the labor force, the state of technology, and the stock of human and tangible capital. The first two are usually assumed to grow smoothly at rates determined exogenously, by noneconomic factors. The accumulation of capital is governed by the thrift of the population, and in equilibrium the growth of the capital stock matches the growth of labor-cum-technology and the growth of output. Simple as it is, the model fits the observed trends of economic growth reasonably well. . . .

In the early 1960s growth became a proclaimed objective of government policy, in this country as elsewhere. Who could be against it? But like most value-laden words, growth has meant different things to different people and at different times. Often growth policy was simply identified with measures to expand aggregate demand in order to bring or keep actual output in line with potential output. In this sense it is simply stabilization policy, only more gap-conscious and growth-conscious than the cycle-smoothing policies of the past.

To economists schooled in postwar neoclassical growth theory, growth policy proper meant something more than this, and more debatable. It meant deliberate effort to speed up the growth of potential output itself, specifically to accelerate the productivity of labor. Growth policy in this meaning was not widely understood or accepted. The neoclassical model outlined above suggested two kinds of policies to foster growth, possibly interrelated: measures that advance technological knowledge and measures that increase the share of potential output devoted to accumulation of physical or human capital.[1] The standard model also suggested that, unless someone can find a way to accelerate technological progress permanently, policy cannot raise the rate of growth permanently. One-shot measures will speed up growth temporarily, for years or decades. But once the economy has absorbed these measures, its future growth rate will be limited once again by constraints of labor and technology. The level of its path, however, will be permanently higher than if the policies had not been undertaken.

Growth measures nearly always involve diversions of current resources from other uses, sacrifices of current consumption for succeeding generations of consumers. Enthusiasts for faster growth are advocates of the future against the present. Their

1. The variety of possible measures, and the difficulty of raising the growth rate by more than one or two percentage points, have been explored by E. F. Denison in his influential study *The Sources of Economic Growth in the United States and the Alternatives before Us* (Committee for Economic Development, 1962).

case rests on the view that the market economy, left to itself, will short-change the future by saving too small a fraction of current output. But it is ironical that the anti-growth men of the 1970s believe that it is they who represent the interests of future generations in opposition to a market economy which is biased toward growth and the wasting of our natural resources. We turn now to the question of whether the growth process inevitably wastes our natural resources.

GROWTH AND NATURAL RESOURCES

Faced with the finiteness of our earth and the exponential growth of economy and population, the environmentalist sees inevitable starvation. The specter of Malthus is haunting even the affluent society. There is a familiar ring to these criticisms. Ever since the industrial revolution pessimistic scientists and economists have warned that natural resources ultimately limit the possibilities of economic expansion and that society only makes the eventual reckoning more painful by ignoring resource limitations now.

In important part, this is a warning about population growth. But taking population developments as given, will natural resources become an increasingly severe drag on economic growth? We have not found evidence to support this fear. Indeed, the opposite appears to be more likely; growth of output per capita will accelerate slightly even as stocks of natural resources decline.

The prevailing standard model of growth assumes that there are no limits on the feasibility of expanding the supplies of non-human agents of production. It is basically a two-factor model in which production depends only on labor and reproducible capital. Land and resources, the third member of the classical triad, has generally been dropped. The simplifications of theory carry over into empirical work. The thousands of aggregate production functions estimated by econometricians in the last decade are labor-capital functions. Presumably the tacit justification has been that reproducible capital is a near-perfect substitute for land and other exhaustible resources, at least in the perspective of heroic aggregation customary in macro-economics. If substitution for natural resources is not possible in any given technology, or if a particular resource is exhausted, we tacitly assume that "resource augmenting" innovations will overcome the scarcity.

These optimistic assumptions about technology stand in contrast to the tacit assumption of environmentalists that no substitutes are available for natural resources. Under this condition, it is easily seen that output will indeed stop growing or decline. It thus appears that the degree of substitutability between capital and labor on the one hand and natural resources on the other is of crucial importance to future growth. Although this is an area needing much future research, we have made two forays to see what the evidence is.

First we ran several simulations of the process of economic growth in order to see which assumptions about substitution and technology fit the "stylized" facts. The important facts are: growing income per capita and capital per capita; relatively declining inputs and income of natural resources; and slowly declining capital-output ratio. Among the various forms of production function considered, the following assumptions come closest to reproducing the stylized facts: (1) Either the elasticity of substitution [2] between land and other factors is high—significantly greater than unity—or land-augmenting technological change has proceeded faster than over-all productivity; (2) the elasticity of substitution between labor and capital is close to unity.

After these simulations were run, it appeared possible to estimate the parameters of the preferred form of production function directly. Econometric estimates confirm proposition (1) directly and seem to prefer the case of high elasticity of substitution between land and neoclassical factors.

Of course it is always possible that the future will be discontinuously different from the past. But if our estimates are accepted, then continuation of substitution during the next fifty years, during which many environmentalists foresee the end to growth, will witness a small increase—perhaps in the order of 0.1 percent per annum—in growth of per capita income.

2. [Elasticity of substitution is a quantitative measure of the ease with which one factor input can be substituted for another in production or the degree to which production is characterized by a diminishing marginal rate of technical substitution. *Editors.*]

Is our economy, with its mixture of market processes and governmental controls, biased in favor of wasteful and shortsighted exploitation of natural resources? In considering this charge, two archetypical cases must be distinguished, although many actual cases fall between them. First, there are appropriable resources for which buyers pay market values and users market rentals. Second, there are inappropriable resources, "public goods," whose use appears free to individual producers and consumers but is costly in aggregate to society.

There seems to be little reason to worry about the exhaustion of resources which the market already treats as economic goods. We have already commented on the irony that both growthmen and anti-growthmen invoke the interests of future generations. The issue between them is not whether and how much provision must be made for future generations, but in what form it should be made. The growthman emphasizes reproducible capital and education. The conservationist emphasizes exhaustible resources—minerals in the ground, open space, virgin land. The economist's first presumption is that the market will decide in what forms to transmit wealth, by the requirement that all kinds of wealth bear a comparable rate of return. Now, stocks of natural resources—for example, mineral deposits—are essentially sterile. Their return to their owners is the increase in their prices, relative to prices of other goods. In a market economy they will be exploited at such a pace that their rate of price appreciation is competitive with rates of return on other kinds of capital. Many conservationists have noted such price appreciation with horror, but if the prices of these resources accurately reflect the scarcities of the future, they must rise in order to induce the proper speed of exploitation. Natural resources *should* grow in relative scarcity—otherwise they are an inefficient way for society to hold and transmit wealth compared to productive physical and human capital. Price appreciation protects resources from premature exploitation.

How would an excessive rate of exploitation show up? We would see rates of relative price increase above the general real rate of return on wealth. This would indicate that society had in the past used precious resources too profligately, relative to the tastes and technologies later revealed. The scattered evidence we have indicates little excessive price rise. For some resources, indeed, prices seem to have risen more slowly than efficient use would indicate *ex post*.

The nightmare of a day of reckoning and economic collapse when all fossil fuels are forever gone seems to be based on failure to recognize the existing and future possibilities of substitute materials and processes. As the day of reckoning approaches, fuel prices will provide—as they do not now—strong incentives for such substitutions, as well as for conserving supplies. The warnings of the conservationists and scientists do underscore the importance of continuous monitoring of the national and world outlook for energy resources. Conceivably both the market and public agencies can be too complacent about the prospects for new and safe substitutes for fossil fuels. The opportunity and need for fruitful collaboration between economists and physical scientists has never been greater.

Possible abuse of public natural resources is much more serious a problem. It is useful to distinguish *local* and *global* ecological disturbances. Local disturbances include transient air pollution, water pollution, noise pollution, visual disamenities. It is certainly true that we have not charged automobile users and electricity consumers for their pollution of the skies, or farmers and housewives for the pollution of lakes by the run-off of fertilizers and detergents. In that degree our national product series have overestimated the advance of welfare. But our investigations indicate that the overestimate is but a few percent of total consumption.

But there are other serious consequences of treating as free goods things which are not really free. This practice gives the wrong signals for the directions of economic growth. The producers of automobiles and of electricity should be given incentives to develop and to utilize "cleaner" technologies. The consumers of automobiles and electricity should pay in higher prices for the pollution they cause, or for the higher costs of low-pollution processes. If recognition of these costs causes consumers to shift their purchases to other goods and services, that is only efficient. At present, overproduction of these goods is uneconomically subsidized as truly as if the producers received cash subsidies from the Treasury. The mistake of the anti-growthman is to blame economic growth *per se* for the misdirection of economic growth. The misdirection is due to a defect of the pricing system—a serious but by no means irreparable defect and one which would in any case be present in a stationary economy.

As for the danger of global ecological catastrophes, there is probably very little that economics can say. Maybe we are pouring pollutants into the atmosphere at such a rate that we will melt the polar icecaps and flood all the world's seaports. Unfortunately, there seems to be great uncertainty about the causes and the likelihood of such occurrences. These catastrophic global disturbances must be of higher priority for research than the local disturbances to which so much attention has been given.

The Limits to Growth

DONELLA H. MEADOWS, DENNIS MEADOWS, ET AL.

While on the faculty at the Massachusetts Institute of Technology, Dennis Meadows directed the research team which produced the widely publicized and controversial book The Limits to Growth *in 1972. He is now associate professor of business and engineering at Dartmouth College.*

OUR WORLD MODEL was built specifically to investigate five major trends of global concern—accelerating industrialization, rapid population growth, widespread malnutrition, depletion of nonrenewable resources, and a deteriorating environment. These trends are all interconnected in many ways, and their development is measured in decades or centuries, rather than in months or years. With the model we are seeking to understand the causes of these trends, their interrelationships, and their implications as much as one hundred years in the future. The model we have constructed is, like every other model, imperfect, oversimplified, and unfinished. We are well aware of its shortcomings, but we believe that it is the most useful model now available for dealing with problems far out on the space-time graph. . . .

The following conclusions have emerged from our work so far.

1. If the present growth trends in world population, industrialization, pollution, food production, and resource depletion continue unchanged, the limits to growth on this planet will be reached sometime within the next one hundred years. The most probable result will be a rather sudden and uncontrollable decline in both population and industrial capacity.

2. It is possible to alter these growth trends and to establish a condition of ecological and economic stability that is sustainable far into the future. The state of global equilibrium could be designed so that the basic material needs of each person on earth are satisfied and each person has an equal opportunity to realize his individual human potential.

3. If the world's people decide to strive for this second outcome rather than the first, the sooner they begin working to attain it, the greater will be their chances of success.

MODELING GROWTH

A quantity exhibits *exponential* growth when it increases by a constant percentage of the whole in a constant time period. A colony of yeast cells in which each cell divides into two cells every ten minutes is growing exponentially. For each single cell, after ten minutes there will be two cells, an increase of 100 percent. After the next ten minutes there will be four cells, then eight, then sixteen. If a miser takes $100 from his mattress and invests it at 7 percent (so that the total amount accumulated increases by 7 percent each year), the invested money will grow much faster than the linearly increasing stock under the mattress. The amount added each year to a bank account or each ten minutes to a yeast colony is not constant. It continually increases, as the total accumulated amount increases. Such exponential growth is a common process in biological, financial, and many other systems of the world. . . .

A French riddle for children illustrates another aspect of exponential growth—the apparent suddenness with which it approaches a fixed limit. Suppose you own a pond on which a water lily is growing. The lily plant doubles in size each day. If the lily were allowed to grow unchecked, it would completely cover the pond in thirty days, choking off the other forms of life in the water. For a long time the lily plant seems small, and so you decide not to worry about cutting it back until it covers half the pond. On what day will that be? On the twenty-ninth day, of course. You have one day to save your pond. . . .

Exponential growth is a dynamic phenomenon, which means that it involves elements that change over time. In simple systems, like the bank account or the lily pond, the cause of exponential growth and its future course are relatively easy to understand. When many different quantities are growing simultaneously in a system, however, and when all the quantities are interrelated in a complicated way, analysis of the causes of growth and of the future behavior of the system becomes very difficult indeed. Does population growth cause industrialization or does industrialization cause population growth? Is either one singly responsible for increasing pollution, or are they both responsible? Will more food production result in more population? If any one of these elements grows slower or faster, what will happen to the growth rates of all the others? These very questions are being debated in many parts of the world today. The answers can be found through a better understanding of the entire complex system that unites all of these important elements.

Dynamic modeling theory indicates that any exponentially growing quantity is somehow involved with a *positive feedback loop*. A positive feedback loop is sometimes called a "vicious circle." An example is the familiar wage-price spiral—wages increase, which causes prices to increase, which leads to demands for higher wages, and so forth. In a positive feedback loop a chain of cause-and-effect relationships closes on itself, so that increasing any one element in the loop will start a sequence of changes that will result in the originally changed element being increased even more.

We can begin our dynamic analysis of the long-term world situation by looking for the positive feedback loops underlying the exponential growth in the five physical quantities we have already mentioned. In particular, the growth rates of two of these elements—population and industrialization—are of interest, since the goal of many development policies is to encourage the growth of the latter relative to the former. The two basic positive feedback loops that account for exponential population and industrial growth are simple in principle. The many interconnections between these two positive feedback loops act to amplify or to diminish the action of the loops, to couple or uncouple the growth rates of population and of industry. These interconnections constitute the rest of the world model.

In 1650 world population numbered about 0.5 billion, and it was growing at a rate of approximately 0.3 percent per year. That corresponds to a doubling time of nearly 250 years. In 1970 the population totaled 3.6 billion and the rate of growth was 2.1 percent per year. The doubling time at this growth rate is 33 years. Thus, not only has the population been growing exponentially, but the rate of growth has also been growing. We might say that population growth has been "super"-exponential;

the population curve is rising even faster than it would if growth were strictly exponential.

The feedback loop structure that represents the dynamic behavior of population growth is shown below.

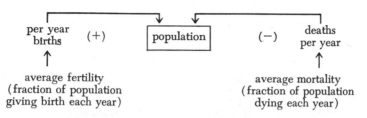

On the left is the positive feedback loop that accounts for the observed exponential growth. In a population with constant, average fertility, the larger the population, the more babies will be born each year. The more babies, the larger the population will be the following year. After a delay to allow those babies to grow up and become parents, even more babies will be born, swelling the population still further. Steady growth will continue as long as average fertility remains constant. If, in addition to sons, each woman has on the average two female children, for example, and each of them grows up to have two more female children, the population will double each generation. The growth rate will depend on both the average fertility and the length of the delay between generations.

There is another feedback loop governing population growth, shown on the right side of the diagram above. It is a *negative feedback loop*. Whereas positive feedback loops generate runaway growth negative feedback loops tend to regulate growth and to hold a system in some stable state. They behave much as a thermostat does in controlling the temperature of a room. If the temperature falls, the thermostat activates the heating system, which causes the temperature to rise again. When the temperature reaches its limit, the thermostat cuts off the heating system, and the temperature begins to fall again. In a negative feedback loop a change in one element is propagated around the circle until it comes back to change that element in a direction *opposite* to the initial change.

The negative feedback loop controlling population is based

upon average mortality, a reflection of the general health of the population. The number of deaths each year is equal to the total population times the average mortality (which we might think of as the average probability of death at any age). . . .

WORLD MODEL BEHAVIOR

As the world system grows toward its ultimate limits, what will be its most likely behavior mode? What relationships now existent will change as the exponential growth curves level off? What will the world be like when growth comes to an end?

There are, of course, many possible answers to these questions. We will examine several alternatives, each dependent on a different set of assumptions about how human society will respond to problems arising from the various limits to growth.

Let us begin by assuming that there will be in the future no great changes in human values or in the functioning of the global population-capital system as it has operated for the last one hundred years. The results of this assumption are shown in Figure 1. We shall refer to this computer output as the "standard run" and use it for comparison with the runs based on other assumptions that follow. The horizontal scale in Figure 1 shows time in years from 1900 to 2100. With the computer we have plotted the progress over time of eight quantities:

> population (total number of persons)
> industrial output per capita (dollar equivalent per person per year)
> pollution (multiple of 1970 level)
> nonrenewable resources (fraction of 1900 reserves remaining)
> crude birth rate (births per 1,000 persons per year)
> crude death rate (deaths per 1,000 persons per year)
> services per capita (dollar equivalent per person per year)

Each of these variables is plotted on a different vertical scale. We have deliberately omitted the vertical scales and we have made the horizontal time scale somewhat vague because we want to emphasize the general behavior modes of these computer out-

FIGURE 1. *World Model Standard Run*

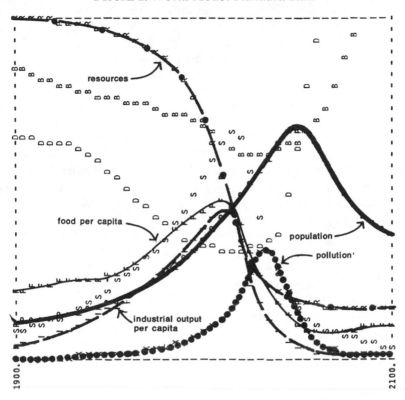

puts, not the numerical values, which are only approximately known.

All levels in the model (population, capital, pollution, etc.) begin with 1900 values. From 1900 to 1970 the variables plotted in Figure 1 (and numerous other variables included in the model but not plotted here) agree generally with their historical values to the extent that we know them. Population rises from 1.6 billion in 1900 to 3.5 billion in 1970. Although the birth rate declines gradually, the death rate falls more quickly, especially after 1940, and the rate of population growth increases. Industrial output, food, and services per capita increase exponentially. The resource base in 1970 is still about 95 percent of its 1900 value, but it declines dramatically thereafter, as population and industrial output continue to grow.

The behavior mode of the system shown in Figure 1 is clearly that of overshoot and collapse. In this run the collapse occurs because of nonrenewable resource depletion. The industrial capital stock grows to a level that requires an enormous input of resources. In the very process of that growth it depletes a large fraction of the resource reserves available. As resource prices rise and mines are depleted, more and more capital must be used for obtaining resources, leaving less to be invested for future growth. Finally investment cannot keep up with depreciation, and the industrial base collapses, taking with it the service and agricultural systems, which have become dependent on industrial inputs (such as fertilizers, pesticides, hospital laboratories, computers, and especially energy for mechanization). For a short time the situation is especially serious because population, with the delays inherent in the age structure and the process of social adjustment, keeps rising. Population finally decreases when the death rate is driven upward by lack of food and health services.

The exact timing of these events is not meaningful, given the great aggregation and many uncertainties in the model. It is significant, however, that growth is stopped well before the year 2100. We have tried in every doubtful case to make the most optimistic estimate of unknown quantities, and we have also ignored discontinuous events such as wars or epidemics, which might act to bring an end to growth even sooner than our model would indicate. In other words, the model is biased to allow growth to continue longer than it probably can continue in the real world. *We can thus say with some confidence that, under the assumption of no major change in the present system, population and industrial growth will certainly stop within the next century, at the latest.*

The system shown in Figure 1 collapses because of a resource crisis. What if our estimate of the global stock of resources is wrong? In Figure 1 we assumed that in 1970 there was a 250-year supply of all resources, at 1970 usage rates. But let us be even more optimistic and assume that new discoveries or advances in technology can *double* the amount of resources economically available. In this case the primary force that stops growth is a sudden increase in the level of pollution, caused by an overloading of the natural absorptive capacity of the environment. The death rate rises abruptly from pollution and from lack of food. At the same time resources are severely depleted, in spite of the doubled amount available, simply because a few more years of exponential growth in industry are sufficient to consume those extra resources.

Is the future of the world system bound to be growth and then collapse into a dismal, depleted existence? Only if we make the initial assumption that our present way of doing things will not change. We have ample evidence of mankind's ingenuity and social flexibility. There are, of course, many likely changes in the system, some of which are already taking place. The Green Revolution is raising agricultural yields in nonindustrialized countries. Knowledge about modern methods of birth control is spreading rapidly. Let us use the world model as a tool to test the possible consequences of the new technologies that promise to raise the limits to growth. . . .

TECHNOLOGY AND THE LIMITS TO GROWTH

In another run, the world model assumes *both* a reduction in resource depletion *and* a reduction in pollution generation from all sources by a factor of four, starting in 1975. Reduction to less than one-fourth of the present rate of pollution generation is probably unrealistic because of cost, and because of the difficulty of eliminating some kinds of pollution, such as thermal pollution and radioisotopes from nuclear power generation, fertilizer runoff, and asbestos particles from brake linings. We assume that such a sharp reduction in pollution generation could occur globally and quickly for purposes of experimentation with the model, not because we believe it is politically feasible, given our present institutions.

The pollution control policy is indeed successful in averting the pollution crisis of the previous run. Both population and industrial output per person rise well beyond their previous peak values, and yet resource depletion and pollution never become problems. The overshoot mode is still operative, however, and the collapse comes about this time from food shortage.

As long as industrial output is rising, the yield from each hectare of land continues to rise (up to a maximum of seven times the average yield in 1900) and new land is developed. At the same time, however, some arable land is taken for urban-industrial use, and some land is eroded, especially by highly capitalized agricultural practices. Eventually the limit of arable land is reached. After that point, as population continues to rise, food per capita decreases. As the food shortage becomes apparent, industrial output is diverted into agricultural capital to increase land yields. Less capital is available for investment, and finally the industrial output per capita begins to fall. When food per capita sinks to the subsistence level, the death rate begins to increase, bringing an end to population growth. . . .

Although we have many reservations about the approximations and simplifications in the present world model, it has led us to one conclusion that appears to be justified under all the assumptions we have tested so far. *The basic behavior mode of the world system is exponential growth of population and capital, followed by collapse.* As we have shown in the model runs presented here, this behavior mode occurs if we assume no change in the present system or if we assume any number of technological changes in the system.

The unspoken assumption behind all of the model runs we have presented in this chapter is that population and capital growth should be allowed to continue until they reach some "natural" limit. This assumption also appears to be a basic part of the human value system currently operational in the real world. Whenever we incorporate this value into the model, the result is that the growing system rises above its ultimate limit and then collapses. When we introduce technological developments that successfully lift some restraint to growth or avoid some collapse, the system simply grows to another limit, temporarily surpasses it, and falls back. Given that first assumption, that population and capital growth should not be deliberately limited but should be left to "seek their own levels," we have not been able to find a set of policies that avoids the collapse mode of behavior. . . .

DELIBERATE CONSTRAINTS ON GROWTH

We have seen that positive feedback loops operating without any constraints generate exponential growth. In the world system two positive feedback loops are dominant now, producing exponential growth of population and of industrial capital.

In any finite system there must be constraints that can act to stop exponential growth. These constraints are negative feedback loops. The negative loops become stronger and stronger as growth approaches the ultimate limit, or carrying capacity, of the system's environment. Finally the negative loops balance or dominant the positive ones, and growth comes to an end. In the world system the negative feedback loops involve such processes as pollution of the environment, depletion of nonrenewable resources, and famine.

The delays inherent in the action of these negative loops tend to allow population and capital to overshoot their ultimately sustainable levels. The period of overshoot is wasteful of resources. It generally decreases the carrying capacity of the environment as well, intensifying the eventual decline in population and capital.

The growth-stopping pressures from negative feedback loops are already being felt in many parts of human society. The major societal responses to these pressures have been directed at the negative feedback loops themselves. Technological solutions have been devised to weaken the loops or to disguise the pressures they generate so that growth can continue. Such means may have some short-term effect in relieving pressures caused by growth, but in the long run they do nothing to prevent the overshoot and subsequent collapse of the system.

Another response to the problems created by growth would be to weaken the *positive* feedback loops that are generating the growth. Such a solution has almost never been acknowledged as legitimate by any modern society, and it has certainly never been effectively carried out. What kinds of policies would such a solution involve? What sort of world would result? There is almost no historical precedent for such an approach, and thus there is no alternative but to discuss it in terms of models— either mental models or formal, written models. How will the world model behave if we include in it some policy to control growth deliberately? Will such a policy change generate a "better" behavior mode? . . .

The positive feedback loop generating population growth involves the birth rate and all the socioeconomic factors that influence the birth rate. It is counteracted by the negative loop of the death rate.

The overwhelming growth in world population caused by the

positive birth-rate loop is a recent phenomenon, a result of mankind's very successful reduction of worldwide mortality. The controlling negative feedback loop has been weakened, allowing the positive loop to operate virtually without constraint. There are only two ways to restore the resulting imbalance. Either the birth rate must be brought down to equal the new, lower death rate, or the death rate must rise again. All of the "natural" constraints to population growth operate in the second way—they raise the death rate. Any society wishing to avoid that result must take deliberate action to control the positive feedback loop —to reduce the birth rate.

In a dynamic model it is a simple matter to counteract runaway positive feedback loops. For the moment let us suspend the requirement of political feasibility and use the model to test the physical, if not the social, implications of limiting population growth. We need only add to the model one more causal loop, connecting the birth rate and the death rate. In other words, we require that the number of babies born each year be equal to the expected number of deaths in the population that year. Thus the positive and negative feedback loops are exactly balanced. As the death rate decreases, because of better

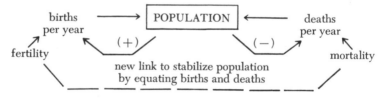

food and medical care, the birth rate will decrease simultaneously. Such a requirement, which is as mathematically simple as it is socially complicated, is for our purposes an experimental device, not necessarily a political recommendation.[1] The result of inserting this policy into the model in 1975 is that the positive feedback loop of population growth is effectively balanced, and population remains constant. At first the birth and death rates are low. But there is still one unchecked positive feedback loop

1. This suggestion for stabilizing population was originally proposed by K. E. Boulding in *The Meaning of the 20th Century* (New York: Harper and Row, 1964).

operating in the model—the one governing the growth of industrial capital. The gain around that loop increases when population is stabilized, resulting in a very rapid growth of income, food, and services per capita. That growth is soon stopped, however, by depletion of nonrenewable resources. The death rate then rises, but total population does not decline because of our requirement that birth rate equal death rate (clearly unrealistic here).

Apparently, if we want a stable system, it is not desirable to let even one of the two critical positive feedback loops generate uncontrolled growth. Stabilizing population alone is not sufficient to prevent overshoot and collapse; a similar run with constant capital and rising population shows that stabilizing capital alone is also not sufficient. What happens if we bring *both* positive feedback loops under control simultaneously? We can stabilize the capital stock in the model by requiring that the investment rate equal the depreciation rate, with an additional model link exactly analogous to the population-stabilizing one.

The result of stopping population growth in 1975 and industrial capital growth in 1985 with no other changes is that severe overshoot and collapse are prevented. Population and capital reach constant values at a relatively high level of food, industrial output, and services per person. Eventually, however, resource shortages reduce industrial output and the temporarily stable state degenerates.

What model assumptions will give us a combination of a decent living standard with somewhat greater stability? We can improve the model behavior greatly by combining technological changes with value changes that reduce the growth tendencies of the system. Different combinations of such policies give us a series of computer outputs that represent a system with reasonably high values of industrial output per capita and with long-term stability. One example of such an output is based on the following policies:

1. Population is stabilized by setting the birth rate equal to the death rate in 1975. Industrial capital is allowed to increase naturally until 1990, after which it, too, is stabilized, by setting the investment rate equal to the depreciation rate.

2. To avoid a nonrenewable resource shortage, resource consumption per unit of industrial output is reduced to one-fourth

of its 1970 value. (This and the following five policies are introduced in 1975.)

3. To further reduce resource depletion and pollution, the economic preferences of society are shifted more toward services such as education and health facilities and less toward factory-produced material goods.

4. Pollution generation per unit of industrial and agricultural output is reduced to one-fourth of its 1970 value.

5. Since the above policies alone would result in a rather low value of food per capita, some people would still be malnourished if the traditional inequalities of distribution persist. To avoid this situation, high value is placed on producing sufficient food for *all* people. Capital is therefore diverted to food production even if such an investment would be considered "uneconomic."

6. This emphasis on highly capitalized agriculture, while necessary to produce enough food, would lead to rapid soil eroison and depletion of soil fertility, destroying long-term stability in the agricultural sector. Therefore the use of agricultural capital has been altered to make soil enrichment and preservation a high priority. This policy implies, for example, use of capital to compost urban organic wastes and return them to the land (a practice that also reduces pollution).

7. The drains on industrial capital for higher services and food production and for resource recycling and pollution control under the above six conditions would lead to a low final level of industrial capital stock. To counteract this effect, the average lifetime of industrial capital is increased, implying better· design for durability and repair and less discarding because of obsolescence. This policy also tends to reduce resource depletion and pollution.

In this run the stable world population is only slightly larger than the population today. There is more than twice as much food per person as the average value in 1970, and world average lifetime is nearly 70 years. The average industrial output per capita is well above today's level, and services per capita have tripled. Total average income per capita (industrial output, food, and services combined) is about $1,800. This value is about half the present average U.S. income, equal to the present average European income, and three times the present average world income. Resources are still being gradually depleted, as they must be under any realistic assumption, but the rate of depletion is so slow that there is time for technology and industry to adjust to changes in resource availability.

The numerical constants that characterize this model run are not the only ones that would produce a stable system. Other people or societies might resolve the various trade-offs differently, putting more or less emphasis on services or food or pollution or material income. This example is included merely as an illustration of the levels of population and capital that are *physically maintainable* on the earth, under the most optimistic assumptions. The model cannot tell us how to attain these levels. It can only indicate a set of mutually consistent goals that are attainable. . . .

Many people will think that the changes we have introduced into the model to avoid the growth-and-collapse behavior mode are not only impossible, but unpleasant, dangerous, even disastrous in themselves. Such policies as reducing the birth rate and diverting capital from production of material goods, by whatever means they might be implemented, seem unnatural and unimaginable, because they have not, in most people's experience, been tried, or even seriously suggested. Indeed there would be little point even in discussing such fundamental changes in the functioning of modern society if we felt that the present pattern of unrestricted growth were sustainable into the future. All the evidence available to us, however, suggests that of the three alternatives—unrestricted growth, a self-imposed limitation to growth, or a nature-imposed limitation to growth—only the last two are actually possible.

Accepting the nature-imposed limits to growth requires no more effort than letting things take their course and waiting to see what will happen. The most probable result of that decision, as we have tried to show here, will be an uncontrollable decrease in population and capital. The real meaning of such a collapse is difficult to imagine because it might take so many different forms. It might occur at different times in different parts of the world, or it might be worldwide. It could be sudden or gradual. If the limit first reached where that of food production, the nonidustrialized countries would suffer the major population decrease. If the first limit were imposed by exhaustion of nonrenewable resources, the industrialized countries would be most affected. It might be that the collapse would leave the earth with its carrying capacity for animal and plant life undiminished, or it might be that the carrying capacity would be reduced or destroyed. Certainly whatever fraction of the human population remained at the end of the process would have very little left with which to build a new society in any form we can now envision.

Achieving a self-imposed limitation to growth would require much effort. It would involve learning to do many things in new ways. It would tax the ingenuity, the flexibility, and the self-discipline of the human race. Bringing a deliberate, controlled end to growth is a tremendous challenge, not easily met. Would the final result be worth the effort? What would humanity gain by such a transition, and what would it lose? Let us consider in more detail what a world of nongrowth might be like. . . .

THE EQUILIBRIUM STATE

By choosing a fairly long time horizon for its existence, and a long average lifetime as a desirable goal, we have now arrived at a minimum set of requirements for the state of global equilibrium. They are:

1. *The capital plant and the population are constant in size.* The birth rate equals the death rate and the capital investment rate equals the depreciation rate.

2. *All input and output rates—births, deaths, investment, and depreciation—are kept to a minimum.*

3. *The levels of capital and population and the ratio of the two are set in accordance with the values of the society.* They may be deliberately revised and slowly adjusted as the advance of technology creates new options.

An equilibrium defined in this way does not mean stagnation. Within the first two guidelines above, corporations could expand or fail, local populations could increase or decrease, income could become more or less evenly distributed. Technological advance would permit the services provided by a constant stock of capital to increase slowly. Within the third guideline, any country could change its average standard of living by altering the balance between its population and its capital. Furthermore, a society could adjust to changing internal or external factors by raising or lowering the population or capital stocks, or both, slowly and in a controlled fashion, with a predetermined goal in mind. The three points above define a *dynamic* equilibrium, which need not and probably would not "freeze" the world into the population-capital configuration that happens to exist at the present time. The object in accepting the above three statements is to create freedom for society, not to impose a straight jacket.

What would life be like in such an equilibrium state? Would innovation be stifled? Would society be locked into the patterns of inequality and injustice we see in the world today? Discussion of these questions must proceed on the basis of mental models, for there is no formal model of social conditions in the equilibrium state. No one can predict what sort of institutions mankind might develop under these new conditions. There is, of course, no guarantee that the new society would be much better or even much different from that which exists today. It seems possible, however, that a society released from struggling with the many problems caused by growth may have more energy and ingenuity available for solving other problems. In fact, we believe that the evolution of a society that favors innovation and technological development, a society based on equality and justice, is far more likely to evolve in a state of global equilibrium than it is in the state of growth we are experiencing today.

GROWTH IN THE EQUILIBRIUM STATE

In 1857 John Stuart Mill wrote:

It is scarcely necessary to remark that a stationary condition of capital and population implies no stationary state of human improvement. There would be as much scope as ever for all kinds of mental culture, and moral and social progress; as much room for improving the Art of Living and much more likelihood of its being improved.[2]

Population and capital are the only quantities that need be constant in the equilibrium state. Any human activity that does not require a large flow of irreplaceable resources or produce severe environmental degradation might continue to grow in-

2. J. S. Mill, "Principles of Political Economy," in *The Collected Works of John Stuart Mill*, ed. V. W. Bladen and J. M. Robson (Toronto: University of Toronto Press, 1965), p. 754.

definitely. In particular, those pursuits that many people would list as the most desirable and satisfying activities of man—education, art, music, religion, basic scientific research, athletics, and social interactions—could flourish. . . .

EQUALITY IN THE EQUILIBRIUM STATE

One of the most commonly accepted myths in our present society is the promise that a continuation of our present patterns of growth will lead to human equality. Present patterns of population and capital growth are actually increasing the gap between the rich and the poor on a worldwide basis. The ultimate result of a continued attempt to grow according to the present pattern will be a disastrous collapse.

The greatest possible impediment to more equal distribution of the world's resources is population growth. It seems to be a universal observation, regrettable but understandable, that, as the number of people over whom a fixed resource must be distributed increases, the equality of distribution decreases. Equal sharing becomes social suicide if the average amount available per person is not enough to maintain life. FAO studies of food distribution have actually documented this general observation.

Analysis of distribution curves shows that when the food supplies of a group diminish, inequalities in intake are accentuated, while the number of undernourished families increases more than in proportion to the deviation from the mean. Moreover, the food intake deficit grows with the size of households so that large families, and their children in particular, are statistically the most likely to be underfed.[3]

In a long-term equilibrium state, the relative levels of population and capital, and their relationships to fixed constraints such as land, fresh water, and mineral resources, would have to be set so that there would be enough food and material production to maintain everyone at (at least) a subsistence level. One barrier to equal distribution would thus be removed. Furthermore, the other effective barrier to equality—the promise of growth—could no longer be maintained, as Dr. Herman E. Daly has pointed out:

3. U.N. Food and Agricultural Organization, *Provisional Indicative World Plan for Agricultural Development* (Rome, 1970), p. 490.

For several reasons the important issue of the stationary state will be distribution, not production. The problem of relative shares can no longer be avoided by appeals to growth. The argument that everyone should be happy as long as his absolute share of wealth increases, regardless of his relative share, will no longer be available. . . . The stationary state would make fewer demands on our environmental resources, but much greater demands on our moral resources.[4]

There is, of course, no assurance that humanity's moral resources would be sufficient to solve the problem of income distribution, even in an equilibrium state. However, there is even less assurance that such social problems will be solved in the present state of growth, which is straining both the moral and the physical resources of the world's people.

4. H. E. Daly, "Toward a Stationary State Economy," in *The Patient Earth*, J. Harte and R. Socolow, eds. (New York: Holt, Rinehart, Winston, 1971), pp. 236–37.

The Limits to Growth: A Review

PETER PASSELL, MARC J. ROBERTS,

and LEONARD ROSS

The authors are economists. Peter Passell and Leonard Ross teach at Columbia University and Marc Roberts is on the faculty at Harvard University. This review appeared in the New York Times Book Review.

THE BOOK IS *The Limits to Growth,* and its message is simple: Either civilization or growth must end, and soon. Continued population and industrial growth will exhaust the world's minerals and bathe the biosphere in fatal levels of pollution. As the authors summarize, "if the present growth trends . . . continue unchanged, the limits of growth on this planet will be reached sometime within the next hundred years."

The Limits to Growth, in our view, is an empty and misleading work. Its imposing apparatus of computer technology and systems jargon conceals a kind of intellectual Rube Goldberg device—one which takes arbitrary assumptions, shakes them up, and comes out with arbitrary conclusions that have the ring of science. *Limits* pretends to a degree of certainty so exaggerated as to obscure the few modest (and unoriginal) insights that it genuinely contains. Less than pseudo-science and little more than polemical fiction, *The Limits to Growth* is best summarized not as a rediscovery of the laws of nature but as a rediscovery of the oldest maxim of computer science: Garbage In, Garbage Out.

Limits approaches the problem of predicting the future straightforwardly enough, employing the time-honored technique of mathematical simulation. Simulation has proved invaluable as a device for testing engineering designs at little cost and no risk to lives. For instance, instead of simply building a prototype aircraft and seeing if it flies, the airplane's characteristics are condensed to a series of computer equations which simulate the airplane in flight. The Apollo moon rocket made thousands of trips in an I.B.M. 360 before it was even built. Economists also use simulation, though their successes have been modest. Simulation models have a rather spotty record in using current data to predict national income, unemployment, and inflation even a year or two in advance.

But *Limits* is cast from a more heroic mold than any engineering or economic study to date. The Meadows team focuses its attention on the whole world and extends its time horizon to centuries. Factors the researchers believe influence population and income are boiled down to a few dozen equations. The crucial variables—population, industrial output, raw materials reserves, food production, and pollution—all interact in ways that are at least superficially reasonable: Population growth is limited by food output, health services, and pollution; industrial growth and agricultural growth are limited by resource availability and pollution. *Limits* is thus able to create a hypothetical future based on knowledge of the past.

As a first approximation of the future, the authors assume that the world is utterly incapable of adjusting to problems of scarcity. Technology stagnates and pollution is ignored, even as it chokes millions to death. A shortage of raw materials prevents industry and agriculture from keeping up with population growth. World reserves of vital materials (silver, tungsten, mercury, etc.) are exhausted within 40 years. Around 2020 the pinch becomes tight enough to cause a fall in per capita income. A few decades later, malnutrition and lagging health services abruptly reverse the climbing population trend. By the year 2100 the resource base has shrunk so badly that the world economy is unable to sustain even nineteenth-century living standards.

Scientists should have few objections to this grim scenario, even though it is based on what the Meadows team admits are crude assumptions. The scenario does plausibly illustrate the need for continued scientific progress to sustain current levels of prosperity. The quality of life in the future surely depends on the progress of technology and, to a lesser extent, on our willingness to limit population growth. But that should come as no surprise to a world that is already enormously dependent on modern techniques: If the telephone company were restricted to turn-of-the-century technology 20 million operators would be needed to handle today's volume of calls. Or, as British editor

Norman Macrae has observed, an extrapolation of the trends of the 1880s would show today's cities buried under horse manure.

By the same measure, the simulation provides some small insight into the probable hazards of continued indifference to pollution and population growth. Current industrial and agricultural practices dump vast quantities of debris into the biosphere which would ultimately leave the air unfit for humans and water unfit for fish. Unchecked, the world's population is likely to double by the year 2000, with most of the burden on less developed countries. The future would be grim indeed if Con Ed were indefinitely allowed to ignore what comes out of its stacks or if Colombia permitted 20 million people to jam the barrios of Bogatá. Had the *Limits* team concluded on this note, they would have had an acceptable point—but one quite independent of their elaborate computer simulation. It doesn't take a $10-million machine to figure out that only science—and the will to use it intelligently—could keep us ahead of population growth.

The authors, however, have much more in mind. They are out to show that pollution and malnutrition cannot be attacked directly, but only by stopping economic growth. They argue that any reasonable modification of their equations to account for new technology, pollution, and population control might postpone collapse but would not avoid it. Under the most sanguine conditions imaginable, they say, growth must end within 100 years. Even if technology doubled known resources and crop yields, pollution were cut by three-fourths, and birth control eliminated all unwanted pregnancies, growth would turn out to be self-limiting. In no more than a century, the collective weight of food shortages, raw material depletion, and pollution would reverse expansion. Hence the only way to avoid collapse and its attendant miseries is to halt growth now. *Limits* preaches that we must learn to make do with what we already have.

It is no coincidence that all the simulations based on the Meadows world model invariably end in collapse. As in any simulation, the results depend on the information initially fed to the computer. And the *Limits* team fixes the wheel; no matter how many times you play there is only one possible outcome. Critical to their model is the notion that growth produces stresses (pollution, resource demands, food requirements) which multiply geometrically. Every child born is not only another mouth to feed but another potential parent. Every new factory not only drains away exhaustible resources but increases our capacity to build more factories. Geometric growth must eventually produce spectacular results.

While the team's world model hypothesizes exponential growth for industrial and agricultural needs, it places arbitrary, non-exponential, limits on the technical progress that might accommodate these needs. New methods of locating and mining ores, or recycling used materials, are assigned the ability to do no more than double reserve capacity; agricultural research can do no more than double land yields; pollution control can cut emissions from each source by no more than three-fourths. Hence the end is inevitable. Economic demands must outstrip economic capacities simply because of the assumption of exponential growth in the former. . . .

The Limits to Growth is not the first research effort to explore the dangers of exponential growth. Nor, once again, was it necessary to use fancy computer techniques to justify what so obviously follows from the assumptions. The Rev. Thomas Malthus made a similar point two centuries ago without benefit of computer printouts or blinking lights. Malthus argued that people tend to multiply exponentially, while the food supply at best increases at a constant rate. He expected that starvation and war would periodically redress the balance.

Still, *The Limits to Growth* might be excused in spite of its lack of originality and scent of technical chicanery if those dismal assumptions behind the calculations were accurate. It is true that exponential growth cannot go on forever if technology does not keep up—and if that is the case we might save ourselves much misery by stopping before we reach the limits. But there is no particular criterion beyond myopia on which to base that speculation. Malthus was wrong; food capacity has kept up with population. While no one knows for certain, technical progress shows no sign of slowing down. The best econometric estimates suggest that it is indeed growing exponentially. The Meadows team could have performed a service by citing hard evidence to discredit these estimates, if they have any. Instead they simply assume a bleak future for technology, announce that their own estimates are generous, and conclude that under any hypothesis about scientific progress growth must end. Heads you lose; tails you lose.

Natural resource reserves and needs in the model are calculated on the most conservative assumptions about the ability of the world economy to adjust to shortages. This is largely due to the absence of prices as a variable in the *Limits* projection of how resources will be used. In the real world, rising prices act as an economic signal to conserve scarce resources, providing incentives to use cheaper materials in their place, stimulating research efforts on new ways to save on resource inputs, and making renewed exploration attempts more profitable.

In fact, natural resource prices have remained low, giving little evidence of coming shortages. And the reasons are not hard to find. Technical change has dramatically reduced exploration and extraction costs, while simultaneously permitting the substitution of plentiful material for scarce ones—plastics for metal, synthetic fibers for natural, etc. Moreover specialists usually agree that cheap energy is the critical long-run constraint on output of raw materials. Given enough energy, minerals might be reclaimed from under the sea, or from seawater itself. A virtually infinite source of energy, the controlled nuclear fusion of hydrogen, will probably be tapped within 50 years.

Limits also assumes that abatement practices will at best reduce pollution by three-quarters. Yet that goal could be accomplished using techniques that exist today and ignores the promise of innovations still under development. Relatively pollution-free autos are within reach if we have the political will to insist; electric power could be generated with minimal pollution if we are willing to pay a reasonable price. . . .

Stopping growth is a sane way to curb pollution only if society doesn't have the nerve to do the job directly. But a world too timid to require smokestack precipitators would hardly jump at the chance to shut down factories. Conversely, if we ever did have the willpower to halt growth, we could use that resolve affirmatively to enhance the quality of life. The President who could convince Congress to forbid new capital investment could find money for comfortable mass transit and could put teeth into antipollution laws.

Economic and Ecological Effects
of a Stationary Economy

ROBERT U. AYRES and ALLEN V. KNEESE

Robert U. Ayres is a physicist with International Research and Technology Corporation and Allen V. Kneese is an economist with Resources for the Future, Inc. Their article was prepared for the Annual Review of Ecology and Systematics, *1971.*

CONTEMPORARY INTEREST in, and concern with, a stationary economy seems to stem from two general causes: (1) the rapid rise in world population in the last few hundred years and especially in the post–World War II period, and (2) strongly increasing environmental pollution, again at an accelerated pace in the post–World War II period. Both these phenomena are contributing to vast and, many fear, strongly adverse imbalances in ecological systems and irreversible depletion of resources.

Since 1920, the world's population has about doubled and the gross load of materials and energy residuals returned to the environment has probably more than quadrupled. The mirror image of the residuals load on the environment is the extraction of material and energy resources from the earth. The disposition of the types of residuals now emitted to the environment can probably not grow very much beyond present levels without highly adverse effects on ecological systems and human health, and the only imaginable really long-term sustainable equilibrium involves stationary populations and very low levels of net use of nonrenewable resources from earth sources.

These harsh facts have caused some to jump to the conclusion that the world must immediately achieve stable population *and* no-growth economies. But achieving these goals quickly involves complexities and side effects which are starting to be discussed in the recent literature. For example, population growth is the result of complex interactions in a system which is slow to adjust into full equilibrium with current changes in birth rates.

Most of the world has no real choice in the near future but

235

to increase production or face the grim Malthusian checks on population increase. Moreover, production must increase rapidly (5 percent a year or more) if the impoverished state of the masses is to be improved even slightly over the next few decades. What is more distressing to many writers is that birth control programs in most countries with rapidly growing populations are not pursued very vigorously; the currently accepted measures can at best prevent unwanted births. The conclusion is drawn that birth rates cannot be brought under control with accepted measures and that unless more stringent ones are adopted, the world will eventually face massive starvation and disease as well as ecological disaster.

Thus, a stationary economy for most of the world seems clearly out of the question as a policy objective for some decades to come. This does not mean that developing countries dare neglect objectives other than growth, such as environmental quality management. Because of extreme congestion, poor combustion processes, bad local sanitation, and meteorological or hydrological conditions, major cities in developing countries experience some of the most intense pollution in the world. São Paulo, Seoul, Taipeh, Accra, and Mexico City are only a few examples. Moreover, these problems, unless brought under effective management, will get rapidly worse as industrial production grows and the ability of people to buy fuel and throw away things increases. For a period of time, at least, during the development of these countries recycling and reuse will tend to decrease (newspapers will no longer be used to wrap food or serve as toilet paper, for example). Moreover, with increased life expectancy the incidence of the chronic degenerative diseases which appear to be associated with high levels of chemical pollution in the environment will tend to increase. By the end of the century U.N. projections show more than three-quarters of the world's population in the less-developed areas, where population is growing far faster than in the developed countries. Urbanization is also proceeding rapidly. Development planning must finally come to grips with these matters.

We might add that it is the opinion of many ecologists and others, including the authors, that *if* the world does finally manage to arrive at some sort of low birth rate and low death rate equilibrium, it will be at a level of population several times higher—at least in many areas—than would be optimum for the human condition. But there really seems to be nothing that can be done about that—at least not for a very long time to come. It is only in the developed countries—which after all use the lion's share of nonrenewable resources and produce the bulk of residuals—that one can seriously discuss zero growth as a major policy objective in the near future. But the recent literature is beginning to explore some of the complexities and problems associated with this objective, even in developed countries, especially if they strive to achieve it quickly. It is also becoming more widely realized that environmental problems do not have to grow in a one-to-one relationship with either population growth or economic growth. We would, in fact, argue that environmental improvement is compatible with growth in the developed countries and, because of more rapid replacement of obsolete technology and increased economic capacity to meet various objectives, may within limits even be made easier by it. The urgent question is whether advanced countries will adopt the policies necessary to protect the environment. . . .

A reasonable approach to our present and near-future situation seems to call for policies directed at rationalizing the allocation of resources by our society. Four specific approaches come to mind: (1) The private costs of production of material objects and energy should be made to reflect the social costs more completely. If this were done adroitly, a strong incentive to reduce the generation and discharge of residuals would be provided, and consumer demand would tend to some extent to shift away from demand for material things and energy toward services. A corollary effect might be to slow down the *measured* rate of productivity gain since the rate of productivity increase in the services sector is much slower than in the material goods production sector.[1] Economists have long argued that private and social costs can be brought into conjunction most effectively and efficiently by taxing activities which impose costs on the general society, such as pollution. The first report of the President's Council on Environmental Quality suggests that this ap-

1. Direct personal services have not historically been improving rapidly in productivity. However, the application of EDP and communications technology to personal services could well usher in an era of more rapid productivity gain.

proach is now getting serious attention in national policy-making.[2] (2) Technological change should be redirected toward technologies which protect the environment and conserve materials and energy. The present incentive system provides little, if any, private incentive for developing this sort of technology on anything like an appropriate scale. Again, heavily taxing activities which tend to degrade the environment would have a desirable effect.[3] (3) Policy should be considered for obtaining an improved distribution of population. At present, the population problem in the United States seems to be not so much one of gross overpopulation as of crowding in areas desirable from an employment, climatic, scenic, or cultural standpoint. Policies to improve employment opportunities as well as cultural and recreational opportunities in such a way as to achieve a better distribution of population clusters would seem wise, providing this can be done without further aggravating the economic problems of the existing urban areas—we are not enthusiastic about tax benefits or subsidies for "newtowns" as currently envisaged. We use the word clusters advisedly because more compact development of smaller cities would tend to be beneficial from the environmental point of view. This would permit better dilution over all, but not sacrifice scale economies in control measures. (4) Finally, it seems that a good case can be made for reducing our population growth rate to zero, but it appears doubtful this can or should be done very quickly. . . .

It seems to us incontrovertible that the world's population will continue to rise inexorably for several more decades, at least, even if the effectiveness of birth control measures is greatly increased. This means that many countries (containing most of the world's population) will have little choice but to strive hard for economic growth. Also, it will probably not prove desirable for the major developed countries (especially those with youthful populations) to develop policies which will end population or economic growth suddenly. . . .

Even if the relatively favorable results outlined above are achieved, we will not ipso facto have attained a permanently

2. Council on Environmental Quality, *Environmental Quality, 1970: 1st Annual Report,* transmitted to U.S. Congress August 1970.

3. R. U. Ayres, *The Range of Policy Alternatives for Maintaining Environmental Quality, IRT-p-28,* Annual Meeting of the American Association for the Advancement of Science, December 28, 1970.

(or very long-term) sustainable equilibrium. Over the period we are considering here, there will continue to be net use (i.e., dispersion and degradation) of depletable resources and the emission of certain cumulative (e.g., CO_2) residuals of the environment.

Eventually we must face the question of whether it is possible to have a stationary or equilibrium system accommodating 15–20 billion persons, which is the level at which the world population may stabilize without large increases in death rates. This is the subject of our next section. It need hardly be noted that the following discussion is highly speculative.

THE VERY LONG RUN

Input Availability · The subject matter of this section may be epitomized by the questions: What kind of society is compatible with a situation in which population is very much larger than today's, and *what happens when there are no new natural resources—including environmental resources—to exploit?* We are aware, of course, that this is a hypothetical limiting case—an asymptote, so to speak—since there exists a virtually infinite supply of most minerals in infinitesimal concentrations in seawater, granite, shale, or clay. These are essentially inexhaustible, since they are the basic materials of the earth's crust. We are also aware that the prices of mineral commodities (in constant dollars) have remained relatively constant over the last hundred years, even though the quality of available natural sources has declined sharply.[4] In prehistoric times copper was not infrequently found in pure form. Today the average copper content of commercial ores is a fraction of 1 percent. A similar, if less dramatic, decline has occurred for essentially all major minerals including silver and gold, iron ore, tin, lead, and zinc. Much the same story also applies to coal and petroleum. However, the capital and technology purchased by exploiting high-quality mineral sources have enabled us to continue to tap lower and lower quality sources at the same relative unit price, while the costs of raw materials relative to the value of final products has actually dropped steadily.

4. H. J. Barnett and C. Morse, *Scarcity and Growth: The Economics of Natural Resource Availability* (Baltimore: Johns Hopkins Press, 1963).

Why, then, should we not extrapolate this comfortable situation indefinitely? We suggest several reasons, which the reader may evaluate for himself.

1. Lower quality ores in some important materials do not necessarily exist in exploitable quantities. This appears to be the case for lead and zinc.[5] The same is probably true for practical purposes with regard to hydrocarbons *as such* (i.e., for nonfuel purposes) since hydrocarbons are not simply dispersed by consumption but are actually used up—that is, chemically transformed into CO_2 and H_2O. Thus we face the likelihood that hydrocarbons will ultimately become rather scarce resources, being replaceable only from natural photosynthesis or by chemical synthesis involving large expenditures of energy.

2. The increased output of the extractive industries in the last century can be attributed in part to the opening up of previously unexplored areas (e.g., Canada, Siberia, Africa, Brazil, Australia). Except for the ocean bottom—which is not easily accessible or easy to exploit—"new" sources will become rarer and rarer in the future.

3. The prices of mineral commodities historically have not reflected social costs arising from pollution and waste disposal. But these costs evidently increase nonlinearly as the amount of processing increases (requiring more energy and more technological inputs) and human settlement becomes more dense. We anticipate that in the long term social costs of obtaining new materials will mount greatly. Low prices have also been subsidized to some extent by devices such as "depletion allowances."

4. The increased productivity of the extractive industries in the last century is also partly due to economies of scale and·the application of mechanical technology. Both are probably subject to the law of diminishing returns. That is, the effort and investment required to achieve further productivity gains in the future will probably be much greater than has been true in the past.

5. The developed countries (except for the Soviet Union) are rapidly using up their domestic high-grade sources of minerals and fossil fuels and becoming dependent on the less-developed nations. The latter, in turn, rely on raw material exports for

5. D. B. Brooks, "The Lead-Zinc Anomaly," *Society of Mining Engineers Transactions*, June 1967.

foreign exchange to purchase needed technological goods and services. It is not unlikely that raw material exporters will increasingly band together to multiply their bargaining power and increase their revenues from this source (this—apart from successful war by the rich nations on the poor—is, in fact, one of the more plausible scenarios for achieving a fairly radical redistribution of wealth and technology in the world).

We do not believe that energy *as such* will prove to be an ultimate constraining factor. While available reserves of petroleum and natural gas must inevitably begin to run out—probably by the end of the century—there are very large reserves of low-quality coal, lignite, and oil shale. High-quality uranium sources are limited, too, but plutonium breeder reactors should make it possible to vastly extend the availability of nuclear fuel. Thorium, also, is a potential source of nuclear power and vast quantities exist in recoverable quantities in granite. Fusion power may be limited by the availability of lithium-6 (to produce tritium), rather than deuterium, but lithium is not a rare element on the earth's surface. Both solar and geothermal power can also be tapped in large quantities—though not necessarily at relative costs as low as fossil or nuclear power. Technologically speaking, it is probably feasible to capture solar power *outside* the earth's atmosphere and ship it back to earth either in the form of a high-intensity coherent electromagnetic beam or as synthetic chemical fuels. (It must be remembered that we are speaking of a very long-run scenario in which space technology is highly developed and by no means exotic.[6])

For purposes of our paradigm, then, the recovery of mineral substances (other than hydrocarbons) from very low-quality sources by the application of large amounts of energy will not be ruled out, but the mining of fossil fuels and mineral ores as currently practiced will be assumed to be no longer possible. Replacement of any materials which are removed from circulation due to dispersal or disposal will occur (1) by processing large quantities of material on the earth's surface, or (2) by importation from extraterrestrial sources such as the moon or asteroids.

6. An interesting discussion of the possibilities of using space is found in T. B. Taylor, *On the Use of Cislunar Space and the Moon for Improving the Quality of Life on Earth* (Xerox) International Research and Technology Corporation.

Also, we do not believe that food availability *as such* will necessarily be limiting in the very long run if population stabilizes. Food is, basically, biologically available energy—in the form of carbohydrate, protein, or fat—plus some needed chemical building blocks which the human organism cannot synthesize from basic elements. These essential components of food include some twenty amino acids. Food must also include a number of minerals such as sodium, potassium, calcium, phosphorus, and iron, of course.

Much remains to be learned about the chemical synthesis of amino acids and vitamins, but most of the basic steps have already been duplicated in the laboratory. In the long-run future, there is absolutely no reason to doubt that food *could* be manufactured in a chemical plant, given the availability of sufficient energy, capital equipment, and knowledge. This is not to imply that synthetic food would necessarily replace food derived from biological origins. Certainly as far ahead as one can foresee, the latter is likely to be both more palatable and more economical to produce. The second assertion may seem slightly controversial at first, but we emphasize that production processes must (in the long run) internalize all social and environmental costs which are now external to the producer. Thus agriculture is capable of providing a number of valuable benefits or "coproducts" besides food itself—including recycling of organic wastes (say through irrigation with sewage, as is done on a limited scale today), regulation of the climate, scenic beauty, a sense of spaciousness and unity with nature, recreational opportunities, as well as a life experience which many find worthy of preservation. (Many of these benefits are not unique to agricultural use of land, but they are incompatible with industrial, residential, commerical, and many recreational uses.) On the other hand, "industrial" food production as currently practiced, e.g., in feed lots or poultry breeding establishments, tends to damage rather than restore or preserve environment by concentrating large quantities of waste products in one location and causing other disturbances to the natural order. Industrial food production is not much different, in principle, from industrial chemical production or other large-scale materials-processing enterprises. It matters little, in this perspective, whether the raw materials originated from farms, forests, or mines. But like these other industrial chemical processes it would probably pose very serious waste control problems.

Food production, whether based on photosynthesis or chemical synthesis, is evidently energy limited. We are confronted with an apparent paradox here. World food production, based on photosynthesis, is apparently quite limited. Some experts have predicted world-wide famine within a decade or two. Others, citing the "green revolution," are much more optimistic. But it is painfully clear that conventional agriculture is beginning to approach its limits and that while the present world population could probably be fed adequately (though two out of three people on the globe are now receiving *in*adequate diets), and conceivably even the year 2000 population and beyond could be supported if new strains of grain and the use of fertilizers spread rapidly enough through Asia and Latin America, it is almost impossible to see how conventional agriculture could support 15–20 billion people at the present U.S. or European dietary standard, with 40 percent (or more) of dietary calories derived from animal sources. But unconventional agriculture perhaps could.

By unconventional agriculture, we mean a system based mainly on harvested or recycled cellulose—rather than carbohydrates—which is converted by bacterial action into feed for cattle, hogs, poultry, or fish. All solid organic wastes—cornstalks and cobs, brush, grass clippings and leaves, food processing wastes, waste paper, animal manure, and even sewage—can be converted into animal feed and thus recycled without benefit of additional photosynthesis. The overall efficiency of conversion of solar energy to food can thus be increased manyfold—probably by an order of magnitude—without increasing the intensity of cultivation or altering the primary ecology. Whatever agricultural processes might be found compatible with the indefinite high-level maintenance of a population of 15–20 billion, one thing is clear—they must be arranged so that much less pesticide and plant nutrient is lost to the environment relative to output than is true of present "developed" agriculture. The results of not achieving this would be profoundly destructive to ecological systems.

Technology in the "Stationary" Economy · At first sight there seems to be no inherent reason why *technology* should not continue to improve in a "stationary" state, nor does there seem to be any basic reason why *wealth* should not increase—provided the material inventory remains unchanged. Even material goods may increase in value (i.e., by offering more services to the user) without increasing their basic resource inputs. A good example of this evolution is the history of radio and TV; 30 years ago even a crude AM radio was both expensive and bulky. Today, the same or better services (i.e., quality of sound reproduction and accessibility of programs) are available in a miniature transistorized radio at a far lower price requiring only a tiny fraction of the physical resources.

Actually, it is easy to see that in a stationary economy (in the above sense) the only *possible* source of increased wealth is better technology—including both hardware and "software" under this rubric. If wealth is to grow without increasing the requirements for resources, it will be necessary to find ways of greatly reducing the physical resources "frozen" in material objects. That is to say, the material component of physical wealth must decline sharply. What is embodied must be carefully maintained and extensively reused both to reduce the use of resource inputs and to control the discharge of residuals.

The use of energy as well as materials in the postulated stationary economy would naturally have to be far more conservative than is now the case in so called "developed" countries, among other reasons because the residual energy "rejected" to the atmosphere might become a severe problem. Present emission of energy is about 1/15,000 of the absorbed solar flux. But if the present rate of growth continued for 250 years emissions would reach 100 percent of the absorbed solar flux. The resulting increase in the earth's temperature would be about 50°C —a condition totally unsuitable for human habitation.

It is almost axiomatic in the conventional wisdom that energy consumption per capita is an index of wealth. It is perfectly true, of course, that rising GNP and rising energy consumption have been historically correlated. It is true, also, that the current pattern of increased output of fabricated goods derived from extractive industries tends to result in a *nonlinear* increase in demand for energy, since the declining quality of raw materials necessitates greater expenditures of energy for processing.

On the other hand, in an economy based on nearly total recycle of nonreplaceable materials, the energy expended on materials processing would depend upon the specific manufacturing and fabricating technology in use. These, in turn, would presumably evolve (given the appropriate incentive structure) in such a way as to reduce both the energy and dollar cost of reprocessing. Most tasks currently carried out by complete machines built for the purpose, would, in such a society, be carried out by programmed modular assemblies of flexible multipurpose *components*. These modules would be, increasingly, electronic or fluidic rather than mechanical in mode of operation. These modules would be replaceable and reparable individually. Since the most efficient form of recycling (from a materials and energy point of view) is that which involves the least change in form or composition, it is apparent that *repair or rebuilding of modules would be highly favored over replacement* by new different types, since the latter would involve the use of virgin materials. Here is one reason why a stationary economy would probably tend to be technologically rather static.

Also the population distribution characteristics of a stationary state would be much older than present populations. The median age would increase to perhaps 35—or even older, if further major extensions in life expectance occur. The labor force would not be growing and, as noted above, increased wealth could only have its origin in technological change. On the other hand, there are grounds for believing that technological change is likely to slow down, rather than speed up, in a society where most physical resources are nonrenewable and must therefore be conserved and recycled. It appears, then, that one cannot expect a continued rapid increase in wealth in a stationary society unless special incentives are created to "institutionalize" technological innovation.

Apart from this possibility, however, a stationary society would not allow for economic growth and *would, therefore, cut down on the possibilities of personal advancement in relative status which a growing economy permits.* This prospect is likely to be horrifying and repugnant to an upward mobile society such as ours, though it is obviously perfectly acceptable in many "traditional" cultures. Of course, most traditional cultures are technologically primitive, so it is very difficult to guess what a future culturally static society, based on a highly sophisticated technology, might be like to live in. We shall not attempt this feat of imagination. We do, however, wish to point out that the values of a society are likely to adapt to its circumstances, and the lack of opportunity for personal advancement in status may not necessarily involve serious deprivation to those who are born in that society.

There is, as we have mentioned, the possibility that technological progress could be institutionalized. The usual notion is that technological change is a consequence of research and invention. If this were so, it would be simple enough to institutionalize technological change by diverting a significant amount of economic resources into research and development. Historically, one observes a strong correlation between periods of rapid technological change and periods of great fertility of invention, as measured for instance by numbers of patents filed. However, examination of the historical evidence does indeed suggest that invention may be stimulated by rapid change, rather than the reverse.[7] In any case, there is no guarantee that inventions and discoveries will be implemented simply because they exist. Innovation is often a fairly painful process which corporations and institutions embrace reluctantly, if at all.

Under the present "rules of the game," technological progress is one of several mechanisms for gaining a competitive advantage or an increased return on investment. Technological progress often stagnates, however, when the market is *not* competitive (i.e., in a monopoly or oligopoly) or when other competitive strategies, such as heavy advertising, are more effective. On the other hand, even a natural monopoly may be quite innovative if for some reason it is constrained from raising prices for the same product and can only increase its earnings by cutting operating costs or providing new services which can be sold at a higher price. The telephone company seems to be an example of this. This pattern may be generalizable. A more reliable guarantee of institutionalizing technological change, at least in a

7. J. Schmookler, *Invention and Economic Growth* (Cambridge, Mass.: Harvard University Press, 1966).

regulated industry, would be to depreciate the rate base as the "embodied" technology ages. Various revisions of the incentive system might be devised to induce innovation even in a relatively static system.

SOME CONCLUDING THOUGHTS ABOUT THE VERY LONG RUN

The foregoing discussion suggests that the view that a stable world population of 15–20 billion persons could ultimately be supported at a comparatively high level of living in a quasi-stationary economy is not on the face of it ridiculous. One can visualize technologies which, if they could be satisfactorily improved, developed, and applied, would make this possible. They would, of course, be highly energy using and require very low rates of dispersal of materials into the environment. But we cannot conclude on this slightly optimistic note without calling attention to some truly major reservations about the ability of humankind to achieve this *relatively* favorable outcome.

The first is the suspicion that scientific research and development is subject to what the economist calls diminishing returns. Simply put, this principle states that as an input of a particular type is increased relative to others, the returns obtained from each successive increment will ultimately decline. The classical economists of the eighteenth and nineteenth centuries felt that economic growth would be brought to an end as an increasing amount of labor was applied to a fixed resource stock so that, eventually, further increments of labor would not yield any additional output. Actually, technology turned out to be the main factor which permitted this dismal result to be avoided— or at least put off for a long time. Labor productivity has been rising fast and almost steadily since the beginning of the industrial revolution. In fact, increased productivity has been the main element in economic growth. To get this result we have been increasing technology as a production factor faster than the other inputs for a long period of time. Most projections of economic activity and use of resources implicitly assume that we will continue to enjoy at least constant returns from scientific and technological input. In other words, labor productivity will continue to rise as it has in the past few decades. In the United

States this means at about 3 percent per year. This may be quite justifiable if one is looking a relatively few decades into the future. But on the longer-time scale we have considered in the final sections of this paper, doubts may well arise, even if institutional arrangements are made to sustain a higher level of scientific enterprise.

The noted classical economists Malthus and Ricardo were products of the Enlightenment, which restored Western man's confidence in his ability to understand the workings of the world through reason. And their works are strong testimonials to the power of this confidence. But the Enlightenment's systematic, analytic engine, the scientific method, was just starting to evolve. A method of discovery was being discovered. It is not hard to understand why the classical economists could not grasp fully the implications of this other product of the Enlightenment. The industrial revolution at first produced enormous productivity gains through the application of reason and ingenuity to mechanical devices without the benefits of systematic science. For example, Cartwright, who made the first power loom and other important textile equipment, was a clergyman who wrote verses, and Benjamin Huntsman, who first made cast steel, was a clockmaker. It was only gradually that industrial innovation moved beyond the basically mechanical and began to incorporate more esoteric accomplishments of formal science, such as chemistry.[8] But once it took hold, science continued to propel productivity forward although some of the more obvious improvements permitted by the spirit of the Enlightenment had been made. As Sir John Hicks, the eminent British economist, has stated in his recent commentary on economic history, "There might have been no Crompton and Arkwright, and still there could have been an industrial revolution; in its later stages it would have been much the same. The impact of science, stimulating the technicians, developing new sources of power, using power to create more than human accuracy, reducing the cost of machines until they were available for a multitude of purposes; this surely is the essential novelty . . ."[9]

8. A fascinating account of this process is found in G. D. H. Cole, "Machines and Men," *Introduction to Economic History, 1750–1950* (London: Macmillan, 1952), chap. 11.

9. J. Hicks, *A Theory of Economic History* (London: Oxford University Press, 1969), p. 147.

The application of science to industry has continued to increase the productivity of labor and more or less steadily push back resource scarcity, despite huge increases in labor and capital inputs. Perhaps it will continue to do so for a long time to come. But it would seem strange if the application of effort to science and technology were entirely immune from diminishing returns. One may speculate that the return from the application of resources to scientific discovery and technological development, in certain important instances, has already begun to diminish. For example, most of the basic mathematical concepts which are used in today's applied science were well known by the beginning of this century. In this connection it is worth noting that Bentley Glass, the outgoing president of the American Association for the Advancement of Science, has forecast in a speech before the 1970 AAS meetings that we cannot expect continued basic scientific discoveries on the scale of the last 100 years.

While new discoveries always remain to be made, although not necessarily at an undiminished pace, there are some basic reasons why quantitative technological improvements may require greater efforts and why the percentage rate of improvement in many fields, as measured in terms of functional indices, will inevitably begin to decline. The efficiency of energy conversion is a good illustration of the point. Power plants have increased in efficiency from 1 or 2 percent in the days of Savery and Watt to upwards of 40 percent in the most advanced power plants today. Thus we have already experienced a 40-fold improvement in two centuries. The next 30 years may conceivably see a further increase to 60 percent overall efficiency, but this only represents a 50 percent improvement over the present level. Obviously the rate of advance thereafter must slow down markedly if only because 100 percent efficiency is the absolute upper limit, and it can never be actually reached. In many other areas, also, this same phenomenology holds true.[10]

Should we encounter strongly diminishing returns to scientific technological development, it may well prove to be impossible to converge to a stable, sustainable economy of 15–20 billion persons in which labor productivity is relatively high. Indeed

10. For a more detailed discussion, see R. U. Ayres, *Technological Forecasting and Long Range Planning* (New York: McGraw-Hill, 1969).

it may not be possible to indefinitely sustain that level of population at *any* level of living. Thus, as far as we can see, science and technology is not the villain but the potential hero of the piece, if it can be properly developed and directed.

A second nagging doubt has its basis in the imperfections of social organization and social institutions. It is a commonplace that industrialization has increased interdependence. So while it can produce high levels of material welfare, it can do so only if a high degree of social order is maintained. The system becomes not only vulnerable to breakdowns in the technological chain, but also to human error and malevolence. Some of the foreseeable technologies for simultaneously increasing productivity over the long-run future and reducing dependence on nonrenewable resources seem to carry with them huge extensions of interdependency in both space and time. An important example is power production from fission reactions. Fissionable material is very abundant (when breeder reactors come into use) and in some respects atomic power makes much lesser demands on the environment than fossil fuels. Even should fusion power become eventually feasible (as we feel sure it will), an intermediate large-scale reliance on fission power will leave humanity with the legacy (curse?) of a large amount of material which must be kept in *permanent* storage. The release of this radioactive material would end human life on earth. It is hard to be encouraged about the demands this makes on humankind's ability to sustain social order. Careful and highly sophisticated control must be exercised over a period "longer," in the words of AEC Commissioner Wilfred E. Johnson, "than the history of most governments that the world has seen." The payoff situation here seems to be one in which we trade a high probability of some productivity gain, a reduction in demand for nonrenewable resources, and improvement in some aspects of environment for an unknown but not necessarily slight probability of ultimate total disaster.

A less extreme but still important example is provided by the technologies for capturing extraterrestrial energy we described earlier. A loss of social order within a country with attendant loss of control or lack of maintenance of the satellites could make it impossible to sustain adequate economic activity anywhere in the land. At the levels of population and dependency on electricity we are envisioning, sustained breakdowns would be huge disasters. Moreover, these monster devices would presumably be extremely vulnerable to hostile attack. There comes to mind at least one historical example of civilization which collapsed utterly as a result of damage to an elaborate physical system on which it depended and which could not be repaired. We refer to the destruction of the Tigris-Euphrates irrigation system by Tamerlane in the fourteenth century.

The large world population of a century or more from now might be sustainable at relatively high levels if the technologies one can optimistically foresee can be successfully applied. For some of the major ones, this assumes that "everything goes right" with social and political institutions, nationally and internationally and for very long periods of time. This is quite an assumption, for historically everything has gone right only momentarily in terms of the time scales we are discussing. Moreover, the incentives to violence may be immense. By the first decades of the twenty-first century now-rich countries will have become heavily dependent on now-poor countries for resource inputs. In Asia poor and extremely densely populated countries (the mainland portion of East Asia will probably by then have a population of at least one and a half billion) will be cheek to jowl with a rich and relatively spacious one. Extremely potent war weapons will by then be available to every country of any size. Perhaps after some bad experiences or as a result of cool judgment, those in a position to guide the applications of technology will decide not to maximize the expected value of productivity gain, but to give heavy emphasis to the risks of disastrous losses as well—something more akin to the minimax criterion of game theory. This might well preclude use of technologies which hold the greatest promise of combining high productivity with low use of nonrenewable natural resources— but which make unacceptable demands on social order.

Can mankind converge monotonically toward a state in which human life is both pleasant and more or less indefinitely viable? This is a very open question, it seems to us. The uncertainties are so great that it is difficult to see how we could rationally influence present policies to take account of possibilities on this time scale. The only clear signal seems to be that if we fail to bring world population under control soon—very soon—humanity's future problems may be totally insoluble. If we do succeed, there is a chance.

The dangers that perhaps impress us most are subtle ones. They revolve around the probability that, as human society makes greater and greater demands on available resources, margin for error decreases. As it decreases a more and more interdependent, elaborate, and fail-safe organization is required simply to prevent the system from collapsing at the first perturbation. Recent unhappy experiences with massive breakdowns or tieups of essential public services—electric power, telephones, sanitation, transportation—suggest very clearly the magnitude of potential instabilities inherent in a system which depends, for example, on maintaining regular communications in space or beneath the ocean. The elemental need to prevent catastrophic breakdowns or holdups may conceivably result in the development of a rigidly structured, rather inhuman "1984" type of social system which subordinates individual talents, needs, or desires to the survival of the social organism as a whole. Or else, the world may "solve" its otherwise insoluble problems by war, famine, or anarchy. We hesitate to dwell on this possibility and it is distasteful to us to end on such a note. We cannot help but hope that others will soon begin to find positive answers where we have uncovered grounds for pessimism. In any case we feel that analyses which address the questions of the longterm viability of a very numerous humanity solely in terms of potential technological, or even economic, capabilities miss some of the most central questions.

PART FOUR   The Economy vs.

Environmental Preservation

Some Environmental Effects
of Economic Development

JOHN V. KRUTILLA

John V. Krutilla is an economist and directs the Natural Environment Research Program at Resources for the Future, Inc. This article was prepared in 1967 for an issue of Daedalus devoted entirely to problems in the American environment.

AMERICAN CULTURE and character have been influenced profoundly by the open rural countryside and the wilderness beyond. The further we are removed from the conditions of a more primitive America, the greater is our nostalgia for the conditions of earlier times. But despite the many influential and eloquent advocates for preserving the American scene—and especially the wilderness and rural countryside—the assaults upon America's landscape and the erosion of its natural environment continue.

In the past, the degradation of the landscape has been associated principally with mining, logging, and agricultural activities. Open pits abandoned after completion of strip-mining operations seriously deface a natural landscape. Occasionally, as in the case of zinc-recovery operations, escape of flue gases destroys the vegetation in the surrounding area. Ducktown, Tennessee, and Sudbury, Ontario, are the classic examples here, and more recent experience in the Trail, British Columbia, area reminds us that mine-mill activities threaten the maintenance of the vegetative cover and topographic equilibrium in surrounding areas.

Together, logging and agricultural activities, including livestock grazing, have most probably had a more extensive effect on natural environments than mining. Where soils were initially thin, or slopes so steep that clearing and converting to cropland was, at best, questionable, early ignorance of or disregard for the equilibrium of topography, soil, and vegetation transformed many an Appalachian landscape into a series of denuded slopes and gullied ridges. Clear-cutting in some private forest holdings often fails to ensure the maintenance of bases for viable biotic communities. In the western portions of North America, the pressure of grazing on the carrying capacity of the range is transforming, and in some cases has transformed, grasslands into areas of desert shrubs, forbs, and other wasteland vegetation.

Such activities are not alone in changing the character of the landscape. Highways, dams, reservoirs, railroads, and utilities all alter the landscape, and their effects on the natural environment are probably greatest in primitive or wilderness areas. Ironically, recreationists, many of whom are lovers of nature, and students of natural history pose the greatest threat to some fragile ecosystems by the intensity of recreation activities in areas of unique geologic, biotic, or recreational interest, in national parks and forests.

Rural areas that lie within easy reach of urbanites are subject to a variety of different factors. The refuse of our increasingly "containerized" society litters the landscape along the corridors between urban places. . . .

Americans often observe that the European landscape appears to be graced by reason of human habitation. Structures erected for their utility to man are often disguised ingeniously or blended into the landscape so that they do not mar the harmony of the pastoral setting. And certainly some of New England, notably the Dorset Valley, also exhibits pastoral scenes that provide a landscape aesthetically more pleasing in some respects than the original forest. But in areas of submarginal agriculture, in New England no less than elsewhere, America is strewn with the unsightly evidence of deteriorating farmsteads and dying and dilapidated communities.

The opening up and development of the country has, of course, affected the natural environments for the survival and reproduction of wildlife. Changes in the landscape have wrought fundamental changes in habitat, thereby altering greatly the numbers, distribution, and character of wildlife in the United States. Some species adaptable to village and farm conditions have increased in numbers since the advent of the white man in America, but these represent a small minority. . . . For the large game mammals, as well as for such fowl as turkey (which are deep-woods species), logging and, perhaps even more, the conversion of forest to cropland altered the conditions of survival beyond immediate retrieval. Not only did these practices change the character of the vegetation, they broke the continuity of the range. Even when large areas of forest land remained, the species that require conditions remote from human habitation disappeared from these areas. . . . The condition of some species, on the other hand, has improved during the last several decades. The whitetail deer and the raccoon have made an excellent adjustment to conditions associated with rural human habitation, and the opossum has even adapted to modern urban conditions. . . . Except for the few species mentioned, however, not only has the original range been reduced drastically, but the survival of the species itself is threatened. A systematic survey by the U.S. Fish and Wildlife Service has identified seventy-eight species of mammals, birds, fishes, and reptiles that are endangered, forty-four others that have become rare, and twenty-one whose occurrence in the United States represents the outer edges of their natural ranges.

THE PROBLEM IN PERSPECTIVE: PAST AND CURRENT

Large, and in many cases, irreversible changes in the American landscape and biota have taken place, but one should not conclude that all of these changes should not have occurred. The extractive activities that have contributed to the deterioration of the natural environment have promoted in a significant way the growth of the national economy and the material well-being of human society. Without them, a modern industrial nation could not have developed.

Earlier in the nation's history, the level of material well-being was quite low relative to present standards, technology was in its infancy, and the wilderness was large in relation to the lands under cultivation and the domesticated varieties of plant and animal life. Under these circumstances, the reduction in the size of the wilderness and the wildlife populations represented a conversion of resources that were abundant, and hence of limited value *at the margin,* into goods and services of high marginal value for the development of the economy. Today we have a large accumulation of capital and a level of living unparalleled in other cultures and previous periods. Moreover, the sophisticated technology that has made this possible appears to have reached a stage where the rate of advance can be manipulated, within limits, by research and development. The continued advance in material well-being now seems to depend more on programming technological advance than on converting the remaining wilderness into material inputs for agricultural and industrial production. If this is so, may we now relax, satisfied that the preservation of the remaining natural environments is assured? On the contrary, there are reasons to fear that additional and unnecessary degradation of natural environments may continue. This is due partly to the imperfection in the economic organization of production and partly to the imperfection with which the governmental processes work.

The organization of industrial production by means of the free market spins off *some* consequences for natural environments that would not be accepted by members of the community were they to have a choice, even if the choice involved costs that they would be required to share. Certain economic choices threaten the continued existence of an irreplaceable asset, while others create nuisances or fail to take advantage of feasible opportunities for enhancing human welfare, primarily because there is no incentive mechanism to reward entrepreneurs for taking action.

Consider first a natural environment that is unique and non-reproducible: Let it be a landscape of commanding beauty overlying mineral deposits of commercial value. To harvest the timber, to work the mineral deposits, and to beneficiate the ores at the site of the mining activity would irreparably destroy the aesthetic quality of the landscape. Preserving the landscape would, however, have no irreversible consequence. It would provide opportunity to harvest the timber and mine the minerals in the future *were circumstances to warrant.*

A private entrepreneur could realize a return from his investment either by marketing the aesthetic features of the landscape and associate biota as a scientific resource or recreational product, or by resorting to mining and logging. In a private-enterprise system, a rational profit-motivated entrepreneur would choose the alternative from which he expected the highest returns. His choice would be based on market values, but the market would register the full value only in a competitive situation.

Under competitive conditions, the value of the output of a good or service is measured by the price of the commodity and the amount sold. There are enough sellers and buyers so that no one seller or buyer can affect the price of the good or the supply appreciably by entering or withdrawing from the market. But when there is no close substitute for a commodity, no alternative source of supply, the value of the output is greater than the product of the price and the quantity, because the price represents only the value per unit that the marginal buyer attaches to the commodity. All buyers who would be willing to pay more than the market price rather than do without receive a bonus represented by the difference between the price and their valuations. This value is not captured by the seller.[1] Thus, if a unique commodity is removed from the market, the social loss is not what the seller could have received, but the sum of the maximum each buyer would have been willing to pay rather than go without. If in our hypothetical example the receipts from mining and other extractive activities correspond to competitive returns, while the receipts from the use of the resources for scientific and recreational purposes correspond to returns from sale of rare commodities for which no adequate substitutes exist, the returns expected by the entrepreneur from the two alternatives are not comparable indices of social value. What do economic observations tell us about the two possibilities?

The continuous decline in the price of natural-resource commodities relative to prices of commodities in general suggests the existence of numerous alternative sources of supply and roughly competitive conditions in the extractive industries.[2] But

1. The student of economics will recognize this as Jules Dupuit's discovery and the value in excess of the entrepreneur's receipts as Alfred Marshall's consumer surplus, a real part of the social valuation of the services of the resource in question. Of course, if there were no substitute for the services of the resources used in one way, monopoly pricing could be practiced, but this would not alter the result that pricing would not appropriate the total social value of the resources in their specialized uses.

2. N. Potter and F. T. Christy, Jr., *Trends in Natural Resource Commodities: Statistics of Prices, Output, Consumption, Foreign Trade, and Employment in the United States, 1870–1957* (Baltimore: Johns Hopkins Press, 1962).

conditions of extreme congestion at scenic landmarks in the national parks suggest that there are no adequate substitutes for these unique natural environments.

The market has another potential deficiency as the mechanism for allocating rare natural environments among competing uses. Individuals who have no definite plans to visit a particular natural wonder may be willing to pay some price in order to retain the option. Large sums change hands in commercial transactions trading in options of one sort or another, not all of which are ultimately exercised. This is a way of hedging against uncertainty by postponing a decision in the hopes that some of the uncertainty will be reduced with time. In the present context, there is a value associated with deferring a decision that will have an irreversible consequence potentially inimical to human welfare. A decision in favor of converting the landscape through commercial exploitation by extractive industries permanently forecloses the opportunity to use the landscape itself as an amenity that gratifies aesthetic interests or psychological needs.

A parallel rationale can be advanced for protecting species threatened with extinction or an entire ecosystem essential to the survival of a species. Such biotic communities represent banks of genetic information required by a species for survival as it competes for the finely graduated niches in nature. Such competition is absent in domestic counterparts; indeed, modern agriculture provides so highly protected an environment that the energy released from some of the genetic characteristics no longer needed for survival is redirected toward productivity. At the same time, the instability that results from progressive reduction of biological diversity through monoculture and the application of pesticides occasionally requires a reintroduction of some genetic materials that have been lost in the domestic strains.

Substantial use is also made of biological specimens for medicinal purposes; indeed, approximately half of the new drugs being produced have botanical sources. Because only a small part of the potential medicinal value of biological sources has been realized, preserving the opportunity to examine all species among the natural biota for this purpose is a matter of no little importance.

There may be substantial commercial value in preserving wild species and natural environments, but the market cannot communicate the option demand nor can the resource owners appropriate the option value. The conventional market operation does not provide adequate information or rewards to ensure the preservation of rare and irreproducible natural phenomena.[3] If the disposition of irreproducible natural environments is determined through normal market transactions, we cannot be confident that the results will represent the most highly valued disposition—either economic or social. At the same time, it must be recognized that only a small proportion of the market allocation of resources involves rare natural environments. And the deficiencies of the market's organization of industrial production detailed above occur only when a rare and irreplaceable asset is involved.

Certain cases of resource use threaten no irreplaceable asset, but neither do the prices by which the economy responds in organizing production reflect the social costs and benefits of such use. These situations have external, offsite, or spillover effects that compromise the efficiency of the market in allocating resources to their highest socially valued uses. . . .

Where external effects occur—and they appear to be concentrated in the natural resources field—benefits are enjoyed by some without cost to themselves, and uncompensated costs are inflicted on others. These costs and benefits do not get reflected in market prices of goods and services to which entrepreneurs respond in making their production decisions. Accordingly, when the spoliation of a natural environment occurs to the advantage of, but without cost to, the despoiler, the market offers no incentive to do otherwise. Without public supervision, continued assaults on the natural environment can be expected. . . .

The market mechanism does not everywhere provide entrepreneurs or resource owners with appropriate information or incentives to adopt actions that are socially optimal while still privately remunerative. Thus, there are imperfections in the way the market organizes production, and the government usually intervenes in particular situations to offset this deficiency. The prime example is the need for public action to offset the absence of adequate market signals or incentives in the field of water-resources development. Development, however, almost always conflicts with the preservation of the natural environment. In

3. J. V. Krutilla, "Conservation Reconsidered," *American Economic Review*, September 1967.

such situations, the implementing of collective decisions by public agencies may itself spawn difficult problems which neither the market nor the government is yet equipped to handle adequately. Reservoirs of the Bureau of Reclamation's proposed Bridge and Marble Canyon Dams would, for example, encroach on the Grand Canyon National Park.

When a public agency undertakes a mission necessitating the resolution of conflicting interests, a decision in favor of the predominant viewpoint as a reflection of majority rule often appears to be required. This reasoning does not hold, however, when public intervention is made in order to improve the allocation of resources because often it would lead to an uneconomic allocation contrary to the justification for public intervention. Nevertheless, a public agency will generally provide a good or service that appeals to many over an alternative that pleases a small minority. If such decisions come up *one at a time,* and each decision in favor of the commonly held preference pre-empts one of the remaining opportunities for indulging an esoteric taste, all of the resources or configurations of land forms and biota necessary to indulge less common tastes will be extinguished over time.[4]

No adequate mechanism exists in the public sector for automatically allocating among the qualitatively different demands in their relative proportions. Since the government is deeply involved in the resources field and dominates, to a large extent, the remaining wildlands, many of the grand panoramic landscapes, and all navigable streams, such machinery is required if we wish to safeguard rare natural environments. It is not just a question of, say, adjusting the margins between hydro-power production and more water-based recreation. Catering to the mass demand for lakes for swimming, boating, and water-skiing is not all of the problem. Provision should also be made for those who prefer to canoe in white water or to fish in free-flowing streams, even if such activities require some resources of use in the more popular water sports.

While public servants might be expected to respond to the predominant viewpoint when they consider a given case, the problem can be structured more meaningfully. We can visualize

4. For an interesting development of a similar point, see A. E. Kahn, "The Tyranny of Small Decisions: Market Failures, Imperfections, and the Limits of Economics," *Kyklos* 19 (1966), fasc. 1, 23–47.

an explicit policy that takes into account the intensity of both the dominant and minority demands as well as the number of individuals nurturing each. *This procedure requires viewing resource configurations not as individual cases but as parts of systems with an appropriate allocation of resources within the system to accommodate the widest range of demands in proportion to their representation.*

Earlier I suggested that the modern industrial economy is winning its independence from the conventional resource base through advances in technology. The more optimistic students of the problem, in fact, hold that ultimately only mass and energy are relevant inputs to an ever increasing production of goods.[5] Yet even these optimists acknowledge that the quality of the environment is deteriorating. Implicit in this paradox of plenty and impoverishment is the asymmetry in the implication of technological advance for manufacturing goods, on the one hand, and for producing natural environments, on the other. In spite of the remarkable advances in technology, rare natural features cannot be created. Producing a replica of the Grand Canyon or Yosemite Valley is as out of the question as the resurrection of an extinct species. Technology can make only a limited contribution to re-establishing *natural* environments. Modern earth-moving technology can help remedy the ravages of open-pit mining, but even so it takes time and the co-operation of nature to restore the landscape and its natural fauna. Technology thus promises liberation from dependence on natural environments as a source of industrial inputs, but not from dependence on natural environments for the amenities associated with personal contacts with nature.

The differential capability for increasing the supply of industrial goods as compared to natural amenities has important implications. As manufactured goods become more abundant and natural amenities more scarce, the trade-off between them will progressively favor the latter. Natural environments, hence, represent assets of appreciating future value. . . .

The change in the face of North America by reason of industrial man's dominance has resulted in a high standard of

5. H. J. Barnett and C. Morse, *Scarcity and Growth: The Economics of Natural Resource Availability* (Baltimore: Johns Hopkins Press, 1963), p. 238.

material well-being, but the ecological consequences may not yet be understood fully nor the ultimate cost appreciated. Some of the degradation—but certainly not all—is the necessary price of the high material standard of living achieved through industrialization. There have been unintended or socially unwarranted side effects of the organization of industrial production that we should have avoided. Yet the information on which decisions are made is not always adequate, nor are the incentives to individuals always in harmony with the larger public interest, often because the mechanisms for harmonizing private and public purposes have not been developed. Some of the environmental deterioration, although sought by no one, cannot be avoided by individual action. Thus, public authority must help to achieve collectively what cannot be attained individually. This involves, in part, the acquisition of greater knowledge in the natural as well as the behavioral sciences. Such knowledge would enable both private and public managers of natural resources to make more discriminating judgments about matters that might have adverse and irreversible consequences. It also involves a need for the creation of social institutions or mechanisms that will not produce results inimical to the preservation of natural environments simply because of the way the machine is assembled.

The Grand Canyon Controversy; or, How Reclamation Justifies the Unjustifiable

ALAN CARLIN*

Alan Carlin is now director of the Implementation Research Division, U.S. Environmental Protection Agency, Washington, D.C., but was an economist with the RAND Corporation, Santa Monica, California, at the time this article was written.

THE NEWS that the Administration no longer recommends the construction of either of the two proposed dams in the Grand Canyon represents a major although as yet incomplete victory by the increasingly influential and activist conservation groups, particularly the Sierra Club. Although by no means all of the proponents have abandoned hope as yet, the amazing thing is not that the dams have finally received what may prove to be a death blow, but that they ever received the support that they have until recently enjoyed. When asked if the Administration's change of heart represented a victory for the Sierra Club, Secretary of the Interior Stewart Udall said that the Administration's decision on the dams represented a "victory for common sense."

The appropriate question would seem to be how it happened that there ever had been such strong Administration support for at least one of the projects that it now admits do not make "common sense." On the basis of earlier statements by Secretary Udall and other Interior Department spokesmen concerning the desirability of examining alternative means of power generation as substitutes for the dams (particularly nuclear alternatives), and of adopting better procedures to insure that alternatives are adequately considered in the future, it seems likely that one important answer is to be found in the economic guidelines used by the Bureau of Reclamation and other federal water resource agencies for the evaluation of projects. In many ways these

* Any views expressed in this paper are those of the author and should not be interpreted as reflecting the views of his employers or the official opinion or policy of any governmental agency. The author is indebted to William E. Hoehn, William A. Johnson, and Richard Nelson for their comments.

guidelines, known as Senate Document 97, are used more as a means of justifying projects economically than their ostensible function of discriminating between economically "good" and "bad" projects. Once a project is declared to have satisfactorily met the "test" (self-administered by the agency that would build the project), the results of this "test" are used to build support for the project, first in the department concerned and then in the Administration as a whole, and later possibly in Congress. But even if it is assumed that the agencies involved have developed a foolproof honor system that eliminates cheating during the examination, there is carefully documented evidence that the test itself does not accurately measure the economic merits of projects, but rather is strongly biased in favor of the proposed projects.

Perhaps the best way to illustrate the shortcomings of these guidelines is to review the economic controversy over the Grand Canyon dams. These procedures have been under attack for many years and particularly by economists over the last decade, but few cases provide a better illustration of how little effect these suggestions have had than the economic controversy over the dams. The Grand Canyon controversy probably represents the first time that a federal water resource agency has had to make a serious public defense of its economic justification for a project prior to its authorization as a result of an attack based on the improved evaluation procedures long advocated by many economists.

The Grand Canyon controversy arose as a result of the proposal that the Bureau of Reclamation build two dams in the canyon as part of the proposed Colorado River Basin Project (CRBP), one at Marble Gorge and the other at Bridge Canyon. Bridge Canyon Dam (which would now be called Hualapai Dam) would be located 53 miles downstream from Grand Canyon National Monument but would back water throughout the length of the monument and 13 miles into Grand Canyon National Park. Marble Gorge Dam would be located 13 miles above the park and would flood the inner gorge of the Grand Canyon 40 miles upstream to Lee's Ferry. The threat to alter the natural state of the canyon, park, and monument led to vigorous opposition by conservationists to the CRBP.

The CRBP was also strongly opposed by the Pacific Northwest. Although the publicly stated purpose of the dams is to provide revenue to subsidize the other principal feature of the CRBP, the Central Arizona Project (which would bring Colorado River water to the Phoenix-Tucson area from the *existing* Lake Havasu impounded by Parker Dam), the real intent is somewhat different. It has been shown (and admitted with certain reservations by the Bureau of Reclamation and now, in effect, by Secretary Udall) that the dams are not needed to finance the Central Arizona Project at all, and that their real but little publicized purpose is to build a fund for the possible future importation of water into the Colorado River (presumably from the Columbia River) if and when this should prove to be politically and economically feasible. Other features of the CRBP were directed to the same end.

Perhaps a few words should be added here concerning the wisdom of using revenue (hopefully) generated by one federal enterprise to subsidize another. Although this is sanctioned by federal reclamation law, it is far from evident that economically unjustified federal activities that cannot pay their own way are any more justified if they can be subsidized by other more profitable federal enterprises. The intent is apparently to avoid the necessity for annual appropriations directly from the federal Treasury and the accompanying congressional scrutiny, even though the actual effect on the Treasury is exactly the same.

Before proceeding into the basic disagreements on the economic issues involved in the Grand Canyon controversy, it is necessary to say a few words about how hydroelectric projects are evaluated. Since few doubt the wisdom of providing the electric power demanded, the principal issue is how this can most economically be carried out. The basic method is therefore to compare the cost of the project with that of other alternatives that will generate the same quantity of electricity by other means. The cost of a suitable alternative, converted into an equivalent annual cost, is termed the "benefits" of the project. The criterion accepted in federal water projects (but generally not by the economics profession) is that a project is economically acceptable if the ratio of these "benefits" to the annual "costs" of the project is greater than one-to-one. The economic significance of this is that a ratio of greater than one-to-one indicates that the total benefits from the project, no matter who receives them, are greater than the total loss, no matter who pays them. It thus says nothing about the redistribution of income involved —just whether the total gained by those who benefit is larger or smaller than the total lost by those who pay the cost.

Last May at a stormy session of a House Interior subcommittee, a careful economic case against the dams was presented over the unusual objections of Representative Craig Hosmer, the leading southern California congressional proponent of the dams, to its even being heard. The economic study in question showed that the benefit-cost ratios for both dams are less than one-to-one when compared with nuclear alternatives. This compares with estimates nearer two-to-one by the Bureau, which used conventional, thermal alternatives.

An analysis of these sharply conflicting conclusions on the economics of the two dams reveals that there are at least three principal differences reflecting the basic cost-benefit procedures used by the Bureau of Reclamation (and other federal water resource development agencies): the type of alternative to be chosen, the relationship between the interest rates used to evaluate the project and the alternative, and the transmission costs of an alternative. In addition, although there was no difference between the analyses in the interest rate actually used to evaluate the dams, the study questioning the economic justification of the dams raised a question as to whether the basic interest rate used to evaluate both the projects and the alternatives should not be higher.

"MOST LIKELY" ALTERNATIVE AND HIGHER INTEREST RATES

In its economic evaluations of the Grand Canyon dams, and in subsequent presentations of them to Congress, the Bureau did not use what for several years has been the lowest-cost alternatives or cost the alternatives that they did use on the same basis as they did the dams. The Bureau defended these practices by citing a set of economic guidelines for analyzing federal water projects known as Senate Document 97. This propounds the curious doctrine that a project should be compared with the "most likely" alternative, and costed in the same way as it would be. By picking a sufficiently expensive "most likely" alternative one could justify any project, however uneconomic it may be. The only economically meaningful comparison is with the lowest-cost alternative rather than with the imprecise and subjective "most likely" alternative.

In this case, the Bureau insisted on comparing the dams to fossil-fueled thermal plants rather than to lower-cost (and by now proven) nuclear plants. And instead of evaluating this high-cost alternative on the basis of the same rates of interest and taxes, the Bureau evaluated them at a substantially higher rate, which they claim represents the average rate that would be paid by private and municipal utilities if they built the "most likely" alternative. The federal government, the Bureau argues, is unlikely to build anything but a hydroelectric plant in the western states for political reasons.

An evaluation carried out on such a basis has no economic meaning. It is as if someone attempted to compare the cost of constructing two brick buildings by pricing face brick for the first building while pricing common brick for the second, except that the price differences involved are very much greater than would be found among types of brick. The use of higher capital charges (higher brick prices) in the form of interest rates and taxes for the alternative than for the dams biases the comparison in favor of the dams.

TRANSMISSION COSTS

The second major area of difference is on the question of the transmission costs to be charged to the alternative. The Bureau insists that roughly the same transmission costs be charged to the alternatives as to the dams despite the obvious savings involved in the fact that the alternatives can be placed close to the major load centers that would use most of the electricity generated. The Bureau claims that the alternatives must serve exactly the same customers as the dams, which they allege would be scattered throughout a five-state area. The Bureau's transmission costs for the alternatives would be necessary if they were also located in the Grand Canyon. But by letting other plants and transmission facilities (that already exist or are planned) provide the minor amounts of power required in areas closer to the Canyon, the nuclear plants can be located near the major load centers, with negligible transmission costs to provide the same service to these load centers as would the dams.

INTEREST RATES

Even at the same low rate of interest used in evaluating the dams (3⅛ percent) the nuclear alternatives were shown to be more economic. However, this rate of interest is below even that of current government borrowing. At higher, real rates of interest, the dams would look even worse. The Bureau justifies this unrealistically low rate of interest on the basis of the same Senate Document 97.

The reasons for this feature of the Document are not difficult to understand. One of the characteristics of public water projects is that they typically substitute what the economist calls capital—usually new construction in this case—for labor, fuel, and other resources. Hydroelectric projects usually have much higher capital costs than coal-burning electric generating plants. But they have low operating costs relative to the coal station, which must budget a large proportion of its annual expenses to the purchase of fuel. Similarly, canals and other inland waterway improvements usually have very heavy initial costs compared to the expansion or continued use of existing rail facilities, but provide the shipper with lower operating costs compared to rail freight.

Clearly the cost of capital used in comparing such projects with alternative ways of accomplishing the same purpose is very important. If the cost is low it is much more attractive to build such capital-intensive projects than if it is high. Thus it is not surprising to find that Senate Document 97 approves the use of a low cost of capital, or interest rate. It does this by establishing a formula based on the average interest rate paid by the Treasury on *long-term* bonds. This sounds innocent enough until it is considered that Congress established a ceiling in 1918 on the rate that the government can pay on bonds of five years or more maturity. Hence when interest rates are high, as is now the case, and the Treasury cannot issue long-term bonds, these high rates never affect the average rate computed according to the formula. At first glance a more appropriate rate would seem to be the current rate for Treasury borrowing.

But then the question arises whether even the current rate paid by the Treasury for capital is a reasonable rate to use. Anyone who has tried to borrow money has noticed that the interest rate paid is substantially above what the government is willing to pay on savings bonds. The reason is also obvious: the lender does not regard him as being as good a risk as the average holder of U.S. savings bonds regards the government. There is much more risk to the lender that the average borrower will not repay his debt. So the lender charges a little more to compensate himself for the higher risk involved.

The relationship of all this to the interest rate used by the government in evaluating water resource projects is that the economic risks involved in the typical water project have proven over the years to be quite substantial. Many projects, through miscalculations or overoptimism, or both, have failed to repay their costs to the Treasury (even at heavily subsidized rates of interest). The best way of allowing for this higher risk is to use an appropriately high interest rate, just as the private lender does in dealing with the average citizen. In this case, the result will be that only very attractive capital-intensive projects will be built and fewer costly mistakes will be made. Some students of the subject have recommended rates as high as 10 percent.

Although the transmission dispute revolves around some of the more technical issues of benefit-cost analysis, it is already evident that most of the problems stem directly from the basic cost-benefit procedures currently used in the evaluation of water resource projects by the Bureau of Reclamation and other federal agencies. The immediate culprit, Senate Document 97, has already been identified. Some of its other features, not relevant to these particular projects, such as the customary inclusion of usually imaginary "secondary benefits" and the differing price levels to be used for evaluating project benefits and costs, are equally as unjustified economically.

But the underlying problem in all this is the fusion of interests between federal water agencies looking for business and congressmen anxious to obtain projects for their districts. Grossly generous guidelines for evaluating water projects serve the interests of both, as does the practice of having the individual agencies concerned carry out the evaluations of particular projects. Since Congress itself is really the principal body charged with reviewing these evaluations, and the individual taxpayer is rarely effectively represented even at the public hearings held by Congress, the outcome is inevitably large public works expenditures. Until such time as the executive branch takes available steps to curb the activities of its water agencies, or the taxpayers organize an effective lobby to protect their interests on public works appropriations, there can be little hope of altering the present state of affairs. At present it is only when other interests, such as conservation, are affected that effective opposition is organized.

The Trans-Alaska Pipeline: An Economic Analysis of Alternatives

CHARLES J. CICCHETTI and A. MYRICK FREEMAN III

Charles J. Cicchetti was research associate at Resources for the Future, Inc., when he did the research on which this paper is based. He has prepared evaluations and analyses of the Alaskan oil development question for congressional committees and for submission as part of the public record relating to the Department of the Interior's decision to permit construction of the Trans-Alaska Pipeline. Professor Cicchetti now teaches economics and environmental studies at the University of Wisconsin, Madison. Professor A. Myrick Freeman III also prepared an analysis of the Environmental Impact Statement for the public record. This paper was prepared for this volume and is based on the authors' earlier analyses.

INTRODUCTION

Two initially unrelated developments in the late 1960s have now become intertwined in one of the nation's most significant environmental preservation and energy development controversies. First, during 1968–70, successful exploratory efforts resulted in the discovery of a major oil field on the North Slope of Alaska. By the end of 1970, the American Petroleum Institute estimated the proved reserves in this Prudhoe Bay field to be approximately 9.6 billion barrels. A field of such size makes this discovery one of the single most important in the history of the domestic crude oil industry.

The second development was the enactment by Congress of the National Environmental Policy Act of 1969 (NEPA) as a declaration of national environmental policy. NEPA requires that all agencies of the federal government develop procedures "which will insure that presently unquantified environmental amenities and values may be given appropriate consideration in decision-making along with economic and technical considerations," that they shall "utilize a systematic interdisciplinary approach which will insure the integrated use of the natural and social sciences . . . in decision-making which may have an impact on man's environment," and that "alternatives to the proposed action" be considered and evaluated. In furtherance of these purposes the act requires that agencies prepare detailed statements on the environmental impacts of major federal actions.[1]

The two developments became intertwined when the consortium of oil companies sought permits from the Department of the Interior to construct a 789-mile pipeline from the Arctic coast to Valdez on the Gulf of Alaska, from which the oil would be shipped by tankers to Puget Sound and California. After the courts ruled that the issuance of permits came under the provisions of NEPA, the Department of the Interior prepared a Draft Impact Statement in January 1971, held public hearings later in the year, and issued an eight-volume Final Environmental Impact Statement and Supplementary Analysis of Economic and Security Aspects of the proposed project in March 1972. In May 1972 the Secretary of the Interior announced his decision to issue the permits for the pipeline, and the decision is now being appealed in the courts by environmental groups, including Friends of the Earth and the Environmental Defense Fund.[2]

The environmentalists involved in this legal battle agree that the magnitude of the North Slope oil pool and its potential contribution to meeting a growing demand for energy probably warrant the development and transportation of this oil to the "South 48." The question is "How?" And the debate on the issue has sharpened this question to one of a comparison of two alternative pipeline routes.

The route which is currently proposed by the oil companies would run south across Alaska through two major mountain ranges. The southern part of this route (TAP) crosses the most seismically active region in North America. The pipeline would terminate in the port city of Valdez, where storage and terminal facilities would be built for shipping the North Slope oil to final markets on the West Coast. The alternative considered most likely would be a pipeline from the North Slope to the Canadian city of Edmonton, following the natural corridor of the Macken-

1. National Environmental Policy Act of 1969, Title I, Sec. 102.
2. [When this book went to press, the environmentalists had won their court appeal. The issue is now before Congress. *Editors.*]

zie River Valley. This route (MVP) would move generally eastward across Alaska and the Yukon to the Mackenzie River and then southeast to Edmonton, covering a distance of 1,600–1,800 miles depending on the exact route chosen. Existing pipelines already connect Edmonton with the U.S. Midwest (Chicago) and Pacific Northwest. Thus although additional capacity would be required, the environmental impact of transporting Alaskan oil to its final destination beyond Edmonton would be minimal.

In this paper we will first outline the kind of analytical framework which is necessary for bringing together technical, economic, and environmental information and insuring its integrated use in decision-making. We will then review available environmental and economic information in the context of this analytical framework. The final task is one of interpretation of the results and discussion of the policy implications of the analysis.

AN INTERGRATED FRAMEWORK FOR ANALYSIS

The ultimate objective of our analysis is to choose from among alternative courses of action so as to maximize social or human welfare. Assume for the moment that we know just what that means, and that we have some unit for measuring welfare (inches, dollars). Then all that would be necessary is to measure each alternative's welfare, compare the measurements, and choose the one with the highest figure.

Now suppose that welfare has two components, economic benefits measured in dollars, which represent the value individuals attach to what is produced, and the number of robins in the world, which we assume for a moment is a proxy for environmental quality. Assume that we face a choice between two mutually exclusive alternatives A and B. Choice A might represent preservation of a wild area, and Choice B its development for economic gain. Suppose that the measurements of the two dimensions of welfare for the two choices were as follows:

	Choice A	Choice B
Economic benefits ($)	100	200
Number of robins	50	60

Clearly there is no difficulty in choosing. Choice B dominates A in that it entails more of both dimensions of welfare.

Now suppose a second case with the following measures of welfare components:

	Choice A	Choice B
Economic benefits ($)	100	110
Number of robins	50	10

In this case development (Choice B) has both benefits (dollars gained) and costs (robins lost), and they cannot be compared unambiguously to determine whether the benefits outweigh the costs. If we had a dollar price tag for robins, the problem would be solved, because the above information could be reduced to a single measure of welfare for each choice.

In practice such problems are ultimately resolved when some agency, commission, elected official, legislative body, or the electorate as a whole takes responsibility and makes the choice. In whatever manner the choice is made, the choice reveals an important piece of information, the implicit value or price placed on robins. In the example, choosing B implies that whoever made the choice is willing to give up 40 robins to gain $10. In other words, society revealed that its implicit valuation of robins was less than 25 cents apiece. (If the outcomes of Choice B were $200 and 49 robins, one would have to place a value of over $100 per robin in order to prefer Choice A.)

NEPA's requirements for an "integrated use of the natural and social sciences" can be met if specialists gather information on the consequences of alternative choices and place it in a framework such as that described here. This framework does not make choices for us, but it organizes information in a way which reveals more clearly the real consequences of the choices we ultimately make.

With respect to the pipeline question, there are in principle three basic alternatives: no development, development through TAP, and development through MVP. As noted above, however, even the environmentalist groups concede the strong case for some form of development. Thus in practice the choice becomes "Which route?" For the two alternatives, a table compiling all available information on relevant effects should be drawn up. Information should be included on economic benefits and costs, national security effects, impact on the balance of international payments, equity (who gets the benefits), and the whole range of unavoidable and threatened environmental impacts. It is beyond the scope of this paper to examine national security and balance of payments questions.[3] Attention will be confined to a table as follows:

	TAP	MVP
Net economic benefits (benefits minus costs)		
Environmental costs		
Equity		

AN ENVIRONMENTAL COMPARISON

The principal concerns of environmentalists have been related to the wilderness character of the territory to be traversed by the pipeline, the fragile nature of the ecological systems, and the uncertainties and risks associated with constructing and operating a pipeline carrying hot oil across permafrost and through earthquake zones. Of further concern has been the threat of oil pollution associated with tanker and terminal operations and possible disasters of the *Torrey Canyon* variety.

The Department of the Interior, in its Environmental Impact Statement, chose to evaluate impacts in six categories:

*Unavoidable Impacts Associated with
Normal Conditions*

   1. Terrestrial Abiotic (non-living) Environment · Damages associated with construction, grading and filling, erosion, etc.

   2. Terrestrial Biotic Environment · Vegetation, fresh-water fisheries, wildlife.

   3. Socioeconomic Environments · Effects on native communities, changes in recreation opportunities, aesthetics, etc.

   4. Marine Environment · Effects associated with the regular

3. Although the Department of the Interior placed heavy reliance on a contrived national security argument to justify its choice of TAP, objective analysis shows little difference between the routes, but with MVP slightly favored on the basis of delivering oil to a higher need area and the greater security of an overland route. If Canada were to collect royalty payments for the use of MVP, TAP would be slightly favored on balance of payments grounds.

operation of tankers and terminal facilities, including oil pollution from tank cleaning.

Threatened Impacts Due to Accident or Natural Disaster

5. *Terrestrial Environments* · Breaks or leaks in the pipeline, including those which might be caused by earthquakes.

6. *Marine Environment* · Tanker accidents or oil spills from other causes.

Some insights regarding the comparisons of the two routes can be gained by examining the distances covered by TAP and MVP under different conditions such as terrain. The data can be summarized as follows:

	TAP	*MVP*
Total distance (miles)	3,039	1,705
Tanker route	2,250	0
Total overland	789	1,705
Distance over permafrost	770	1,205
Distance through earthquake zone	260	0

These data show that the two routes are likely to be different in the kinds of environmental damages associated with them. In attempting to rank the two routes on the basis of environmental harm, one must weigh the greater overland distance of MVP and the disruption associated with it against the hazards of marine transportation and the risks of earthquake damage accompanying TAP.

The Department of the Interior's own analysis reflects these difficulties. The Impact Statement concluded that, "No single generalized route appears to be superior in all [environmental] respects to any other." But in comparing TAP and MVP in each of the six categories, the Impact Statement found MVP to be superior in every respect except unavoidable impacts on terrestrial abiotic environments.[4] The superiority of TAP in this one category is directly related to the shorter overland distance of TAP. But the Impact Statement concedes that this advantage for TAP is lost if, as seems likely, a natural gas pipeline is built from the Alaskan North Slope along the MVP corridor. In this case all six categories of environmental impact of the combined

4. Department of the Interior, *The Final Environmental Impact Statement on the Proposed Trans-Alaska Pipeline* (Washington, D.C., 1972), vol. 1, pp. 320–22.

oil/gas pipeline systems would be lessened by choosing the Mackenzie Valley corridor for both pipelines.

In summary, these considerations would point to MVP as the preferred route on environmental grounds unless one were to place very low weight on (be relatively unconcerned with) effects on the marine environment and the threat of earthquake damage to the pipeline. In the discussion which follows, we assume that any reasonable weighing of the diverse environmental impacts of the two projects would show that MVP has lower environmental costs than TAP.

NET ECONOMIC BENEFITS

The principles of benefit-cost analysis can be utilized first to evaluate the question: What are the net economic benefits of TAP (B_T) compared with the alternative of no development? If B_T is positive, a decision whether or not to develop would be based on a comparison of B_T with the other project effects such as environmental costs. Similarly, the benefits of MVP (B_M) can be evaluated. If both development alternatives have positive net benefits, then the question *might* become one of which project to develop. Then the relevant comparison is between the differences in benefits (the economic advantage of one project) and the differences in environmental and other costs (the environmental disadvantages of that project).

The first step is to define net economic benefit. If it can be assumed that the output of the project (in this case oil) replaces an equal quantity of output from an alternative source without affecting the total supply from all sources or changing market price, then the net benefit is the resource saving realized by developing the project. In other words, for TAP:

$$B_T = C_A - C_T$$

where C_A is the cost of the old source and C_T is the cost of TAP. The cheaper TAP oil is relative to the old source, the greater the net benefits of developing TAP.

Normally in benefit-cost analysis the new source of supply is assumed to displace the *highest cost* alternative supply—which in this case would be production from oil fields in the continental United States. But a variety of public policy measures and private actions, including the oil import quota system and cartel price and output controls, serve to maintain an artificially high price for oil in the U.S. market. This in turn provides a protective umbrella for high-cost U.S. producers. Therefore it is more reasonable to assume that North Slope oil would in fact displace low-cost oil imported from the Middle East.

On the basis of presently contracted price agreements and continued improvements in tanker technology, Middle East oil is expected to cost $2.01 per barrel landed in Los Angeles in 1975.[5] On a similar basis, Middle East oil will cost about $2.26 per barrel shipped via tanker and pipeline from the East Coast to Chicago. However, since it is difficult to predict future developments in oil pricing in the Middle East, a more "conservative" set of assumptions was used to calculate landed costs of $2.49 and $2.74 per barrel in Los Angeles and Chicago respectively.

Turning to the costs of the projects, C_T and C_M, we face considerable uncertainty in deriving estimates. Total project costs depend on the discount rate or opportunity cost of capital, the expected life of the project (for amortizing capital costs), the time stream of production, operating costs, and, of course, the costs of construction.

There have been many estimates of the various components of cost for both projects, and at the present time there is still no single estimate of total cost that is agreed to by industry or government sources, to say nothing of the estimates one might expect from environmentalists. Therefore, the strategy we adopted was to use various cost figures which bracket the estimates provided by other sources and make alternative calculations to determine the sensitivity of the results to variations in the assumptions. The results of these calculations have been reported elsewhere.[6] Here we have assumed a 10 percent discount rate, a 25-year life, and the production schedule reported by the oil companies.[7]

5. These and other figures are discussed and justified in C. J. Cicchetti, *Alaskan Oil: An Economic and Environmental Analysis of Alternative Routes and Markets* (Baltimore: Johns Hopkins Press, 1972).

6. *Ibid.*

7. The 10 percent discount rate is assumed to represent the opportunity cost or return forgone on private investment. Using a lower discount rate increases the net economic benefits for both alternatives, but tends to increase MVP's benefits relatively more.

The costs of TAP calculated on a per barrel basis are expected to lie between $.91 and $1.10, based on the above assumptions. Net benefits, B_T, are:

TAP	C_A	C_T	B_T
High cost	$2.49 −	1.10 =	1.39
Low cost	2.49 −	.91 =	1.58
Middle	2.49 −	1.01 =	1.48

Similar figures for MVP are:

MVP	C_A	C_M	B_M
High cost	$2.74 −	1.23 =	1.51
Low cost	2.74 −	.94 =	1.80
Middle	2.74 −	1.09 =	1.65

Although the range of uncertainty precludes strong statements about the comparison of net benefits, it is clear that both alternatives have high net economic benefits. And the figures provide some basis for believing that the net benefits of MVP are between ten and twenty cents per barrel higher than for TAP.[8] This is because the higher value of Alaskan oil in the Middle West (compared to the West Coast) more than offsets the slightly higher cost of shipping the oil there.

As was shown in the preceding section, it appears reasonable to judge MVP as environmentally less hazardous than TAP. And we have now suggested that it has higher net economic benefits. The last element in the analysis to consider is equity, or the redistribution of income, or how much importance to attach to equity in comparing alternative projects. All available information on distribution should be compiled and displayed along with data on economic benefits and environmental effects so that these issues can be debated.

There are two kinds of equity questions which might be of importance in this case. The first is between consumers of oil products and the oil companies, while the second is between oil companies and state and federal governments. If oil companies

8. The benefits to the United States of MVP would be reduced by the amount of any tax or royalty imposed by Canada for use of its right of way. But on the basis of reasonable assumptions, we calculate that Canada could impose a tax of up to 20 percent on the costs of transporting oil across her territory without exhausting the benefits to the United States. Note that for the purpose of simplicity many other categories of benefits, all of which favored MVP relative to TAP, have been omitted.

exercise monopoly power to raise prices and revenues, the result is an expropriation of money from consumers by oil companies. Alternatively, if new low-cost supplies of oil force prices down, consumers benefit. But in the North Slope case, it is expected that existing cartel-like restrictions on supply will prevent price reductions, so that consumers will not benefit directly from low-cost North Slope oil.

Where state or national governments collect income taxes or royalties on production, they "expropriate" some of the monetary gain occuring to oil companies. The principal questions here are: How will the gain associated with North Slope oil be divided between the companies and the State of Alaska, and how does the choice of a pipeline route affect that division?

Under present arrangements, the state will collect royalties of approximately 20 percent of the value of oil production calculated at the wellhead. This figure is known as "wellhead price" and is calculated by deducting all transportation costs from the price at which the oil is sold at its destination. Based on market prices in Los Angeles and Chicago, wellhead prices for the two pipeline routes are:

	TAP	MVP
Market price	$3.17	3.81
Transportation*	− 1.01	− 1.09
Wellhead price	2.16	2.72

* Middle cost.

The difference is striking. The state would collect more than 10 cents per barrel more in royalties if MVP were built. And company net profits (before corporate income taxes) would also be almost 50 cents per barrel higher. Over the lifetime of the pipeline, MVP would generate additional royalties for the state with a present value of close to half a billion dollars, and additional oil company profits in the neighborhood of $2 billion present value.

If MVP is superior on economic and environmental grounds, and yields both higher royalties for Alaska and higher profits for the producers, we must ask: Why has TAP been chosen and fought for by the producers, the State of Alaska, and the Department of the Interior?

OIL COMPANIES ARE NOT IRRATIONAL

The key to understanding the apparently irrational preference of oil producers for TAP is the impact of North Slope oil on the demand-supply balance of the West Coast oil market. Recall that our calculation of net economic benefits was based on the assumption that the new supply displaced one alternative source of supply (imports) without affecting total market supply or market price. In the Midwest market, this is a reasonable assumption. But on the West Coast the story is different. Given present rates of growth of regional production and consumption, the 2 million barrels per day of North Slope oil might not be absorbed at present prices for 15 years. In other words, even with all imports displaced, North Slope oil would be in excess supply well into the 1980s.

This excess supply can be accommodated in one of two ways. One way is for producers to allow the price of oil to fall on the West Coast. This would stimulate an increase in oil consumption and, more important, cause a curtailment of domestic production as high-cost marginal wells were shut down. The alternative is for producers to find other markets for the excess quantity of oil. It would be against the economic interests of producers to allow the West Coast price to fall as long as they can find profitable alternative markets for the oil. In fact, such alternatives do exist.

Two plans for dealing with this excess supply have been discussed. Both of them raise producers' profits higher than with MVP and at the same time drive net efficiency benefits for the nation and the state taxes down further still. These are:

An Export for Import Plan. Under this plan, excess oil would be shipped in foreign-built tankers from Valdez, Alaska, to Japan. In return, if the plan were approved by the federal government, the exporting company would be allowed to increase its imports of low-cost foreign oil on the East Coast barrel for barrel.[9] The lower Japanese price combined with the higher transportation costs would reduce net economic benefits to the nation and royalty payments to Alaska.

9. [In April, 1973 President Nixon ended the Mandatory Oil Import Quota Program. However the price differentials between the East Coast and West Coast referred to in the text are still present. *Editors.*]

Producers' profits on the sale of North Slope oil would be lower, too. But if producers are allowed to import additional oil to the East Coast on a barrel-for-barrel basis, the extraordinary profits more than make up the difference. The figures for TAP to Los Angeles and Export for Import are as follows:

	TAP to Los Angeles	Export for Import
Market prices	$3.17	$2.00
Less: Production costs for North Slope oil	.25	.25
Transportation via TAP and tanker	1.01	.80
Before tax net revenue	$1.91	$ .95
Plus: Profit per barrel on low-cost imports under the import quota system		$1.75
Reduced taxes to the State of Alaska due to reduction of wellhead price of $.96		.19
Per barrel equivalent net revenue	$1.91	$2.89
Difference		+ $.98

A second plan calls for the use of foreign-built and operated tankers to transport North Slope crude oil from Valdez to Central America, where a new pipeline would be built to move oil to another fleet of foreign tankers to carry oil to the Virgin Islands for refining. By selling oil to themselves or engaging in "swaps" at the low world price, the wellhead price and taxes to the State of Alaska would be reduced. After refining, this domestic crude could then be shipped to the East Coast to be sold at the high East Coast price. Since this is domestic oil, the mandatory Oil Import Quota Program would not apply. Calculations reported elsewhere show that with the several variations on this plan, Alaska's royalties are reduced, net economic benefits are reduced because of the resources devoted to roundabout transportation, but producers' profits are increased because of higher selling prices.[10]

In addition to these two plans, there are two other important although less ingenious oil company considerations:

1. Due to monopoly pricing and the favorable tax treatment accorded by federal law, the oil industry experiences unusually high rates of return on invested capital. Rates of return of 10 percent would be regarded as unimpressive by oil company officials, and they could be expected to use a substantially higher

10. C. J. Cicchetti, Alaskan Oil.

discount rate in evaluating their investment alternatives. Accordingly, while delaying a dollar of net economic benefits may cost society or the State of Alaska about 10 cents per year, the oil companies on the North Slope find their opportunity costs to be several times greater than this amount. Possible delays of two or three years in order to build a superior Canadian alternative may double the economic costs to the oil companies. Thus their choice of the route they judged initially to be the fastest possible development is understandable, even if it is not socially justifiable.

2. In addition, British Petroleum, Ltd., has merged with Standard Oil Company of Ohio. In order to complete this merger as agreed, BP must produce 600,000 barrels of oil per day by the end of 1977. Possible delays along with possible loss of pipeline throughput control are doubtless reasons why BP has selected and pursued the TAP alternative in order to develop the speediest alternative, regardless of U.S. and Canadian national interests.

MAKING NEPA WORK

The purposes of NEPA were to establish environmental quality as a policy objective and to improve the procedures for making decisions about the environment. NEPA has been on the books only three years, so it is too early for a complete assessment of NEPA's contribution to environmental policy. Yet the experience with TAP makes some preliminary judgments possible.

The TAP case may typify the kind of problem the drafters of NEPA had in mind. The application for the pipeline permits appeared to pose a conflict between fairly well-defined, narrow economic interests and environmental values difficult to measure. Yet when we examined the available economic and environmental information in a systematic framework and carefully evaluated alternatives, the conflict disappeared. The MVP alternative dominated TAP in that it ranked higher on both environmental and economic grounds. For people who want to make NEPA work the real question is why the Department of the Interior, with access to essentially the same information, came to a different conclusion—supporting TAP over MVP. Or to put it differently: If NEPA's procedures and prescriptions could not produce a better decision in this relatively easy case, what can we expect on a really tough call?

One of the weaknesses of NEPA is that it does not provide for a thoroughly independent and open review of the Impact Statements or the agency decisions. Although current regulations provide that the Impact Statement be transmitted to the Council on Environmental Quality before final decisions are made, CEQ does not have independent review authority. CEQ is only an advisory body to the President. Technically speaking, it can comment on environmental issues only if asked by the President. And it can make its own opinion public only with the President's approval.

Thus while NEPA requires that environmental considerations be given weight, it does not tell us how much weight. More important, it leaves the decision as to how much weight to give to environmental values largely up to those who are drafting the Impact Statement. Yet these are the same agencies and bureaucrats who, along with their special-interest-group clients, may have the most to lose by full adherence to the spirit as well as the letter of NEPA.

NEPA's purposes would be better served by the establishment of a statutorily independent authority which would be required either to prepare or review agencies' Impact Statements, hold public hearings, and issue its own rulings or advisory opinions as to whether NEPA's criteria have been met. Where the agency and the authority disagree, the dispute should be resolved by the President or Congress. The objective of this suggestion is to open up the decision-making process and to provide independent review and evaluations as counterweights to agencies' use of analyses and Impact Statements as *ex post* justifications of decisions already made for other reasons.

The lack of effective review of Impact Statements and agency decisions allows agencies and special-interest groups to hide the real reasons for selecting inferior alternatives behind biased analyses designed to obscure and mislead. It appears that the real issue posed by the TAP case is more than a question of relative economic or environmental superiority. It is a question of building new political and administrative arrangements for environmental decision-making.

Suggested Further Readings

American Chemical Society. *Cleaning Our Environment: The Chemical Basis for Action.* Washington, D.C., 1969.

Barnett, Harold J., and Chandler Morse. *Scarcity and Growth.* Baltimore: Johns Hopkins Press, 1963.

Commoner, Barry. *The Closing Circle.* New York: Knopf, 1971.

Council on Environmental Quality, Annual Reports for 1970, 1971, and 1972.

Ehrlich, Paul R., and Anne H. Ehrlich. *Population, Resources, Environment,* 2nd ed. San Francisco: Freeman, 1972.

Esposito, John. *Vanishing Air: The Ralph Nader Task Force Report on Air Pollution.* New York: Grossman, 1970.

Freeman, A. Myrick, III, and Robert Haveman. "Water Pollution Control, River Basin Authorities, and Economic Incentives: Some Current Policy Issues," *Public Policy* 19, no. 1 (Winter 1971).

_____. "Residuals Charges for Pollution Control: A Policy Evaluation," *Science* 177, no. 4046 (July 28, 1972).

_____, and Allen Kneese. *The Economics of Environmental Policy.* New York: Wiley, 1973.

Kneese, Allen. "Strategies for Environmental Management," *Public Policy* 19, no. 1 (Winter 1971).

_____, and Blair T. Bower. *Managing Water Quality: Economics, Technology, Institutions.* Baltimore: Johns Hopkins Press, 1968.

_____, eds. *Environmental Quality Analysis: Theory and Method in the Social Sciences.* Baltimore: Johns Hopkins Press, 1972.

Krutilla, John V. "Conservation Reconsidered," *American Economic Review,* September 1967.

Landsberg, Hans. "The U.S. Resource Outlook: Quantity and Quality," *Daedalus,* Fall 1967.

Roberts, Marc J. "River Basin Authorities: A National Solution to Water Pollution," *Harvard Law Review,* May 1970.

Schurr, Sam, ed. *Energy, Economic Growth, and the Environment.* Balitmore: Johns Hopkins Press, 1972.